Eph 2 :16

THE KEY CONCEPTS OF ST. PAUL

THE KEY CONCEPTS
OF ST. PAUL

FRANÇOIS AMIOT

HERDER AND HERDER

1962

HERDER AND HERDER NEW YORK

232, Madison Avenue, New York 16, N.Y.

Original edition „Les idées maîtresses de saint Paul", Cerf, Paris

Translated by John Dingle

Grateful acknowledgement is due to the Cardinal Archbishop of Westminster and Messrs. Burns and Oates, Ltd., for their permission to use extracts from Monsignor R. A. Knox's translation of the New Testament; and also to Messrs. Sheed and Ward, Inc., of New York, for allowing quotations to be used from the New Testament in English, in the translation of Monsignor R. A. Knox. Copyright 1944.

Nihil Obstat: Hubertus Richards, S.T.L., L.S.S., Censor deputatus.

Imprimatur: E. Morrogh Bernard, Vic. Gen.

Westmonasterii, die 6a Decembris, 1961.

Library of Congress Catalog Card Number: 61-17458

First published in West Germany © 1962 Herder KG

Printed in West Germany by Herder

SANCTE PAVLE
APOSTOLE
PRAEDICATOR VERITATIS
ET
DOCTOR GENTIVM
INTERCEDE PRO NOBIS
AD DEVM
QVI TE ELEGIT

CONTENTS

CONTENTS

Part Three
PARTICIPATION IN SALVATION. COLLECTIVE ASPECT

Part Four
THE ATTAINMENT OF SALVATION

Translator's Note

Most of the New Testament quotations used in this volume are taken from Monsignor Ronald Knox's translation and the Old Testament quotations are taken from the Rheims-Douai version. In a few cases, however, to establish the author's point more clearly, we have found it necessary to use the Rheims-Douai version for New Testament quotations or to provide our own rendering of the French texts which are the author's version, published in *Gestes et Textes des Apôtres*. The latter passages are marked to that effect.

BIBLIOGRAPHICAL NOTE

Recommended as works of a general character on the thought of St. Paul:

Prat, *The Theology of St. Paul,* Burns & Oates, 1926.

Colon, article *Paul* in the *Dictionnaire de Théologie catholique,* Letouzey.

Cerfaux, *Christ in the Theology of St. Paul,* Herder & Herder, 1959.

Cerfaux, *The Church in the Theology of St. Paul,* Herder & Herder, 1959.

Bonsirven, *L'Évangile de Paul,* Aubier.

LIST OF ABBREVIATIONS

SDB – *Supplément au Dictionnaire de la Bible,* Letouzey.

DT – *Dictionnaire de Théologie catholique,* Letouzey.

DA – *Dictionnaire Apologétique de la foi catholique,* Beauchesne.

RB – *Revue Biblique Internationale,* Gabalda.

RSR – *Recherches de sciences religieuses,* rue Monsieur, Paris.

Bibl. – *Biblica,* Institut Biblique, Rome.

Rev.SR – *Revue des sciences religieuses,* Faculté de Strasbourg.

RSPT – *Revue des sciences philosophiques et théologiques,* Vrin.

Kittel: – *Theologisches Wörterbuch zum N.T.,* Kohlhammer, Stuttgart (Protestant).

FOREWORD

THIS study of St. Paul appeared in France in a series bearing the wisely chosen title of *Lectio Divina*. Patristic and medieval authors liked to use this term to describe a thoughtful and prayerful reading of Sacred Scripture. St. Benedict made this loving study of the inspired word one of the chief monastic occupations, grouping it with the *Opus Dei* and manual labour. Those who followed the Father of Monasticism continued to encourage souls seeking God to devote long hours to the Bible; they taught that *"lectio divina* formed one side of the ascetic triangle of reading, prayer, contemplation".

Father Amiot's book deserves a place in the *Lectio Divina* series, for it enables even the most inexperienced reader to continue the search for knowledge that comes from love and leads to love. He knows St. Paul well. Earlier books on the Apostle to the Gentiles, commentaries on the Pauline epistles, and years of lectures enable him to speak with authority. He understands the beauty of Paul's words as well as their difficulty: the beauty he can deepen, some of the difficulty he can remove. Under this guidance, the study of St. Paul can lead souls along that path leading to light and life, which was so highly recommended in early monastic and in medieval days.

Pope Pius XII has encouraged twentieth century readers to return to Sacred Scripture. Father Amiot, professor at the Seminary of Saint-Sulpice, is one of the scholars who have made this return both pleasant and profitable. Well aware that the overflowing enthusiasm of the Apostle can discourage as well as attract, and knowing from experience that beginners are disconcerted by the exuberant riches of the Apostle's thought, he has been happily inspired to centre his synthesis of Pauline theology about one single idea: salvation. This theme is well chosen, for without it no true understanding of the primitive Church or its teaching is possible.

During Old Testament days, the Israelites considered salvation in a restricted sense. Most of the words they used in this connection were built around a root meaning broad or spacious. They thought of salvation as a state of victorious security in which, with God's help, they were free from danger, disasters, evil powers and death. Unlike the Greeks, they did not think of salvation as deliverance from the miseries of man's human lot, or in the modern theological terms of the salvation of the soul. When through revelation they began to think of life after death, they did so in terms of the resurrection of the body rather than in terms of the immortality of the soul. All these ideas were clarified and transformed by their experiences as a nation and the sufferings of their just men. Prophets and sages contributed to this development but a complete understanding was reserved for the New Testament with its message of Christ's incarnation, ministry, crucifixion, and resurrection. One of the most helpful aspects of this book is the author's understanding of the place of the resurrection in Paul's thought. He does not consider it merely as a proof of Christ's divine mission or the crown of his sufferings, but he shows that it is part of the perfect fulfilment of his sacrificial work.

All this is clearly stated in the soteriology of the Acts of the Apostles and it is with the primitive Church in Jerusalem that Father Amiot begins his study of St. Paul. The surprising story of the vocation of the vehement persecutor is related in the dramatic introductory chapter which serves as the historical setting for the whole book. A second chapter introduces the reader to Paul the preacher and writer, and serves to show his relationships with the intellectual cross-currents of his day.

It is only in Part One that the author begins his examination of the great reality of salvation. He admits that the Pauline writings contain a number of major themes, whose orchestration contributes to the depth and beauty of this doctrine. He considers and rejects the themes of grace, justification, redemption, or incorporation in the dead and risen Christ because he feels that the term salvation with its derivatives, although they may occur less frequently than some of the others, expresses the one really dominant Pauline theme. In his analysis he stresses the gratuitous and universal nature of salvation while never losing sight of the fact that the divine initiative leaves man free to accept or to reject God's gift.

Since this gift is made to men in history and through history, the author, in an understandably but regrettably brief space, describes the preparation for Christ's coming and his saving work. This provides a background for much of Paul's thought, containing as it does so many references to Adam, the fall of man, Abraham, Moses and the Law. The second and third parts are like the two wing panels of a diptych: in the first, Father Amiot develops Paul's teaching about the salvation of the individual; in the second, he shows how this same gift is given man as a member of the Church, Christ's Mystical Body. All this is summed up in the final section in which he deals with Christian hope and eschatology.

Gratitude to God is Paul's response to the message of salvation entrusted to him. Gratitude may well be the burden of the soul who uses this book to begin the *Lectio Divina* so long in honour in the Church.

Mother Kathryn Sullivan, R.S.C.J.
Manhattanville College of the Sacred Heart,
Purchase, New York.

PREFACE

St. Paul attracts us by the splendour of his doctrine and the elevation of his own moral character. But the richness and complexity of his thought, the depth of his intuitions and the quickness and nature of his reasoning processes are liable to deter any reader unprepared for them. Though dazzling, the jewels of his thought are surrounded by darkness and it is only with difficulty that we can assign them their place in a composite whole. The early Christians themselves came up against these difficulties (2 Peter 3:15–16) and even an assiduous study of the Pauline writings does not entirely remove them. We feel the need for an overall approach intended to bring out the principal themes, to show their connection with one another, their consistency and their relationship to a central idea. Such an approach to the work of St. Paul is the aim of this book. The limited space at our disposal constrains us to be brief and to pass over a number of secondary questions. We have striven merely to bring out the cardinal points in the thought of St. Paul, relating them to the main theme of salvation through the crucified and risen Christ. We hope that our work will help towards an understanding of his admirable apostolic message, that it will be to the great benefit of the faith, to a deepening of Christian life, and to the winning of salvation through our Lord Jesus Christ (1 Thess. 5:9).

Easter, 1959.   F. A.

1

UNEXPECTED VOCATION OF A
NEW APOSTLE

*"Christ Jesus has won the mastery
over me"* (Phil. 3:12).

It was Pentecost in the year 57 or 58 and in the heat of this Palestinian springtide Jerusalem was in a sudden ferment. A certain Paul, coming to the Temple to fulfil a vow, had been seized by the Jews from Asia who had raised the crowd against him. They accused him of profaning the holy place by bringing in a pagan and called upon others to help them, crying out loudly: "Men of Israel, come to the rescue; here is the man who goes about everywhere, teaching everybody to despise our people, and our law, and this place. He has brought Gentiles into the Temple too, profaning these sacred precincts." (Acts 21:28). Paul had in fact been seen in the town accompanied by the Ephesian Trophimus and the apostle's enemies alleged that he had taken his companion beyond the wall separating the court of the Gentiles from that of the Israelites. Gentiles were forbidden to enter the part of the Temple reserved for the Jews under pain of death and notices placed at each gate warned any who might be tempted to ignore the ban. Paul had been careful not to lay himself open to so serious a charge, but the accusation against him was itself sufficient to cause great excitement. A crowd came running up from all parts. The levites shut the gates leading to the court of the priests while a fanatical crowd laid hands on

15

Paul and his very life was in danger. Immediately, Roman soldiers intervened. The garrison was stationed at Antonia, a spot
overlooking the Temple from which it had been easy to see what
was taking place. The tribune in command of the citadel rushed
towards the demonstrators, followed by his men. The soldiers
had some difficulty in seizing Paul and manacling him. The
officer then demanded who he was and what he was doing but,
in the tumult, succeeded in obtaining only confused answers. He
had Paul taken to the fortress while the crowd cried out for his
blood. Its violence was such that when they reached the steps
leading to the citadel the soldiers had to carry Paul. Just as they
were about to enter the gates, he succeeded in obtaining the
tribune's permission to speak. He made a sign with his hand and,
once he was heard to be using Aramaic, a deep silence fell. Paul
described himself and gave an account of his conversion to Christ
and of the mission to the Gentiles which had been entrusted to
him. His words did nothing to pacify the demonstrators who
interrupted him and cried out: "Away with such a fellow from
the earth; it is a disgrace that he should live" (Acts 22:22). They
shook their garments, making the dust fly. To end the matter and
establish the cause of the uproar, the tribune ordered the centurion on duty to question the prisoner under the lash. Paul
objected, losing no time in advancing a claim to Roman citizenship, thus saving himself from a scourging. He was not, however, set free and this arrest, soon followed by his transfer to
Caesarea, was the beginning of a long captivity.

Who, then, was this man whose presence caused such a tumult?
His Jewish name was Saul or Saül. In the apocryphal *Acta* of
Paul and Thecla, we are given what appears to be an authentic
picture of his physical appearance. According to this account, he
was small and somewhat bent. He was bald on the crown of his
head but his beard was thick. His legs were bowed, he was pale
and had a slightly aquiline nose. He appeared elderly but had a

charming manner, in spite of a countenance that bore the marks of some ill-defined constitutional weakness (2 Cor. 10:1, 10; 12:7–9). He was born in the Cilician town of Tarsus, probably seven or eight years after our Saviour, about A.D. 3. This is suggested by his epistle to Philemon, written between 61 and 63, in which he speaks of himself as an old man, implying that he was at least sixty. He set out his civil and religious status in the epistle to the Philippians (3:5): "I was circumcised seven days after I was born; I come from the stock of Israel, from the tribe of Benjamin, Hebrew-speaking as my parents were before me. Over the law, I was a Pharisee; to prove my loyalty, I persecuted the Church of God; in observing what the law commands, I was beyond reproach." This implies that he was not one of the Hellenising Jews, who associated freely with the Gentiles. But his education had not cut him off entirely from the Greek world, for the Jews of Tarsus lived in fairly close contact with the Gentiles. He had been greatly influenced by Hellenic culture and his epistles show that he was proficient in Greek,[1] being thus providentially prepared for his vocation among the Gentiles. Paul came indirectly under the influence of the famous schools which made Tarsus the rival of Athens and Alexandria. He had inherited from his father the coveted privilege of Roman citizenship and availed himself of it on a number of occasions (Acts 16:37–38; 22:26–29). We do not know how his father came to acquire this citizenship in the first place.

From the age of five or six, the young Saul was sent to the Jewish school, where the whole teaching was based on the scripture. He became familiar with the Hebrew bible and the Greek version of the Seventy, gradually acquiring that remarkable knowledge of the Old Testament to which his epistles bear witness in almost every line.

[1] The Greek, that is, of everyday speech and of the Septuagint, not the classical Greek of the men of letters.

When nearly thirteen, he was sent to Jerusalem to complete his education. His master there was the celebrated Pharisee Gamaliel, himself the grandson and disciple of Hillel who, during the reign of Herod the Great, had been the famous rival of Shammaï. Under Gamaliel, Saul received additional training, not only in the bible, but in the traditions the rabbis had added to the scriptures, giving rise to the enormous compilation of the Talmud. For these traditions, the doctors claimed an authority equal to that of the law itself, a pretension for which our Saviour was to reproach them bitterly, all the more so since they often misrepresented the spirit of the law and, by their subtle casuistry, led people to transgress its essential precepts (Matt. 15:3–6; 23:16–28; Mark 7:5–13). Gamaliel, however, was a straight-forward and honest man and, late in the day though it was, showed signs of moderation in the Sanhedrin (Acts 5:34–40). At his school, Saul was imbued with a zeal for the law which his fiery temperament pushed to extreme lengths. He does not appear to have known our Lord, for there is no need to interpret in the sense of a meeting the reference in 2 Corinthians 5:16. Paul's exceptional attachment to the traditions of his forefathers (Gal. 1:14) could hardly have predisposed him to accept the teachings of the Galilean prophet when he came to hear them.

He returned to his own country about the age of twenty and may then have started to undertake his duties as a rabbi while at the same time perfecting himself in his father's trade. As far as is known, the latter was a rich maker of goats' hair tents, a spe-ciality of Tarsus. In principle, every Jewish doctor was expected to earn his living by working at a manual trade in order to be able to teach the law without payment while remaining in-dependent. Saul, then, became a tent-maker, either weaving the tent-cloth, or cutting it out and sewing it up. He could have had no inkling of how useful this apprenticeship was to prove by enabling him to preach the gospel without any concern for material reward. At this period, no doubt, he renewed contact with Greek culture and his intellectual gifts would have enabled him to assimilate it without any detriment to his monotheism and without diminishing the abhorrence in which he held the idolatry and moral turpitude of the pagan world.

For reasons that have not emerged, he had returned to Jerusalem not long after the Passion, in 31 or 32. There, he showed himself to be a Pharisee of the Pharisees. Many things had changed in the holy city since his last visit. The death of Jesus had not put an end to the discussion provoked by his teaching and miracles. Far from acting as a discouragement, his ignominious death had stimulated the zeal of his disciples. They insisted that he had risen and that they had seen him in the flesh. They recognized him as the Messiah promised to Israel and as the Son of God and called upon their compatriots to share their own faith in him. Many had joined the new sect, particularly among the Greek-speaking Jews, and there had even been a certain number of priest-converts (Acts 6:7). Those who were apparently the leaders among the disciples performed astonishing cures and the people held them in high honour (Acts 5:13). The Sanhedrin had imprisoned them on two occasions and had in vain forbidden them to speak in the name of Jesus. They had, moreover, quickly been released. Gamaliel, impressed by the course of events, had warned his colleagues against taking a decision that might mean opposing God, if indeed the new sectaries were working in God's name. As soon as they were released, the apostles began once more to preach with joyous zeal and with growing success (Acts 5:34–42; 6:7).

In Saul's eyes, these men represented a mortal threat to Judaism. What was to happen to the holy religion to which he clung with every fibre of his being? Could this poor illuminee who had been condemned by the highest court in the land and had died miserably on a cross be anything but a false Messiah?

Meanwhile, the situation was worsening. A disciple called Stephen, famed as a worker of miracles, had carried the debate into the synagogues where his skill in argument had confounded the Jewish doctors. Taken before the Sanhedrin, he had outlined the history of God's dealings with his people. The attitude of his hearers, however, led Stephen to reproach them and they, angered in turn, gnashed their teeth at him. Stephen was then favoured with a vision which confirmed his faith and could not restrain himself from crying out: "I see heaven opening and the Son of Man standing at the right hand of God" (Acts 7:56). This was too much, and the members of the Sanhedrin, shocked at what they considered blasphemy, fell upon Stephen, thrust him out of the city and stoned him. Saul was there, giving his voice for the murder and holding the clothes of the murderers. He saw Stephen die, pardoning his executioners as Jesus had done on the cross, but his fanaticism was not shaken by the holiness of the first martyr (Acts 7:56 to 8:1; 22:20).

This summary execution marked the beginning of a violent persecution in Jerusalem. Most of the faithful took refuge in the countryside of Judea and Samaria. Saul, prominent because of his zeal for the law and his acute intelligence, rapidly became a leader among the persecutors. He raided the houses of those who had not been able to flee and had men and women thrown into prison (Acts 8:4; 22:4). On occasion, he tried to force them into blasphemy (26:11). His conscience did not trouble him and his good faith remained complete, as he was to claim about himself later in Caesarea when he was brought before King Agrippa: "Well then, I thought it my duty to defy, in many ways, the name of Jesus the Nazarene" (Acts 26:9). It was not long before Jerusalem seemed to him too restricted for his activities. The new sect had spread as far as Damascus, the capital of Syria, and he obtained for himself a commission to go there and take the Christians into custody, bringing them back in chains to Jerusalem. The Roman authorities recognized or at least tolerated the jurisdiction of the High Priest over the Jewish colonies of the dispersion and Saul obtained an official mandate from him, confirmed in writing. Threatening massacre with every breath he drew, Saul then left the holy city for Damascus, accompanied by an escort. On the outskirts of the Syrian capital, he was destined to make an encounter as unexpected as it was decisive. He met Jesus of Nazareth, risen and glorified. The ravening wolf of the tribe of Benjamin was to discover the Master who, by a signal stroke of divine grace, would turn him into an apostle.

The incident, which probably occurred in 32 or 33, is known through three separate passages in the Acts (9:1–18; 22:3–15; and 26:9–18). The first is St. Luke's own account and the other two form part of St. Paul's speeches when he was arrested in Jerusalem and when he appeared before Agrippa at Caesarea. The three accounts are in complete harmony as far as the main features are concerned. The apparent discrepancies relate only to a detail – the attitude of Saul's companions. But, if we look into the matter closely, we see that there is no contradiction.[2] The third account (26:16–18) adds, putting them on the lips of Christ, words that were no doubt addressed to Paul by Ananias, speaking on behalf of the Saviour. This was simply a matter of literary convenience, as Ananias was not mentioned in this last discourse.

Saul was approaching Damascus when, about midday, he was suddenly struck to the ground, together with a number of his companions, by a light that was brighter than the rising sun. At

[2] According to the first account, Saul's astonished companions heard the voice speak but did not see anyone (9:7). According to the second, they saw the light but did not understand the voice (22:9). These descriptions are easy to understand, relating as they do to a confused experience of seeing and hearing. The witnesses saw the light but did not see Christ and heard his voice without understanding what he was saying to Saul.

the same time, a voice, speaking to him in his native tongue, said: "Saul, Saul, why dost thou persecute me? This is a thankless task of thine, kicking against the goad." The proud Pharisee felt himself pierced through and through and dominated by a force which, imperious though it was, still respected his freedom. Dazzled and trembling, he could only reply: "Who art thou, Lord?" The voice resumed, "I am Jesus, whom Saul persecutes". And Saul saw the Son of Man shining in glory – the Son of Man whom Stephen had seen standing at the right hand of the Father at the very moment that he bore witness to him before the Sanhedrin. Saul had before him the one who was crucified at Calvary but was now risen and eternally living. He was invaded by an unfathomable clarity of vision,[3] bringing with it a certainty that was to make a new man of him at a single stroke, changing radically the whole direction of his life. Jesus of Nazareth had overcome his executioners and overcome death itself. His resurrection undeniably proved the truth of his teaching. He was indeed the Messiah promised to Israel, the only begotten Son of God, the Lord equal to Jahveh. In a flash Saul understood all this. He could only submit and stammer, "Lord, what wilt thou have me do?" The reply came at once, "Rise up, and go into the city; and there thou shalt be told what thy work is". He rose up therefore, but the intensity of the light had blinded him. It was necessary for him to be made to feel his own impotence if he was to bend himself entirely to the will of the Almighty. Members of his escort had to take him by the hand and it was in this fashion that he entered Damascus. The man who had expected to arrive as a redoubtable leader and inflexible persecutor did so instead in pitiful array.

[3] The apostle was no doubt thinking of this marvellous light when he later wrote to the Corinthians: "The same God who bade light shine out of darkness has kindled a light in our hearts, whose shining is to make known his glory as he has revealed it in the features of Jesus Christ" (2 Cor. 4:6).

He took lodgings with a certain Judas and, still blind, remained three days without eating. He was bewildered by the blow that had befallen him and, doubtless, even more deeply lost in his own reflections and prayers, but he did not remain for long wrapped in himself. A disciple named Ananias had been warned in a vision to seek him out. Extremely frightened, he replied that he knew all about Saul's persecuting activities and about what he intended to do to the faithful in Damascus. But the Lord answered: "Go on thy errand; this is a man I have chosen to be the instrument for bringing my name before the heathen and their rulers, and before the people of Israel too. I have yet to tell him how much suffering he will have to undergo for my name's sake" (Acts 9:15–16). Ananias obeyed, not without misgivings, but Saul's attitude dispelled his fears. He laid hands on the converted persecutor, who immediately recovered his sight, and he then had a long conversation with him, completing his instruction then and there. Without waiting further, Ananias invited him to be baptized and Saul agreed without hesitation. The sacrament of regeneration completed his consecration to the service of our Lord. From that time forward, to the general astonishment, he began teaching in the synagogues of Damascus that Jesus was the Messiah promised to Israel and the Son of God. By a remarkable paradox of the divine will, however, this fanatical Pharisee was to find that his chief mission was to preach the name of that Jesus whom he had once hated to the Gentiles whom he had despised and detested. This was what he came fully to understand during the two years of recollection and reflection spent "in Arabia" before returning to Damascus. By Arabia was probably meant the Hauran, to the east of the Syrian capital. It was fitting that the future apostle should complete his training in the silence of the desert as Moses, Elias, and even the Master had done.

The moment he became a Christian, Paul was, in fact, made

23

an apostle. His mission was entrusted to him directly by the Almighty and he was able proudly to describe himself as "an apostle not holding his commission from men, not appointed by man's means, but by Jesus Christ, and God the Father who raised him from the dead" (Gal. 1:1). Nevertheless, having left Damascus to avoid the anger of the Jews, he was careful while in Jerusalem to compare his "gospel" with the teaching of Peter and the other apostles, not in order to remove doubts, for these had never troubled him, but to establish his conformity with their doctrine (Gal. 1:18; 2:1–2).

Rationalist criticism has striven hard to eliminate the supernatural elements from the account of the conversion of St. Paul. We hardly dare repeat the allegations of Renan who, laughing no doubt at his own readers, pretended to explain everything by sunstroke, accompanied by a brain storm, to which he attributed a hallucination. Can we seriously look to a passing neurosis for the explanation of a change which strengthened Paul's mental balance, gave full rein to his genius, increased his intellectual grasp, and added greatly to the energy of his temperament? If there had indeed been an illusion, the contradictions and sufferings of a long missionary life would have effectively cured it.

Others have maintained that what happened at Damascus was the sequel to a long preparation. Paul, they argued, had acted reluctantly against Christ's disciples, uncertain of the justice of his cause, secretly drawn towards those whom he was persecuting and, indeed, already half a Christian without knowing it. To this he has himself replied. His sincerity during the persecution was complete and he felt no remorse. He thought it his duty to fight Jesus (Acts 26:9). Once converted to Christ, he had the deepest regret for his past action. He called himself the least of the apostles, not fit to bear the name (1 Cor. 15:9; Gal. 1:13–14), even though he had been shown mercy because he was acting in the ignorance of unbelief (1 Tim. 1:13). He asserted that

Christ Jesus had taken possession of him (Phil. 3:12) and that he had been separated violently from Judaism like a child who comes to birth unexpectedly (1 Cor. 15:8). He attributed his sudden change to a divine intervention as decisive as it was unexpected. It had pleased God, who had set Paul apart from the day of his birth and called him by his grace, to reveal his own Son in Paul, in order that he should preach his gospel among the Gentiles (Gal. 1:15–16). Elsewhere, the apostle adds humbly: "Only, by God's grace, I am what I am, and the grace he has shown me has not been without fruit" (1 Cor. 15:10).[4]

But there is still a mystery and it could hardly be otherwise. This action of divine grace is attested by the very one who was the object of it and who is, moreover, an extremely clear witness. Without hesitation, he puts the apparition on the road to Damascus on the same plane as Christ's appearances to the apostles and the disciples between the resurrection and the ascension (1 Cor. 15:8). Like the disciples, he had indeed *seen* the Lord Jesus and, on this score, claimed with the eleven the rank of apostle: "Am I not an apostle, have I not seen our Lord Jesus Christ?" (1 Cor. 9:1). He makes a distinction between this vision and the other very different visions with which he was later favoured. In the case of at least one of these, he asserts that it threw him into an ecstasy, so that he could not say whether his spirit was in his body or apart from his body (2 Cor. 12:1–4). Do those who try to minimize the importance of the supernatural element realize the extent of the change it operated in Paul? The convinced and stubborn Pharisee, all the more firmly attached to Judaism by the depth of his religious feelings, was separated from Christ by a mountain of prejudices and by a conception of the Messianic future radically different from the one the Saviour had with such

---

[4] At least as far as the rapidity of the conversion is concerned, we can without disrespect compare that of St. Paul with Pascal's famous night, as well as with the conversions of Father Ratisbonne and Claudel.

difficulty persuaded the apostles to accept. In a moment, his suspicions had disappeared in the beams of the divine light. As St. Augustine says, it was Saul who was thrown to the ground and Paul who rose up. His Jewish pride and his pharisaic complacency, neither of which predisposed him to accept any mystical intervention, were suddenly overwhelmed by the reproaches and the vision of Jesus. Henceforth, he reckoned as nothing the privileges of race and of sect of which he had been so proud. "And all this, which once stood to my credit, I now write down as loss, for the love of Christ. For that matter, there is nothing I do not write down as loss compared with the high privilege of knowing Christ Jesus, my Lord; for love of him I have lost everything, treat everything else as refuse, if I may have Christ to my credit.... Him I would learn to know, and the virtue of his resurrection, and what it means to share his sufferings" (Phil. 3:7–8, 10). If one still had doubts about the objectivity of such a witness, it would be necessary to set them aside on judging the tree by its fruits. Who, we must once again ask, could be made to believe that Paul's astonishing apostolic career, with all its courage and unconquerable serenity, confirmed as it was by miracles, and crowned by the religious and moral transformation of countless souls, could have proceeded from an illusion, or been the result of a dramatic mistake capable of standing up to so much opposition and persecution?

The conversion of Paul was a determining factor in the spread of Christianity. If the young Church had not possessed this genius, it would have risked being bogged down in an introspective Judeo-Christianity. Without neglecting his own countrymen, Paul was destined in particular to be the apostle of the Gentile nations (Gal. 2:7–9). No one was to play a greater part than he in eliminating the differences of outlook and the hatred that threw Israel into opposition with the uncircumcised and that were so vividly recalled within the Temple by the wall separating the court of the Gentiles from that of the Israelites (Eph. 2:14). At the height of the struggle against the Judaists, who wanted to impose the Mosaic precepts on all converts, he was to show that the law was henceforth superseded and to cry in triumphant accents: "No more Jew or Gentile, no more slave and freeman, no more male and female; you are all one person in Jesus Christ" (Gal. 3:28).[5] Where did the apostle derive a certitude so fundamental, so assertive, and yet so difficult to accept for those who had come to Christianity through Judaism? Its origin must lie in the apparition on the road to Damascus in which the light of Christ illumined for him the essentials of the gospel he was to announce to the world.

The important element was the manifestation of the risen Christ. The resurrection was the great sign, the "sign of Jonas", that the Saviour had himself announced as decisive (Matt. 12:39–40). The vision of the Crucified shining in glory must have burned into the mind of Saul an idea of the teaching of Jesus of which he had already obtained a glimmering in the course of his persecuting activities and this had given his soul an unshakeable certainty. Ananias and the other members of the faithful doubtless helped him in his life-giving meditations, dominated and clarified as they were by the heavenly vision with which he had just been favoured. The resurrection brought with it the authentication, the confirmation by God, of what Jesus had said of himself and of his redemptive mission. Later, Paul was to write to the Corinthians: "If Christ has not risen, then our preaching is groundless, and your faith, too, is groundless.... You are back in your sins" (1 Cor. 15:14,17). He immediately

---

[5] Many pagans converted to the God of Israel had such an aversion to circumcision that they preferred to remain all their lives "fearers of God", "proselytes at the gate", imperfectly assimilated to the Jewish people. Had they become Christians they would hardly have been willing to undergo circumcision.

adds with a note of exultation, "But no, Christ has risen from the dead, the first-fruits of all those who have fallen asleep" (ibid. 20). Christ had conquered death, thus giving an unshakeable foundation to the faith of all those who were to believe in him. He was, therefore, the glorious Messiah that he had proclaimed himself to be before Caiphas. He was the Lord, possessing divine dignity and rank – the glory in which he appeared did not leave Saul any room for doubt on the subject. He was the Son of God, not only in the state in which he then was as the risen Christ, but during his earthly life and in his eternal pre-existence. He was, as he had stated, the Redeemer of the world by his sacrifice of which his glorification demonstrated the efficacy. He was the source of forgiveness, justice, grace, holiness, resurrection and eternal life. Jesus bore witness, moreover, to the closeness of the union between himself and his disciples: to attack them was to persecute him. Saul at last came to understand that salvation was available to men through faith in Jesus and not through the observance of the Mosaic law. The terrible antagonism between Jews and Christians was resolved in favour of the new religion. "I will be thy deliverer from the hands of thy people, and of the Gentiles, to whom I am now sending thee... so that they may receive, through faith in me, remission of their sins and an inheritance among the saints" (Acts 26:17–18). This doctrine – the universality of the call to faith and salvation so that Christ would be all in all – was what he was later to call the "mystery" (Eph. 3:2 et seq.) and it was he who was destined to be the privileged announcer of it.

St. Paul's theology was to reflect his own religious experience and this clearly cannot be explained in terms of subjective impressions but was founded on the action of Christ both in the apparition on the road to Damascus and in the revelations that followed it and was also based on the enlightenment and habitual guidance of the Holy Spirit. When the apostle describes the role of faith, it must not be forgotten what faith constitutes for him – a complete gift, the commitment of his entire being. If we look upon it in any other way, we risk misrepresenting his thought. When he comes to speak of Christ, Paul will be found to concentrate for preference on the glorified state in which our Lord presented himself to him, appearing as the principle of unity and the crown of all things. But the apostle does not forget the cross and never separates it from the glorification of the Saviour, which lies with the cross at the centre of his teaching.[6]

It seems then that, right from his conversion, Paul was aware of the most important elements of what was to prove his "gospel". But this was a general and intuitive acquaintance and the various parts, at first dimly seen, were to be brought out more clearly later. His prolonged thought, his missionary career, his contacts with the other apostles, the needs of the churches, and the controversies all led him to clarify the details and work out the consequences that followed from them. The claims of the Judaists were to form the occasion for a formal demonstration of the abolition of the old law. Against the beginning of Gnosticism, he emphasized Christ's divinity and pre-existence, his role in creation and his eternal reign. The life and even the irregularities of the Christian communities brought him to lay down the requirements of evangelical morality and to dwell with predilection on the doctrine of the Mystical Body. But the most elaborate expositions, such as those recurring in the epistles written during the captivity, had been preceded in the earlier epistles by brief statements and allusions, containing the doctrines concerned in embryo. There had been some progress in

[6] He was to describe the Passion in such moving terms that he was able to write to the Galatians (3:1) that he had, so to speak, placed before their eyes Jesus crucified. And it was with the cross that he was to begin his preaching to the sceptical and corrupt people of Corinth (1 Cor. 2:2).

the form of expression, but no change in the sense of an introduction of fresh elements. Paul's theology continued to follow
the same line and, as it grew more complete, the elements existing
in it from the beginning became more and more explicit. Indeed,
from the moment of Paul's conversion, God made his Son known
in him (Gal. 1:16). But as with the others engaged with him
in spreading Christianity, the gradual apprehension and formulation of the great mystery revealed by Jesus came to Paul
only after a certain amount of going back over the same ground
and of hesitations and at first he expressed himself imperfectly, incompletely and implicitly. Such gropings were inevitable. But if we take Paul's thought as a whole, we see in
it a deep unity and discern the admirable action of the Holy
Spirit who, in accordance with Christ's promises, brought to
the Church during the apostolic age what, at the time of the
Passion of the Saviour, the disciples were not yet in a position
to furnish (John 14:26; 15:11–13). The convert of Damascus
had been one of the privileged instruments of this marvellous
illumination.[7]

From the moment he had given himself to Christ and received baptism, Paul had been, as he himself liked to say,
clothed in the new self (Eph. 4:24). He had become a new
creature (2 Cor. 5:17). His reply to the Saviour, "What must
I do, Lord?" (Acts 22:10), was the key to his whole life. He
belonged without reserve to the one whose imperious call he had
answered. He was to press on, forgetful of what was behind
him, and intent on what lay ahead (Phil. 3:13). The fanatical
persecutor was replaced by an apostle, consumed with love for
Christ and for his brethren, one who would make the world ring
with the transcendental wisdom and power of the gospel, though
up to that time the world had seen in the gospel nothing but
scandal and folly (1 Cor. 1:23–24).

[7] See Benoit, RB, 1947, 608–12.

The worker was providentially prepared for the task God was to entrust to him. Genius that he was, he was outstandingly endowed with gifts of mind and heart, and employed them with unfailing devotion in the service of his new faith and of him who was the object of that faith, Jesus Christ, universal Lord and Saviour of the world. Seized by the almighty hand of the Saviour, Paul was ready in his name to forsake all things. His one desire was to know the Lord ever more deeply, to know him "and the virtue of his resurrection, and what it means to share his sufferings" (Phil. 3:10), his "unfathomable riches" and the plan of the redemptive mystery (Eph. 3:8–9). He centred everything on Christ's adorable person, in a love that was humble, grateful, enthusiastic and generous, and expressed this love in burning passages in his epistles and in the incessant labours of a lifetime. He never separated love of Christ from his love for those to whom he preached the gospel. He would spend himself without counting the cost (2 Cor. 12:15), wishing even to go so far as to give his life for them, so much did he love them (1 Thess. 2:8), happy to suffer and to pay off the debt which the afflictions of Christ still left to be paid (Col. 1:24). Had it been necessary, he would have been ready to be anathema and to be separated eternally from Christ for the sake of his own kinsmen by race, the unbelieving Jews (Rom. 9:3). He was to make himself all things to all men with complete unselfishness, working with his hands in order to be a burden to none (2 Cor. 11:7–10) and to be able to give freely what he had freely received, making himself everybody's slave, to win more souls (1 Cor. 9:15–22), and ready to hand over to other preachers, provided only that Christ was proclaimed (Phil. 1:15–18).

His apostolic zeal took complete hold of him, pouring itself out in tumultuous accents and spreading like a torrent of burning lava. But he remained thoughtful and balanced. His multifarious activities, energetic and sometimes anxious though they were, remained always carefully thought out. He was vehement yet tender, bold yet prudent, frank yet appreciative of others' feelings, not rushing blindly forth to conquer the world, but attacking at strategic points, making for the great towns such as Athens, Corinth, Ephesus and Rome, and addressing Jews and Gentiles in turn. He organized new communities, established a hierarchy over them and settled, with great wisdom and a never-failing apostolic sense, the delicate moral problems arising. His intellectual gifts and the inspiration of the Holy Ghost gave him an unequalled understanding of the light of Christ and the revelation of the redemptive plan which he was engaged in spreading everywhere. He preached at the same time by force of example, living what he taught. He was able to offer himself as a model with a pride that still remained humble (Eph. 5:1; Phil. 3:17), so completely did he realize that it was not he who was at work but the grace of God working with him (1 Cor. 15:10). His enthusiastic temperament and extreme sensitivity made it more difficult for him than for others to bear the burden of misunderstandings, contradictions, misbehaviour and ingratitude. The trials sometimes weighed so heavily that he thought he was on the verge of death (2 Cor. 1:8). But he recovered himself and set to work with renewed energy, never allowing himself to be overwhelmed. In the evening of his life, with martyrdom near and oppressed with a sense of almost universal abandonment, he confided to his disciple, Timothy, that the Lord had helped him and given him strength (2 Tim. 3:11) and he declared proudly, "He, to whom I have given my confidence, is no stranger to me.... The time has nearly come when I can go free. I have fought the good fight; I have finished the race; I have kept the faith; I look forward to the prize that is waiting for me, the prize I have earned. The Lord, the judge whose award never goes amiss, will grant it to me" (2 Tim. 1:12; 4: 6–8).

We are forced to admire the nobility of character, the great intelligence, the generosity, the profoundly religious mind and absolute integrity of such a man. He was indeed the instrument of choice that the Lord prepared for himself to bring his name "before the heathen and their rulers, and before the people of Israel too" (Acts 9:15). His anxious temperament, his interior struggles, his indomitable courage and the care with which he adapted himself to the most varied circumstances all bring Paul closer to us and increase our love for the persecutor turned apostle whose teaching continues to enlighten the world and whose sanctity invites the imitation of all those who believe in Christ Jesus.

2

THE HERALD OF CHRIST AND THE WRITER

*"Grace and peace be yours from God, our
Father, and from the Lord Jesus Christ."*

PAUL began his preaching of Christ immediately on his return
to Damascus after his retreat in Arabia, but the traps laid for him
by the Jews forced him after a while to flee from the Syrian
capital, having himself let down along the wall in a hamper
(Acts 9:23–25; 2 Cor. 11:32–33). He then went up to Jerusalem
to meet Peter for the first time (Gal. 1:18). Barnabas presented
him to the apostles after overcoming with some difficulty the
fears aroused by the former persecutor. In this respect, too, he
was, like the Master himself, a sign which men would refuse to
acknowledge. The Hellenising Jews tried to put him to death.
He had to leave for Caesarea and eventually returned to his
native city (Acts 9:26, 30). He evangelized Cilicia up to the
time when, towards 44, Barnabas, who had been sent from Jerusalem to organize the Christian community in Antioch, wanted
his help and came to look for him at Tarsus. This was the start
of the great missionary journeys, whose principal episodes are
so well recounted by St. Luke in the Acts. They were eventually
to bring Paul to Rome. After further missions, which followed
an early period in captivity and of which we know little, his
apostolic career seems to have been brought to a close by a
glorious martyrdom, which took place in the capital of the
Empire, probably in A.D. 67.

Paul preached with unflagging energy throughout most of the Greco-Roman world. St. Luke has left a few examples of his oral teaching in the reports of the speeches at Pisidian Antioch (Acts 13:16–41, 46–47), Lystra (14:14–16), Athens (17:22–31), and Rome (28:23–28). His teaching is, however, known to us chiefly through his epistles, which were written as circumstances dictated in answer to the needs of the different Christian communities. Providentially, they give an almost complete picture of Pauline doctrine in spite of the episodic and fragmentary character of most of them. They are one of the chief treasures of the Church and, with the gospels, form the most attractive part of the inspired writings. But all the evidence goes to show that they constituted only a tiny part of Paul's apostolic labours. The earliest, the letter to the Galatians, was probably written in 49, about the middle of Paul's missionary life, after fourteen years of reflection and apostolic activity. Most of the epistles stand out like signposts through the second part of his apostolate. The last of all, the second to Timothy, was not written until shortly before his martyrdom. In these letters, we can see right from the beginning the complete maturity of his thought, which he later developed only slightly in one or two particulars, as events dictated.

The Pauline epistles, fourteen in number, are extremely varied in length and importance, ranging as they do from what is little more than a note to Philemon to the great theological fresco of the epistle to the Romans. They were authentic letters, addressed to communities or to specific individuals, but they were also intended to be given a certain publicity (Col. 4:15–16). They were circulated rapidly throughout the churches and the second epistle of St. Peter (3:15–16), written about 64 or a little later, already indicates the existence of a corpus of Pauline writings. In accordance with ancient custom, each epistle has an address at the beginning and a salutation at the end, written in the apostle's own hand (2 Thess. 3:17–18; Gal. 6:11 et seq.), the rest being dictated to a secretary (Rom. 16:22). The body of the epistle consists in many cases of a dogmatic survey, in which the emphasis is chiefly on doctrine, and a moral section in which the dominant note is one of exhortation. At other times, the style is more epistolary and difficult to analyse (2 Corinthians, Philippians, Philemon).

The only epistles whose authenticity has been contested are the second to the Thessalonians, the epistle to the Ephesians and the pastorals (1 and 2 Timothy and Titus). The arguments against the first named have been well refuted. It is more difficult to deal with the challenge to the pastoral epistles but they are generally agreed to contain at least fragments of Pauline writings. The rest may have been the work of a secretary or of an immediate disciple of the apostle and if that is so the connection with St. Paul may be considered sufficiently close. Many scholars are, however, prepared stoutly to defend the complete authenticity of these particular epistles.[1]

Like the other New Testament authors, St. Paul wrote, not in classical Greek, but in the *koine* dialect, used in commerce and business. Its wide diffusion throughout the Greco-Roman world was one of a large number of factors favouring the spread of Christianity. Through his familiarity with the Old Testament, the apostle frequently uses words and turns of phrase that are Hebrew or, to be more precise, biblical. This scriptural atmosphere gives his writings a character of their own. The style, moreover, reflects the man perhaps more than in the case of any other writer and this makes it both attractive and difficult. There

[1] The epistle to the Hebrews, which is the work of an unknown disciple, must be put in a category of its own. The Church has, however, always accepted it as Pauline because it follows St. Paul's teaching, and that is why we refer to it as readily as to the others. See Bonsirven, *Épître aux Hébreux* (Verbum Salutis), Beauchesne, 1943; Spicq, *Épître aux Hébreux* (Études Bibliques), Gabalda, 1952, I, 197–219.

is a fullness of thought and doctrine in the writings of the apostle that makes the words burst, as it were, under a pressure they are incapable of sustaining. This explains the abrupt and elliptical turns of phrase and the unexpected digressions that are such a trial to the reader, but it also explains the wonderful metaphors, glistening like diamonds.

The apostle's quick, penetrating and intuitive mind creates an added difficulty. St. Paul does not always allow himself time to express every stage in his argument but goes straight to the essential points and to the ultimate consequences,[2] leaving his opponent battered even if unconvinced. Paul trembles with eagerness, becomes heated, thinks of a hundred things at once, enlarges the meaning of words and opens tremendous vistas. Sometimes, he is content with a simple allusion. It is not easy, for instance, to tell what errors he has in mind in the epistles written during his captivity and in the pastoral epistles and we can do no more than guess at the nature of the baptism for the dead about which he writes to the Corinthians (1 Cor. 15:29). He gives one-sided accounts, pressing to the limit a single aspect of a question, the other side of which he will deal with later. The Mosaic law, so severely criticized because of the transgressions to which it gave rise (Gal. 3:19 et seq.), is later described as holy and just (Rom. 7:12). Marriage, at first apparently unfavourably

---

[2] Examples: If the Mosaic law remains necessary for salvation, Christ's death was needless and in turning people away from the law he served the cause of sin (Gal. 2:21,17). A group in Corinth had become exaggeratedly attached to Paul himself: was it Paul who was crucified for his disciples (1 Cor. 1:13)? Against impurity: Were they to take the members of Christ and make them one with the members of a harlot? (1 Cor. 6:15). In respect of meat sacrificed to idols: Were they to scandalize a brother for whom Christ had died? (1 Cor. 8:11). If the dead do not rise, nor is Christ risen and the teaching of the apostles and the faith become groundless (1 Cor. 15:14, etc.). Perhaps we must also take into account the distaste shown by the great mystics for methodical reflection and their difficulty in expressing what they have experienced (2 Cor. 12:4).

compared with virginity (1 Cor. 7:25–38), is later praised in a magnificent comparison between the marital union and the union of Christ with his Church (Eph. 5:22–33). God shows mercy where he wills and where it is his will he hardens men's hearts, but man nevertheless remains free and responsible (Rom. 9:14 et seq.). The unbelief of the Jews led the apostles to evangelize the heathen, thus exciting the emulation of Israel which will one day return to Christ (Rom. 11:11 et seq.). The reader has to take into account polemical exaggerations, bring together complementary points of view and make a synthesis of thought that is always found to be penetrating and accurate, once all its elements have been assembled. Sometimes subtle reasoning in the rabbinical manner seems to complicate the argument (Gal. 3:16; 4:21–31) and the thought appears to be presented in a series of developments and in a sort of concentric exposition recalling St. John, until it is finally brought to a precise formulation (Rom. 5:12–21; 6:1–11).

There is something vividly alive about this astonishing combination of depth in thought, clarity in intuition, and vigorous, subtle logic in dialectic. The apostle personifies the great realities he is studying. The law, the gospel, sin, death and the cross all take on substance as it were on his lips and come to play their part, sometimes in company with fictitious adversaries who dispute with them after the manner of the Stoics (Rom. 3; 10:14–31, etc.). Dominating everything is a clash of antitheses: law and faith, light and darkness, the letter and the spirit, freedom and slavery, the flesh and the spirit, the old man and the new, Adam and Christ. Here and there, we come across developments presented with an irresistible eloquence (Phil. 2:5–11; Eph. 1:3–14; 4:4–6). The attraction of such an inimitable style is easy to understand, for it gives free rein to all the feelings characteristic of the apostle's powerful personality. We discover the delicacy of a warm heart, animated by a charity universal in its embrace, and a sublimity of doctrine that is nevertheless accompanied by a sense of the practical realities and by consummate prudence. The apostle speaks with a gentle authority but knows at times how to be extremely severe. He shows complete unselfishness and an almost incredible strength of mind in the midst of trials of all kinds. His soul is on fire with the love of Christ (Gal. 2:19–21; Phil. 1:18–26; etc.). Paul is a great mystic and a man of action, a great writer and at the same time a man of great practical achievements. His mind instinctively tends towards higher things which inspire him with deep admiration and enthusiasm. His thought then takes on a lyrical form which dazzles and conquers the reader (1 Cor. 13; 15:21–28, 50–57; Rom. 8:31–39; 1 Tim. 3:16; etc.). Sometimes again, a great sweeping passage, rich in doctrine, suddenly and unexpectedly appears among exhortations (1 Cor. 6: 3, 17, 19, 20; 8:11; 10:31; 2 Cor. 8:9; etc.).

He normally draws his comparisons from everyday life – the yeast which is kneaded into the lump (1 Cor. 5:6–8), the games in the stadium (1 Cor. 9:24–27), the equipment of the Roman soldier (Eph. 6:13–17), the human body (1 Cor. 12:14–30), grafting (Rom. 11:17–24), building (1 Cor. 3:10–11), and the marriage bond (Eph. 5:25–32). Great traveller though he was, Paul seems to have remained indifferent to the beauties of nature and in this respect we can almost regret his gospel task. His apostolic mission closed his mind to everything else. He wanted only to be the ambassador of Christ (2 Cor. 5:20). His life was Christ (Phil. 1:21; Gal. 2:20). His constant care was for the churches (2 Cor. 11:28) and to make himself all things to all men (1 Cor. 9:21–22). But his care for the inner realities was accompanied by a gift of sympathy, well analysed by Newman, that gives him such a strong appeal and will continue to gain for him countless disciples, anxious to steep themselves in his teaching.[3]

[3] See Thils, *Pour mieux comprendre s. Paul,* de Brouwer, 1941; Brunot, *Le génie littéraire de saint Paul,* Éditions du Cerf, 1955.

This teaching was not based exclusively on the revelations received from Christ, rich though they were. Paul clearly owed much to his early training and to the different circles in which he moved. It will therefore be useful to enquire briefly into the influences to which he was subjected and which necessarily left a mark on his intellectual attitude and his teaching.

Like every rabbi, St. Paul was a man of the bible. He had a wonderfully deep knowledge of the Old Testament and was constantly alluding to it even when he was not directly quoting. His direct references to the sacred texts take on a variety of forms.[4] Often, he recalls the events and prophecies in accordance with the literal sense of the passages concerned,[5] sometimes, however, adding detail relating to the general context,[6] or again interpreting the sacred text so as to bring out the figure concerned, starting from the principle that the scriptures reach their fulfilment in Christ and that the history and institutions of Israel are all ordered towards Christ and tend towards him, prefiguring the more perfect realities for which they prepare.[7] The scriptures contain the shadows of future events (Col. 2:17) and it is in this perspective that their full, underlying sense can be understood and that the letter can be surpassed by the spirit. It is thus that Adam is the figure of Christ (Rom. 5:12–19), and that the justification of Abraham, obtained through faith, foreshadowed

[4] His readers did not know Hebrew and Paul usually quotes scripture from the Greek of the Septuagint. Sometimes, he quotes the general sense of a passage from memory and, at other times, combines a number of texts, perhaps making use of existing anthologies. See for example Rom. 3:10–18; 9:25–29; 2 Cor. 6:16–18; Gal. 3:7–14.

[5] For example, speaking of the Passion and the resurrection: Gal. 3:13; 1 Cor. 15:3–4.

[6] For example, texts from Habacuc (2:4) and the psalms (143:2) dealing with justification by faith, and Gal. 2:16; 3:11 and Rom. 1:17 and 3:20.

[7] This principle was not unknown to Judaism, ancient events being regarded as a preparation for Messianic times. See de Lubac, *A propos de l'allégorie chrétienne*, RSR, 1959, 5–44.

Christian justification (Gal. 3:6 et seq.; Rom. 4). Probably no one has been more enlightened by God than St. Paul on the continuity of the divine plan and on the outline and announcement contained in the Old Testament of what the New Testament was later to bring. No one has been granted a deeper insight than he into the abolition of the law by Christ's sacrifice and into the call to all peoples to faith in Jesus Christ. Certain details of the allegories used may seem to us artificial – as for instance in the opposition between Sara and Agar (Gal. 4:21–32) or when St. Paul is speaking of the significance of the veiling of Moses's face (2 Cor. 3:13–16) – but that does not affect the validity of the general principle. Holy scripture does not look to the past but must be interpreted in the light of Christ.

Thus we find scriptural texts used in the epistles, as indeed throughout the whole of the New Testament, for a wide range of purposes. Sometimes scripture is quoted merely as a literary embellishment, without concern for the sense.[8] Sometimes details are quoted to introduce an illustration of the writer's thought rather than to provide the basis for a real argument.[9] Nevertheless, St. Paul always has present in his own mind the essential point of the unity of the redemptive design, conceived by God from all eternity, prepared over the centuries and accomplished in Jesus Christ. This idea, which is at the root of his typology, induces him to make free use of the scriptures, unhampered by detailed exegesis and vain controversy, but always remaining faithful to the real spirit of the Old Testament, of which Christ is the fulfilment and the ultimate reason (Rom. 10:4). Certainly, no one could deny that St. Paul owes much to rabbinical methods, but he manages to avoid sterile argument and even more is he

[8] For instance, Rom. 10:18, quoting Ps. 19:5, 2 Cor. 8:14–15, quoting Exod. 16:18.

[9] Gal. 3:16; the singular collective noun used in Genesis to describe the posterity of Abraham prefigures Christ better than would a plural.

exempt from arbitrary interpretations, which would falsify the real meaning of the texts concerned. He derives something, again, from the Judaism of Alexandria, though more through the canonical Book of Wisdom than through the philosophical and theological speculation of Philo. There can be no doubt, too, that his teaching on the last things is influenced both in matter and form by the apocalyptic passages of the Old Testament and by certain extra-canonical Jewish apocalypses. It is also possible that Paul borrowed from the Essenes of Qumrân and Damascus. He may have been in contact with the latter and made some conversions among them. But all this is no more than speculation. There are some striking similarities of language between the epistles and the writings of the Essenes – for instance the use of expressions such as "earthen vessels" and "a share in the heritage of the saints". Other similarities are to be found in the links between the ideas of mystery, revelation and knowledge, in the names of Belial and Angel of Light attributed to Satan, in the distinction between light and darkness, and in the theology of the Holy Spirit.[10] Here and there we come across references to the fall and there is a deep sense of sin. The doctrine of justification is linked with the prophecy of Habacuc (2:14), but that is as far as the analogies take us. Qumrân attributed justification to the law and not to faith and there is nothing in the texts to remind us of the universality of Christianity (the sons of darkness are doomed to destruction). Even less is there any reminder in the writings of Qumrân of the teaching that Christ is the Son of God and Redeemer.[11]

Besides an appreciation of the significance of the prophecies,

[10] See Schmitt, *Les Écrits du N.T. et les textes de Qumrân*, Rev. S.R., 1956, 281.

[11] Vermès, *Les manuscrits du désert de Juda*, Desclée, 1953; Carmignac, *Le Docteur de justice et Jésus Christ*, L'Orante, 1957; Daniélou, *Les manuscrits de la mer Morte et les origines du Christianisme*, L'Orante, 1957, 94–8.

which he owed to his conversion, Saul had from childhood up derived from the scriptures a knowledge of the fundamental truths that gave Israel its enormous spiritual superiority over all other nations, in spite of its minor importance in the political scale. There was the essential dogma of one God, transcendent and creating; there were the doctrines of Providence and the divine ordering of the world, and those of original sin and of punishment extending beyond the tomb, the doctrine of the resurrection, and the precepts of the decalogue, taken up and epitomized in the precepts of charity towards God and one's neighbour. Paul also acquired from the sacred books a deep sense of God, a sense of sin, and the admirable religious spirit that constituted the priceless treasure of the true Israel and must remain the essential foundation of any civilization worthy of the name.

He owed a great deal, needless to say, to his brothers in the faith and received from them his first religious instruction, completing the revelations coming directly from heaven. His contacts with the apostles and the disciples were particularly useful to him for the detailed knowledge they furnished of our Lord's life and they led to a deepening of his understanding of the doctrines of the Trinity, the incarnation, the redemptive death of Christ, the sacraments, the last things, and the moral teaching that stems from them. He did not have the use of the synoptic gospels which, with the exception of the Aramaic gospel of St. Matthew, were written later than most of his epistles, but his use of the documents later collected by the evangelists is proved by the many similarities of language. The details he gives of Christ's earthly life provide a kind of outline biography. His speeches as reported in the Acts and the many references in the epistles (Acts 28:31; Rom. 6:17; 1 Cor. 15:1–11) indicate, too, that he had the benefit of a body of doctrine taught by all the preachers, a παράδοσις to which he was determined to conform his own teaching, lest he should take a useless course (Gal. 2:2; compare 1 Cor. 11:23; 15:11). Vividly original in character, he was still no innovator. Nobody was more careful than he to preserve absolute fidelity to the thought of the one Master, expressed in the common faith which all preachers of the gospel had the overriding duty and firm intention of transmitting in its full purity as a sacred deposit that must be defended from all deterioration.[12]

Although his main training was in the school of the bible, he could not be in touch with the Greek world from childhood upwards and throughout the course of his life without owing something to Hellenistic culture. Its influence seems, however, to have been superficial, so deeply was he marked by Judaism. The Jews had an insurmountable repugnance to Greco-Roman paganism. Paul himself condemns throughout the crude errors of its polytheism and its moral corruption (Rom. 1:18–32). Its false wisdom, expressed in empty rhetoric and closed as it was to the supernatural, met with his scorn. He described it as folly and contrasted it triumphantly with the higher wisdom of the gospel (1 Cor. 1:17–21, 26). Though it was a flourishing school of thought in Tarsus, Stoicism, even in its noblest aspirations, could have little attraction for St. Paul, for it involved a disappointing pantheism and an altogether weak idea of immortality. Hellenism influenced him only through its vocabulary and its literary processes and it is the everyday words rather than the terms of the

---

[12] 2 Thess. 1:10; 1 Cor. 1:6; 2 Cor. 9:13; Rom. 10:9–10; Eph. 4:14–15; Col. 2:7–8; 1 Tim. 2:6; 6:20; 2 Tim. 1:14. St. Paul's fidelity to the common doctrine is recognized by many non-Catholic commentators. This teaching assumed in Jerusalem a form that was more markedly Judeo-Christian than elsewhere but which became less so after the catastrophe of A.D. 70. Traces of it were nevertheless still to be found in the Apocrypha and in the Apostolic Fathers. See Daniélou, *Théologie du Judéo-Christianisme*, Desclée, 1958. Orthodox Judeo-Christianity insisted on the parallels between the first creation and the second, which followed the redemption, and on God's eternal design, rather than on the typology.

philosophers that are to be found in his writings. He partly depended also on a terminology he had built up for himself[13] and gave a fresh significance to a large number of terms current at the time, thus providing the language of Christian theology. The two poetical allusions to be found in his writings[14] do not provide sufficient proof that the apostle was familiar with Greek literature and there are no further indications of such knowledge.

The possibility that Paul borrowed something from the pagan mysteries has also been mooted, especially those mysteries relating to gods who died and were raised to life, and it has been suggested that this may have influenced his teaching on baptism and the Eucharist. To take this view, however, is to forget that the Judeo-Christians would never have tolerated such a contamination of doctrine and that the apostle himself abominated these mysteries and said so in his epistle to the Corinthians (2 Cor. 6:14–16; 1 Cor. 10:20–21). He could have known of them only indirectly from the testimony of initiates converted to Christianity, since the secrets were jealously guarded and, obviously, he had never had himself initiated. Like all Jews, he held idols in complete contempt (1 Cor. 8:4; 10:19) and the first thing he required of converts was that they should renounce them in order to devote themselves to the worship of the living God (1 Thess. 1:9). It is hard to see how such a determined attitude could be reconciled with an acceptance of pagan influences. It should be added that the amalgam of Greek and oriental religions in which one school professes to see resemblances with St. Paul's teaching is in fact a late syncretism which did not take on any real consistency until after the advent of Christianity, especially in regard to the Mithraic cult. As for the mysteries concerning gods who died and were raised (Attis and Osiris, the mysteries

[13] For instance, more than thirty words in συν, neologisms intended to express the idea of the Christian's union with Christ.

[14] Acts 17:28; Titus 1:12. See Brunot, op. cit., 75–82.

45

of Eleusis, etc.), these were to begin with no more than symbols of the springtide regeneration of the fruits of the earth. Afterwards, speculation commenced and there was an accretion of mythology, but this was a purely literary development, late to make its appearance. In spite of the respectable enough desire for immortality which may have been reflected in these cults, and leaving aside the question of the morality of the rites themselves, the atmosphere was entirely different from that of St. Paul's teaching. The observance of the rites of initiation was thought to produce an automatic effect, without requiring a turning away from sin or a spiritual change. The initiate aimed simply at earning for himself a pleasant life in the company of the gods, who were not loved for their own sakes. Even less was there any question of redemption and none of the gods died to obtain pardon for sinners. The mysteries were at the antipodes of the Pauline doctrine of a redeeming sacrifice and the uniting of the Christian to Christ in death to sin and in a life that looked towards God (Rom. 6:11 et seq.). The benefits aspired to by the initiates in these pagan mysteries had nothing in common with the supernatural benefit that Paul desired for Christians in the opening phrases of his letters, which christianized the Greek salutation[15] and gave a deeper meaning to the Greek form of address: "Grace and peace be yours from God who is our Father, and from the Lord Jesus Christ".[16]

[15] Using χάρις (grace) in place of χαῖρε (rejoice).

[16] For a study of St. Paul's thought and the factors influencing it, see also the works quoted in the course of this chapter: Bonsirven, *Exégèse rabbinique et exégèse paulinienne,* Beauchesne 1939; SDB, *Citations de l'Ancien Testament dans le Nouveau,* Venard; Lagrange, *Le Judaïsme avant Jésus-Christ* (Études Bibliques), Gabalda, 1931; Festugière, *L'idéal religieux des Grecs et l'Évangile* (Études Bibliques), Gabalda, 1932; Lagrange, *L'Orphisme* (Études Bibliques), Gabalda, 1937; DA, *Les mystères païens et s. Paul,* Jacquier; SDB, *Baptême,* Coppens; Allo, *L'évolution de l'Évangile de Paul,* Vivre et Penser, RB 1941, 48–77; 165–193; SDB, *Mystères dans la Bible* (Prümm).

PART ONE

SALVATION THROUGH CHRIST

3

THE GREAT REALITY: SALVATION

> *"Such prayer is our duty, it is what God, our Saviour, expects of us, since it is his will that all men should be saved, and be led to recognize the truth" (1 Tim. 2:4–5).*

THE Pauline epistles contain a certain number of important themes which are closely interlinked and appear as various aspects of a single, overriding reality. Commentators, who are agreed on fundamentals, do not all look upon these themes in the same light. Some see redemption as the essential idea, while others take it to be the doctrine of incorporation in the dead and risen Christ, or look for it in the doctrine of justification and grace. Each of these approaches is valid enough but incorporation in Christ and grace are consequences of the redemption and the redemption itself is one element in a wider and more comprehensive reality which is the universal salvation wished for by God and brought about by Christ's sacrifice. The term salvation with its derivatives, although less frequently met with in the epistles than "grace" and "justice", seems to express the idea that is really dominant in St. Paul.[1]

Salvation was the great preoccupation in apostolic times. What mattered for the faithful above all else was to be saved (Acts

[1] See Cerfaux, *Christ in the Theology of St. Paul,* Herder and Herder, 1–3.

15:1,11). The gospel was one of salvation, the good news of salvation (Eph. 1:13), the way of salvation (Acts 16:17), a divine force for the salvation of all believers (Rom. 1:16). What is meant by this complex notion?

Interpreting the word in a secular sense, salvation is to be seen first as deliverance from the greatest of evils for one of the faithful – divine vengeance, death and eternal damnation.

In the celebrated passage in which he likens various aspects of the gospel to pieces of Roman armour, Paul speaks of the helmet of salvation (Eph. 6:17), regarding it as an effective protection against the dangers menacing the Christian, and the greatest of these is the danger that he will suffer divine vengeance in the shape of the Creator's well-merited anger with sinful man. This anger fell upon the unbelieving Jews (1 Thess. 2:16) and would not spare the heathen who rejected the gospel (Rom. 2:5–8). Nor would it spare rebel Christians who came to live like pagans (Col. 3:6–8; Eph. 5:6). The times before the coming of Christ were times of wrath, resulting from the universal spread of sin, of which the opening of the epistle to the Romans provides us with such a dark picture. The heathens failed to recognize the Creator in his works and God abandoned them to the aberrations of their foolish hearts and to their guilty lusts. The Jews, who were so proud of their privileges, had not observed the law or kept the high ideal that it prescribed for them. Sin had extended its baneful dominion over the whole human race but the forecast of a new time, one of pardon (2 Cor. 6:2), succeeds this terrible picture. The blood of Christ had obtained the forgiveness of all their sins for those who were eventually to believe in him. God's infinite mercy justifies us through the blood of the redeemer, sinners as we are, and "children of wrath" (Eph. 2:3 [Douai]). Enemies of God, we are reconciled with him by the death of his Son. All the more so shall we be saved by his life, preserved by him from the vengeance that would have irrevocably fallen upon

us on the day of judgement had we remained in our sins (Rom.
5: 9–10). Jesus saves us from the anger which falls on hardened
sinners (1 Thess. 1:10) and Paul is able to cry in triumph, "God
has not destined us for vengeance; he means us to win salvation
through our Lord Jesus Christ" (1 Thess. 5: 9).

By freeing us from sin, salvation preserves us from death at
the same time as it delivers us from vengeance. Through sin
death came into the world (Rom. 5:12), not simply bodily death,
which is its punishment, but also spiritual death, the culmination
of sin's baneful dominion (Rom. 5:21). St. Paul sometimes
speaks of one, sometimes of the other and sometimes of both
at once when he insistently repeats that sin leads to death, that
death is the wages of sin (Rom. 6:16, 21, 23), and that sin
brings death (Rom. 7:11, 13). But he affirms constantly, by
way of contrast, that Christ brings life and that it is our own
choice whether we participate in it. The preachers of the gospel
are "Christ's incense offered to God, making manifest both
those who are achieving salvation and those who are on the
road to ruin; as a deadly fume where it finds death, as a life-
giving perfume where it finds life" (2 Cor. 2:15–16). If we
live a life of nature, we are marked out for death. If we mortify
the ways of nature through the power of the Spirit we live
(Rom. 8:13) and Christ sets us free, if we so wish, from the
domination of sin and of death (Rom. 8:2). It is sin that gives
death its sting (1 Cor. 15:56), and by renouncing sin we escape
death in its spiritual form now and we escape bodily death on
the day of the resurrection.

The horizon extends to the future life. We will not be saved
in the full sense of the word unless we avoid eternal perdition
(2 Thess. 1:9; Phil. 3:19), and the apostle frequently recalls
the eventual possibility of damnation. It is a question of faithfulness to the message committed to him and of a necessary
warning. Hardened sinners are "vessels of wrath, fitted for

destruction" (Rom. 9:22 [Douai]), whereas salvation is promised to those who hold firm in the faith of the gospel (Phil. 1:27–28), whom God has chosen from the beginning to save (2 Thess. 2:13). The others will not escape eternal punishment, "far from the presence of the Lord, and the majesty of his power" (2 Thess. 1:9) and ruin will fall upon them suddenly like the pangs that come to a woman in travail (1 Thess. 5:3). Those for whom the message of the cross is but folly will be lost, while to those who are on the way to salvation, it is the evidence of God's power (1 Cor. 1:18). We shall not be saved unless we live in fear of eternal punishment.

Nevertheless, for the Christian, fear should not be the predominant attitude and still less should it exclude other dispositions. Salvation means freedom from sin and from the evils due to sin, but it is also the possession of the good things promised by Christ in this life and in the other in such a way that hope and love will always be there to temper fear. Preservation from sin and death implies the opening of the way to justice and eternal life. These two aspects are inseparable and, whatever he may do in the actual formulation, the apostle does not separate them in his thought.

The divine promises surpass anything the human heart can conceive (1 Cor. 2:9). To those who love him and persevere in doing good, God promises eternal life (Rom. 2:7) and has intended also "to make known the riches of his glory in respect of those vessels of mercy whom he has already destined for glory" (Rom. 9:23).[2] The divine gifts are offered to the faithful from this life onwards and will be given in their fullness in eternity. There are thus two phases of salvation – beginning and consummation.

The first stage is that of hope, but it already involves a certain measure of real possession, imperfect though it is, of the eternal reward. "It is in hope that we have been saved" (Rom. 8:24).[3]

[2], [3] Translator's own rendering.

The condition of this first phase of salvation is faith understood in its Pauline sense, the essential points being the divinity of Christ and his resurrection: "Thou canst find salvation, if thou wilt use thy lips to confess that Jesus is the Lord, and thy heart to believe that God has raised him up from the dead. The heart has only to believe, if we are to be justified; the lips have only to make confession, if we are to be saved.... Everyone who calls upon the name of the Lord will be saved" (Rom. 10:9, 10, 13). Looked at from a more subjective point of view, this dawning of salvation is life in Christ: "Christ among you, your hope of glory.... Your life is hidden away now with Christ in God" (Col. 1:27; 3:3). So much is this the case that Paul is able to make his admirable assertion: "And yet I am alive; or rather, not I; it is Christ that lives in me" (Gal. 2:20). To describe the new state of the Christian, he repeats again and again that he is *in Christo Jesu.*

Ultimate salvation consists in being with Christ, in living eternally in Christ's blessed company. "And so we shall be with the Lord for ever" (1 Thess. 4:17). This great promise makes us regard our present life as an exile far from the Lord and to long for the future life, accepting death if necessary in order to achieve it. "We take heart, I say, and have a mind rather to be exiled from the body, and at home with the Lord" (2 Cor. 5:8). Only his preoccupation with his apostolic duties could counterbalance for St. Paul the ardour of his desire. He opens his heart on the subject to the Philippians in moving terms: "For me, life means Christ; death is a prize to be won. But what if living on in this mortal body is the only way to harvest what I have sown? Thus I cannot tell what to choose.... I long to have done with it and be with Christ, a better thing, much more than a better thing; and yet, for your sakes, that I should wait in the body is more urgent still" (Phil. 1:21–24).

To be admitted into the company of Christ signifies to enter eternal life and to participate in his glory. "Now that you are free from the claims of sin... you have a harvest in your sanctification, and your reward is eternal life. Sin offers death, for wages; God offers us eternal life as a free gift, through Christ Jesus our Lord" (Rom. 6:22–23). The gift of sanctifying grace brings eternal life (Rom. 5:21), since "our Saviour Jesus Christ... has annulled death, now he has shed abroad the rays of life and immortality, through that gospel which I have been appointed to herald" (2 Tim. 1:10). The justification, mercifully granted by God, makes us heirs, with the hope of eternal life set before us (Titus 3:7). This supreme object of hope is attained by anyone admitted after death into the company of Christ. It implies participation in the very glory of God and of the Saviour. God invites us to the glory of his kingdom (1 Thess. 2:12), and the temporary trial of earthly life "brings with it a reward multiplied every way, loading us with everlasting glory" (2 Cor. 4:17). For the Christian, hope is hope of attaining glory as sons of God (Rom. 5:2). Every Christian ready to suffer will be glorified with him (Rom. 8:17). Possession of Christ during this earthly life implies hope of future glory (Col. 1:27). The elect will "have a share in the salvation that is in Christ, and eternal glory with it" (2 Tim. 2:10).[4] Finally, glorification will transform the body itself, raising it when Christ returns in triumph. "Christ is your life, and when he is made manifest, you too will be made manifest in glory with him" (Col. 3:4). It is then that salvation will be fully realized.

These promises did not come completely unheralded, and the apostle shows that the Old Testament not only foreshadows them but even applies them for the first time in the case of Abraham, who was justified through faith. Their novelty is, however, evident in every aspect. It is shown both in the magnificence of

---

[4] Translator's own rendering.

54

these divine gifts and in two characteristics to which we shall again have to turn later — the universality and the gratuity of salvation. God wishes to save all men. He makes no distinction between Jews and the heathen (1 Tim. 2:4; Rom. 10:12). His gift of salvation is an act of pure generosity on his part to which sinners have no claim (Eph. 2:8; Titus 3:5). Human pride is thus set at naught and the sinner cannot take credit as the author of his own salvation. Paul frequently insists on the necessity of humility (1 Cor. 1:29; 4:7; Rom. 3:24–27; 4:2, 16; Eph. 2:9). He is all the more inclined to stress the point since, in his own conversion, he experienced how completely gratuitous was the divine election that set him apart from the time he was in his mother's womb (Gal. 1:15), as had previously been the case with Jeremias (Jer. 1:5). It is from God and God alone that salvation comes to men through Jesus Christ.

4

DIVINE INITIATIVE IN SALVATION. ITS GRATUITOUSNESS AND UNIVERSALITY

*"The grace of God has dawned, a source
of salvation for all men" (Titus 2:11).*[1]

THE very idea of salvation as expressed in the epistles supposes that God is its author by a providential initiative which leaves man free to give or withhold consent. The supernatural character of salvation shows that it is a free gift and a work of pure mercy.

The salvation of the human race is the fulfilment of a plan formed by God from all eternity. "Blessed be that God, that Father of our Lord Jesus Christ, who has blessed us, in Christ, with every spiritual blessing, higher than heaven itself. He has chosen us out, in Christ, before the foundation of the world, to be saints, to be blameless in his sight, in his love; marking us out beforehand (so his will decreed) to be his adopted children through Jesus Christ" (Eph. 1:3–5). This deeply impressive opening to the epistle to the Ephesians continues with a fresh assertion of the free predestination of the elect which is completed by their election to a heavenly inheritance and followed by the efficacious call of the gospel to Jews and Gentiles alike (1:11–14). An eloquent passage in the epistle to the Romans, in which Paul deals at one and the same time with the past, the present and the future, shows even more clearly the divine plan

---

[1] Translator's own rendering.

and its application: "All those who from the first were known to him, he has destined from the first to be moulded into the image of his Son, who is thus to become the eldest-born among many brethren. So predestined, he called them; so called, he justified them; so justified, he glorified them" (Rom. 8:29–30). God knew and singled out those whom he wished to shower with his gifts, and he predestined them to become like his Son, foreseeing all the means necessary to attain this end. This plan is realized on earth and, through it, God has successively called his elect to the faith and then justified them. Paul boldly anticipates, relying on the certitude furnished by Christian hope: so justified, he glorified them.

These elliptical passages, full as they are of doctrine, indicate through their context with what infinite love God has conceived and executed his eternal plan (Eph. 3:11). He did not spare his own Son but gave him up for us all (Rom. 8:32). It is through love that he marked us out beforehand, according to an interpretation of Eph. 1:5 which is at least probable. It is his goodness that led him to reconcile the world to himself in Christ (2 Cor. 5:19). The effective gift of salvation was inspired by his goodness and his love (Titus 3:4–5). In the same fashion, Christ offered himself for us with an ineffable love (Gal. 1:4; 2:20; Eph. 5:2) from which no earthly power can separate us (Rom. 8:35–38).

There are similar sentiments in many other passages. We are enjoined to thank God our Father "for making us fit to share the light which saints inherit, for rescuing us from the power of darkness, and transferring us to the kingdom of his beloved Son" (Col. 1:12–13). The beloved Son, that is, "who gave himself as a ransom for them all" (1 Tim. 2:6). God has thus acted in the richness of his mercy. "With what an excess of love he loved us.... He would have all future ages see, in that clemency which he showed us in Christ Jesus, the surpassing richness of his grace" (Eph. 2:4,7). His love shone all the more in that we were sinners and enemies of God (Rom. 5:8, 10).

Love implies the complete freedom and gratuitousness of the gift. Paul repeatedly affirms that the plan of salvation and its realization are to be attributed to the free and generous exercise of God's will. He marked us out beforehand, "for so his will decreed...to make known to us the hidden purpose of his will. It was his loving design, for it is he who is at work everywhere, carrying out the designs of his will" (Eph. 1:5, 9, 11). Man had no prescriptive right. The whole work of salvation is gratuitous. The expression is a happy one and the apostle constantly repeats it, for the gratuity of salvation, and of the supernatural gifts which prepare the way for it, is in a way the essential truth.[2] God grants us justification "as a free gift from his grace" (Rom. 3:24). The good works that man had been able to accomplish had been merely a negative preparation and this applied particularly to the works prescribed by the Mosaic law, in which the Jews sometimes took an inordinate pride.[3] Such works do not give any right to expect divine gifts as a salary due in justice, the gifts being of a different order and an expression of divine bounty, freely given. "And if it is due to grace, then it is not due to works; otherwise grace would be grace no longer" (Rom. 11:6).[4] "Has he not saved us, and called us to a vocation of holiness? It was not because of anything we had done; we owe it to his own design, to the grace lavished on us" (2 Tim.

---

[2] It is not, moreover, a new truth. All the acts of divine generosity that studded the Old Testament were also gratuitous — for instance the vocation of Abraham and the patriarchs, the Exodus, the covenant made on Sinai, the Messianic promises, the forgiveness extended so many times to a sinful Israel, and the partial gift of the Spirit. But the gratuitous character of the divine favours is more apparent than ever under the new covenant.

[3] We shall turn to this question again later in dealing with the abolition of the Mosaic law.

[4] Translator's own rendering.

1:9), and "it was not thanks to anything we had done for our own justification. In accordance with his own merciful design he saved us" (Titus 3:5). Man is thus constrained to adopt an attitude of complete humility. He has no right to glorify himself because he counts for nothing in his own elevation to the supernatural order. Self-glorification is out of place for Jew and heathen alike. No creature has any ground for boasting in the presence of God (1 Cor. 1:29). There is nothing of what we have that did not come to us from God and we have no right to take glory in it, as we might have done had it not been a gift (1 Cor. 4:7). "What has become, then, of thy pride? No room has been left for it. On what principle? The principle which depends on observances? No, the principle which depends on faith" (Rom. 3:27). Had Abraham been justified by his works, he would have had something to be proud of, but it was not so. It was his faith in the divine promises, themselves completely gratuitous, that was reckoned virtue in him, "according to God's gracious plan" (Rom. 4:2, 3, 16). In his own case, Paul had a deep understanding of the fact that God had called him by grace (Gal. 1:15). He applies unhesitatingly to everybody what he has already said of Abraham (Rom. 4:4–5). It is determined that no one shall have anything to say for himself (Rom. 3:19) and all vainglory is out of place. Pride, whether it be that of the Pharisee of old or of the rationalist of today, acts as a barrier to salvation offered by God. The condition of obtaining graces is recognition of God's transcendence and of the gratuitousness of the supernatural order. This is the underlying truth that demands the submission of the stiff-necked in a humbly prayerful attitude, respectfully awaiting divine bounty.

Salvation, as we have seen, is always presented as the work of the Father and the Son in common, or rather as the work of the Father through the Son. When the time appointed for the redemption came, God sent out "on a mission to us" his Son born of a woman (Gal. 4:4), "in flesh like sinful flesh in order to overcome sin" (Rom. 8:3).[5] Redemption was obtained and men were reconciled to God by the sacrifice of the blood of Jesus (Rom. 3:24; 5:10). Paul follows the example of Peter (Acts 4:12; 5:31) in attributing to Christ the title of Saviour (Acts 13:23; Titus 1:4; 2:13; 3:6). Jesus came as Saviour to enlighten us on the divine plan of the redemption (2 Tim. 1:9–10). "He can perfectly save those who through him make their way to God" (Heb. 7:25)[6] and we await his coming as Saviour for the final stage of salvation which is the glorification of our own bodies, moulded into the image of his glorified body (Phil. 3:20). But the Father is equally Saviour because he has sent his Son to redeem men and in him has reconciled the world to himself (2 Cor. 5:19). This idea is to be found throughout the epistles and the title of Saviour is specifically given to the Father in the pastoral epistles (1 Tim. 1:1; 2:3; 4:10; Titus 1:3; 2:10–11; 3:4). The mission of the Holy Spirit, too, is several times mentioned in conjunction with that of the Son. The gift of the Holy Spirit makes us children of the Father by adoption and co-heirs with Christ, and the adoption of sons is the fruit of the redemption (Gal. 4:6; Rom. 8:15–17).

God's initiative of salvation has a universal aspect, for he is the God of all. "Is God the God of the Jews only? Is he not the God of the Gentiles too?" (Rom. 3:29). He wishes all men to be saved and to come to a knowledge of the truth. He is the one God and Christ is the one mediator between him and men (1 Tim. 2:4–5). The affirmation of this universal will for salvation was a complete novelty. Judaism had misunderstood the prophecies announcing that all people would one day adore the God of Israel (Isa. 2:1–5; 45:22; 52:10; 60; Ps. 22:28; etc.),

[5] Translator's own rendering.
[6] Ibid.

and the Gentiles, held in scorn by the chosen people, and strangers to the divine promises, were, so to speak, without God in the world (Eph. 2:12). The doctrine of the universal call to salvation, which seems so natural to us, did not prevail without difficulty in the primitive Church.

The pentecostal converts do not seem to have had the remotest idea of associating with Gentiles. Peter himself understood the providential plan only after a vision in which God showed him that the Mosaic law was superseded and when he saw the Holy Ghost come down upon the centurion, Cornelius, and his family (Acts 10). Once back in Jerusalem, he had to meet the criticisms of the Jewish Christians and justify his actions (Acts 11:1–18). Later, in Antioch, where there were many who had come to Christianity from paganism, he refrained from eating with them for fear of offending the Judaists from Jerusalem. This change of attitude seriously threatened divisions within the Christian community and Paul vigorously rebuked the chief of the apostles for his inconsistent behaviour (Gal. 2:11–21).

The law caused Paul himself no hesitations or heart searchings. From the time of his conversion, he was the apostle of the Gentiles and understood that there was no salvation except in Jesus Christ and that the law was abolished, but this did not lead him to turn away from his fellow-countrymen, for whom he never ceased to feel the greatest affection (Rom. 9:1–5). Everywhere he went, he began by preaching the gospel in their midst because it was to the people through whom Christ derived his human nature that the good news must first of all be given (Acts 13:46). But there were never very many conversions and on a number of occasions the Jews were responsible for starting a persecution against the apostle (Acts 13:13–52; 14:1–6, 19–20; 17:1–14; 18:12–17). Only from the Jews of Ephesus and Rome did he get a better reception (Acts 19:10–17; 28:23–29).

The unbelief of Israel was a source of great sorrow to Paul

(Rom. 9:1–3), but in a famous passage in the epistle to the Romans (9–11) he shows not only that the chosen people was not completely rejected (he was himself a living witness of this), but also that it was not to be final and must be regarded as having a providential purpose. God is always able to draw good from the evil he permits. He had not disowned his people and they remained dear to him for the sake of their fathers. He did not repent of the gifts he made (11:2,28). Indeed, the effect of the faithlessness of Israel had been to turn the preachers of the gospel towards the Gentiles, of whom a large number had come to salvation. The result of this would one day be a fruitful example for the Jews. "Blindness has fallen upon a part of Israel, but only until the tale of the Gentile nations is complete; then the whole of Israel will find salvation" (Rom. 11:25–26). The conversion of the Israelites would even be easier than that of the Gentiles for it would be a question of grafting them on to the olive to which they belonged by nature whereas the Gentiles had been cut from the wild olive and grafted unnaturally into a maiden olive (11:23–24). The apostle adds, addressing the converts from paganism:

> You were once rebels, until through their rebellion you obtained pardon; they are rebels now, obtaining pardon for you, only to be pardoned in their turn. Thus God has abandoned all men to their rebellion, only to include them all in his pardon (Rom. 11:30–31).[7]

[7] This expression seems hard and paradoxical and several others could be quoted (9:14–18). But they must be considered in their own context, lest, as has too often happened, they be misinterpreted. God is free both in the disposal of his gifts and in the direction of his call. But no one arouses his anger without having merited it. Lack of faith always remains without excuse and to profit by God's mercy, it is necessary to have avoided resisting him. When he "hardens" men it is through enlightenment and miracles so that the hardening is due to their own bad dispositions. Israel is temporarily rejected, but only through its own fault.

Looked at from this point of view, God's designs are seen to be admirable (Rom. 11:33–36). And when Israel turns to the gospel, it will be a marvel, a resurrection from the dead and the source of innumerable blessings (Rom. 11:15) to be added to those arising from the conversion of the heathen.

While awaiting this ardently desired outcome, Paul boldly proclaims the abolition of the Mosaic law, stressing the point particularly in his epistles to the Romans and the Galatians, and he also emphasizes the call of faith addressed to the Gentiles. His clarity of vision, which had a supernatural origin, enabled the Church to overcome the difficulty involved in the transition from a Jewish to a universal Christianity. After the incidents in Galatia, he is to be found taking a definite stand in a particularly forthright epistle, and before this he had already refused to have his disciple Titus circumcised and had withstood Peter at the time of the trouble in Antioch (Gal. 2:3, 11 et seq.). At the Council of Jerusalem, held a short time afterwards, he succeeded in imposing "the true principles of the gospel"[8] (Gal. 2:5). The view of the Judaists, who contended that circumcision was necessary for salvation, was rejected and it was decided that Gentile Christians were not to be obliged to observe the Mosaic law. A minimum number of provisions of the law were kept in force in order to permit Jews and Gentiles to eat in common and partake together of the Holy Eucharist. These consisted of abstention from meat that had been sacrificed to idols, from the flesh of

While looking at things from God's point of view, St. Paul assumes individual freedom and responsibility and deals, moreover, at much greater length with the lack of faith of Israel taken as a whole than with the predestination of individuals to whom the possibility of conversion is always open (11:14). We must also take into account a characteristic of Semitic writing which readily overlooks secondary causes, relating everything directly to God. See our *Enseignement de s. Paul,* 11, 169–80.

[8] This chronology seems to us probable though it is much debated.

beasts that had been strangled, and from fornication (Acts 15:1–35). This was a liberation, for, as the apostle continually proclaimed, the Greco-Roman world would never have become Christian had it been necessary first of all to become Jewish.

Not satisfied with merely showing that the law was abolished,[9] he contrasted God's true Israel, made up of the community of the faithful, and Israel according to the flesh (Gal. 6:16). He also contrasted the children of Abraham's faith, who were his real posterity, with his children by natural descent (Gal. 3:6; Rom. 9:7–8). In another passage, he makes a distinction between the circumcision achieved in the heart and that according to the flesh (Rom. 2:25–29; Col. 2:11). He links in a further series of comparisons the new rule of the spirit and the old one of the letter (Rom. 7:6), and grace and the law (Rom. 6:14). "Circumcision means nothing, the want of it means nothing; when a man is in Christ Jesus, there has been a new creation" (Gal. 6:15). For Paul, the appeal of faith to the Gentiles is a lofty conception, emanating from God, a mystery only imperfectly understood before the advent of Christ and now revealed through the Holy Spirit. "Through the Gospel preaching the Gentiles are to win the same divine promise, in Christ Jesus" (Eph. 3:6). In accordance with God's eternal plan, Paul was specially charged to announce this mystery and to make known to the heathen the unfathomable riches of Christ and God's infinitely varied wisdom (Eph. 3:8–10). Henceforth, the Gentiles had Christ among them, their hope of glory (Col. 1:27). Jews and Gentiles, formerly enemies, were reconciled as one new man in Christ, united in a single body (Eph. 2:16). By his cross and his blood, he had made a single people out of two peoples and had brought close those who were once far away (Eph. 2:13–14). The Gentiles were no longer foreigners or passing guests. "The saints are your fellow-citizens, you belong to God's household. Apostles and

[9] See ch. 5 below.

prophets are the foundation on which you were built, and the chief corner-stone of it is Jesus Christ himself" (Eph. 2:19–20). In the overriding unity of Christ, different characteristics lose their significance. "Here is no more Gentile and Jew, no more circumcised and uncircumcised, no one is barbarian or Scythian, no one is slave or free man; there is nothing but Christ in any of us" (Col. 3:11). This was a triumphant proclamation of the divine plan of salvation.[10]

While it demonstrated God's mercy and his great love for man (Titus 3:4), this stimulating picture of universal salvation had, as its end and final aim, God's glorification. God had fulfilled his eternal plan "to the splendour of his grace... for the exaltation and praise of his glory" (Eph. 1:6, 12, 14).[11] It could hardly be otherwise, but it is good to hear Paul recall this fundamentally religious thought that was ever in the mind of Christ as he worked for the glory of his Father. At the end of time, the Saviour will return to him his kingdom which will have achieved its completion (1 Cor. 15:24). But even now, writes the apostle to the Corinthians, "everything is for you, whether it be Paul, or Apollo, or Cephas, or the world, or life, or death, or the present, or the future; it is all for you, and you for Christ, and Christ for God" (1 Cor. 3:21–23). His final word as he contemplated the divine mercies was to be: "Honour and glory through endless ages to the king of all the ages, the immortal, the invisible, who alone is God, Amen" (1 Tim. 1:17).

Such is the infinite embrace of the divine plan of salvation. It is being realized in the Church and was prepared over the centuries, before entering through Jesus Christ into its final stage.

---

[10] The parallel between Adam and Christ (1 Cor. 15:21–22; Rom. 5:15 and 18–21) implies the universality of the call to salvation. See the following chapter and SDB, *Mystères dans la Bible*, 189–224.

[11] Translator's own rendering.

5

PREPARATION AND WAITING FOR
SALVATION

*"But, in these days, God's way of justi-
fication has at last been brought to light;
one which was attested by the law and
the prophets" (Rom. 3:21).*

THE salvation brought by Christ was preceded by a long period
of waiting going back to Adam's fall which had precipitated the
human race into sin and made the redemption necessary, provided
that God in his mercy wished to raise fallen humanity and reconcile it with himself. The promise that followed the fall (Gen.
3:16) and the covenant made with Noe after the deluge (Gen. 9:9
et seq.) gave a foretaste of the exercise of this mercy. The covenant
with Abraham and his posterity (Gen. 17) whereby the patriarch
was justified by God because of his faith in the promises (Gen.
15:6), foreshadowed more clearly the ultimate covenant.
Finally, the covenant with Israel, concluded through Moses,
added to the obligation of faith that of observing the law given
by God on Sinai (Exod. 19:6; 24:7–8). Subsequently, the
prophets announced the new and more perfect covenant which
was to extend to the whole of humanity (Jer. 31:31–34; Ezech.
36:26–28; Isa. 55:3; 59:21; 61:8). Besides specific quotations
from the Old Testament, Paul frequently recalls the words of the
prophets in more general terms (Rom. 1:2; 3:21; 16:26; Heb.
1:1). There is an unbroken continuity in God's plan. Paul

66

demonstrated it particularly by laying stress on the three principal stages of religious history before Christ, which were marked by Adam, Abraham and Moses. The epistle to the Galatians mentions only the two last stages, but the letter to the Romans goes right back to the first man.

I. Adam and the Fall

The important text is Rom. 5:12–21, which has to be read in conjunction with 1 Cor. 15:21–22, 45–49 and with other passages of lesser importance. In this as in other cases, we shall have to depart from the chronological order of the epistles, the teachings of which were determined by the problems and needs of the individual churches and do not, from the doctrinal point of view, constitute a composite and well ordered whole.

The doctrine of the fall formed part of Judaism as commonly held at the time of the gospel. The account given in Gen. 3 indicates that the punishment for the first sin was not merely bodily death but also separation from God and the loss of his friendship. Other texts are held by some to suggest the sinful character of the first fault and the universal corruption of humanity. One of these is verse 7 of the Miserere Psalm: "Evil was I born, a sinner did my mother conceive me." And Job 14:4 in the Septuagint reads: "None is free from all stain, did he but live a single day."[1]

The Book of Wisdom (2:24) asserts more explicitly: "But by the envy of the devil, death came into the world: And they follow him that are of his side." The context associates physical and spiritual death, contrasting the lot of sinners with that of the just who are "in the hand of God" and whose death is merely apparent. "In the sight of the unwise they seemed to die... but

[1] Translator's own rendering.

they are in peace... Their hope is full of immortality" (3:1, 2, 4). The death of the sinner is here regarded as a breach with God and as the deprivation of salvation. Moreover, following the lead of the Book of Ecclesiasticus (25:33), several apocryphal books link the fall of man with the sin of Adam or with that of Eve. (Examples are The Life of Adam and Eve, the Apocalypses of Moses and Baruch and, above all, the 4th Book of Esdras, chapter 3). A similar teaching is enshrined in the Qumrân documents (Hymn 4, line 26; Manual of Discipline col. 11). Paul has thus no need to produce proof of the fall. Nevertheless, in a sequence of arguments in which he shows that our unhappy interdependence in Adam is superabundantly compensated for by our interdependence in Jesus Christ, he points out that the fall was in the nature of a sin:

> Just as through one man sin came into the world, and by sin death, and just as in this way death affected all men owing to the fact that (or because) all have sinned.... Even up to the time of the law there was indeed sin in the world, but sin is not imputed where there is no law. Nevertheless, death reigned from Adam until Moses over those who had not committed sin like to the transgression of Adam, who was the type of him who was to come. (Rom. 5:12–14).[2]

The fall of the first man was the sign for the baneful entry into the world[3] of sin, with death as its consequence (Gen. 2:17; 3:19). Judging by the passages in the same epistle in which Paul represents death as the wages of sin, contrasting it with supernatural life and eternal life, and judging by his significant reference to the Book of Wisdom, we are inclined to believe that he is here thinking not simply of bodily death but, in conjunction with it, of spiritual death and eternal death. The passages con-

[2] Translator's own rendering.
[3] St. Paul does no more than allude to Eve (2 Cor. 11:3; 1 Tim. 2:13–14) because she is not the head of the human race (1 Cor. 11:3).

cerned are Rom. 6:21, 23; 7:5, 10, 13; 8:2, 6, and they are to be compared with 1 Cor. 15:56. Verses 17–21 of Rom. 5 express the same antithesis, from which it seems to follow that death is to be regarded as the deprivation of salvation and the final separation from God, of which physical death is a conspicuous accompaniment of obvious importance. Death understood in this sense touches all men, from the fact that all have sinned.[4] Paul is referring here only to adults. They have all sinned. The expulsion from the Garden of Eden was followed by a terrible unleashing of sin among the descendants of the first man. St. Paul has in mind their personal sins but considered in relation to the sin of Adam which they have so to speak ratified, becoming the responsible victims of the power of sin, of the moral disease introduced into the world by sin. This power of sin fell upon men, showing its effect on them through their own personal sins. These sins are not the cause of death but the consequence of the fallen state to which the sin of Adam reduced humanity.

All had in reality sinned until the arrival of Jesus Christ, who was to repair the consequences of the first transgression. The period between Adam and Moses had been marked in a terrible

---

[4] We adopt here the view expressed by Lyonnet in his appendix to Huby's commentary on the epistle to the Romans, pages 523 et seq. He bases himself on the authority of most of the Greek Fathers. Many modern commentators (including the author in his *Enseignement de s. Paul*, I, 142–5) translate the end of verse 12 as "because all have sinned", believing the subsequent verses to show that it is original sin, and not personal sins, that is in question. No one adopts any longer the translation "In him (Adam) all have sinned" given in the Vulgate. Such a rendering would emphasize more directly the transmission of the original sin but does not seem grammatically possible. Moreover, the transmission is formally indicated in verses 18 to 20. Mgr. Cerfaux, in *Christ in the Theology of St. Paul*, 230, suggests another translation, "on account of him by whom all have sinned". St. Paul's thought is complex. For further details see Lagrange, *Épître aux Romains* (Études Bibliques), Gabalda, and particularly Dubarle, *Le péché originel dans l'Écriture* (Lectio divina), 1958, 120–72 (with a full bibliography).

way by the ravages of sin. The overflowing of sin provoked the punishment of the flood and the destruction of Sodom and other guilty cities. It is clear enough that death then reigned in the world and yet it ruled over men "who were not themselves guilty of transgressing a law as Adam was". These men were not, in fact, violating positive precepts carrying with them the sanction of death against transgressors, as had done the prohibition formulated by God in the Garden of Paradise, or subsequently, certain prescriptions of the Mosaic law.[5] Their ignorance may have diminished the malice of actions that were objectively blameworthy. Nevertheless, it is evident that death reigned during that period of history. Its baneful dominion was thus not the consequence of personal transgressions but was indeed that of the sin of Adam.

Later the Mosaic law "intervened, only to amplify our fault" (5:20; compare 3:20; 4:15; 7:7; Gal. 3:19; 1 Cor. 15:56). Even though the law was holy, just, and good in itself (7:12) and set forth a high moral ideal, it had in practice roused the lusts of sinners and multiplied their faults (2:17–19). God had allowed these failings and thus punished the pride of those who claimed to observe the law through their own resources, without calling upon divine help. The first three chapters of the epistle to the Romans describe the terrible state of the world, pagan as well as Jewish, before the coming of the Saviour. The pagans went astray through their basic error about God and their idolatry (Rom. 1:18–23) and these things aroused Paul's horror (Acts 17:16; 2 Cor. 6:16). They had fallen into the most filthy

---

[5] The sanctions of the Mosaic law should not, strictly speaking, be regarded as having caused the death of the transgressors which was, in any case, inevitable. What they did was simply to anticipate the death and give it a violent character. The reference here is not to children who died without sin or to adults free from personal faults. In dealing with these two categories, there was no reason to turn particularly to the period before Moses. See Kittel, ἁμαρτία pp. 311–7 (Grundmann).

practices (Rom. 1:24–32), had become slaves of sin (Rom. 6:6, 17–20; 7:14; Titus 3:3), slaves of the flesh (Rom. 8:5–8; Gal. 5:16–24), under the tyranny of corruption (Rom. 8:21), enemies of God (Rom. 5:10; Col. 1:21), worthy of condemnation (Rom. 5:18; 8:1), and dominated by evil spirits (Eph. 2:2; 6:11 et seq.). The proud Jews observed the law badly and thus shared in the general corruption (Rom. 2:17–24). Man, who had come forth from the hands of his Creator innocent, had become the old man dominated by sin (Rom. 6:6; Eph. 4:22–24). And sin even affected inanimate objects, perverted from their true end by corrupt man (Rom. 8:19–22). This was the time of God's anger (Rom. 1:18; 2:5). But it was also the time of divine patience. God tolerated and permitted sin without calling for a satisfaction in keeping with its enormity.[6] The whole human race was under the domination of sin (Rom. 3:9 et seq.), "deprived of the glory of God" (Rom. 3:23).[7]

This state of things could not last. Adam was "the type of him who was to come" (5:14), and Paul has reminded us of our solidarity with Adam only in order to emphasize our contrasting solidarity with Christ, which is infinitely more efficacious because it sets in motion an infinitely greater force than that of sin and death. On the one hand was the fault of a single man, bringing with it death and a sentence of condemnation for all; on the other hand, the divine and entirely free gift, obtained through Jesus Christ alone — a gift coming after numerous faults, which had been added to that of Adam, and ending in a sentence of justification and in the reign of life over justified sinners. And the apostle concludes in triumphant tones with a passage indicating nevertheless that solidarity in Adam was indeed solidarity in sin:

[6] The flood, the destruction of Sodom and Gomorrah and the Babylonian captivity were only partial punishments which did not restore order.

[7] Translator's own rendering.

71

> Just as a single fault has brought condemnation upon all, so a single act of justice merits for all men the justification that confers life. For, just as by the disobedience of one man all the rest have been constituted sinners, so also by the obedience of one man all the others will be constituted just. The law, it is true, intervened to make sin abound; but where sin had abounded, grace has abounded still more, so that where sin reigned with death in view, grace should also reign through justice unto eternal life through Jesus Christ our Lord (5:18–21).[8]

But, as Paul had briefly indicated some years before in his first epistle to the Corinthians (15:21–22, 45–49), Christ is indeed the new Adam, the source of resurrection, the life-giving spirit, and the heavenly man, whereas the first Adam had been earthly and the cause of death.

The epistles give no explicit account of the conditions necessary for salvation before the coming of Christ, but the situation was not entirely hopeless. The pagans, deprived of the light of a positive law, themselves took the place of the law, and when their conduct was in harmony with the dictates of their conscience, they showed that the essential precepts of the Mosaic law were engraved in their hearts. They were thus able to expect a favourable judgement (Rom. 2:14–16). As for the descendants of Abraham, they could, like him, achieve justification by imitating his faith (4:3).

II. Abraham and Justification by Faith

Paul was obliged quite early to resist the groups of Judeo-Christians who considered the Mosaic law to be still in force and went so far as to maintain that salvation was not possible without circumcision (Acts 15:1). He did so with particular vigour in the epistle to the Galatians and then more fully and

---

[8] Translator's own rendering.

calmly in the epistle to the Romans, after the Council of Jerusalem had proclaimed that the law should not be imposed on converts from paganism. Christ's appearance to him had shown him in an undeniable way that the period of the law had passed and that faith in the risen Christ was alone sufficient to justify man. Moreover, while meditating on the scriptures, he found the doctrine of justification by faith expressed in simple form in Hab. 2:4: "the just shall live in his faith". The prophet was announcing that faith in the divine promises would obtain for Israel delivery from the Babylonian captivity. Faithfulness would be the guarantee of national survival. But the reference was general and could legitimately be applied in a deeper sense, assuming temporal salvation to be recognized as the anticipation and foreshadowing of Messianic salvation and the reference to life to relate to the spiritual life. The point common to the two interpretations was that life would be obtained by an absolute trust in the word and mercy of God. The apostle bases himself on this reading when he starts his argument with the words of Habacuc (Gal. 3:11 and Rom. 1:17). Faith in Jesus Christ will obtain the true liberation which is liberation from sin, and which therefore constitutes the true life.[9]

Strictly speaking, this argument would be sufficient in itself, but there are others, deriving their full force from Paul's familiarity with the scriptures and the extraordinary depth of his thought. It was a stroke of genius on his part to quote the case of Abraham, the venerated patriarch whose children the Jews were so proud to be.

It is evident that Abraham's justification depended on his faith in the divine promises. He "put his faith in God, and it was reckoned virtue in him" (Gal. 3:6 and Rom. 4:3, quoting Gen. 15:6). The Mosaic law was not yet in existence and circumcision was imposed on the Father of the believers only "as the seal of

[9] See Huby, *Épître aux Romains* (Verbum Salutis), 70.

73

that justification which came to him through his faith while he was still uncircumcised" (Rom. 4:11 and Gen. 17:9–14). His faith in the future birth of Isaac was truly admirable, in view of his age which seemed to make the divine promise impossible to fulfil.

> "We are his children in the sight of God, in whom he put his faith, who can raise the dead to life, and send his call to that which has no being, as if it already were.
> "Abraham, then, believed, hoping against hope; and thus became the father of many nations; *like these, he was told, thy posterity shall be.* There was no wavering in his faith; he gave no thought to the want of life in his own body, though he was nearly a hundred years old at the time, nor to the deadness of Sara's womb; he showed no hesitation or doubt at God's promise, but drew strength from his faith, confessing God's power, fully convinced that God was able to perform what he had promised. This, then, *was reckoned virtue* in him" (Rom. 4:17–22; compare Gal. 3:6).[10]

Abraham's faith in God the Creator and in God who raises to life is seen by St. Paul as the foretaste and the type of Christian faith in the resurrection of Christ because it was an act of faith in the vivification of the patriarch's body and of the womb of Sara, which were as though dead. The apostle adds immediately afterwards:

> And the words, *It was reckoned virtue in him*,[11] were not written of him only: they were written of us too. It will be reckoned virtue in us, if we believe in God as having raised our Lord Jesus Christ from the dead (Rom. 4:23–24).

The objective of Christian faith is obviously more precise and fuller. The promise of blessings which were to be extended

---

[10] The author has: "This, then *was reckoned justice in him*." Translator.

[11] The author has: "That was accounted to him." Translator.

through Abraham to all nations is being fulfilled with a magnificence that the patriarch could have done no more than suspect, but in both cases what is fundamentally demanded of man is the same. The patriarch can therefore be regarded as the father of all, of the circumcised who observed the law and who followed in the steps of his faith, and also of the uncircumcised who imitate his faith (Rom. 4:10–12). And the paradoxical conclusion emerges that it is the uncircumcised who are the more perfect imitators since there is a greater similarity between their faith and that of Abraham, justified before the institution of circumcision. Abraham's posterity is thus seen to mean his posterity according to the faith. Inheritance according to the flesh, without faith, does not count: "You must recognize, then, that Abraham's real children are the children of his faith" (Gal. 3:7).[12] God, who could have raised up children of Abraham from the very stones of the desert (Matt. 3:9), has chosen to himself a multitude of children of Abraham from among the heathen who believe in Jesus Christ.

Justification by faith was thus nothing new but reflected an unchanging providential dispensation. Even under the rule of the law, faith was necessary, as we shall point out later. In citing the case of Abraham, the apostle showed the universality of the call to salvation, but he emphasized no less clearly the gratuitousness of this call and of the faith itself.[13]

It can be objected that the doctrine of justification by faith seems at first sight to contradict the gratuity of the faith. The co-operation called for from man may seem to make him responsible for his own justification, but this is not so in reality because there is no common measure between the act of faith and the gift of justice. The apostle shows this, contrasting the case of the

[12] St. Paul indicates at the same time the nature and function of the Mosaic law. See section III below.
[13] These two points have already been touched upon in chapter 4.

Jew who earned a wage by his observance of the law and that of the believer whose situation is altogether different:

> The wage is not reckoned as a favour to him who works to earn it, but it is reckoned as his due, whereas to the one who, performing no work, simply believes in him who justifies the sinner, it is his faith that is reckoned justice (Rom. 4:4–5).[14]

God gave the law to Moses as a kind of bilateral contract, binding himself to shower his people with blessings, particularly in the temporal order, if they fulfilled the precepts of the law. The blessings promised by God thus assume the character of a wage due in justice, whereas the promise made to Abraham was gratuitous and unconditional. The justification which was an essential element in it, was, and remains, a pure favour to which man has no right. The faith upon which depends the opening of the way to justification is reckoned as justice but is not a "work" which would strictly merit justice.

Faith is a necessary preparation, an indispensable condition, but it is not the primary and true source of justification, in spite of what might be called its totalitarian character. Faith in the Pauline sense is, in fact, not simply acceptance by the intelligence of the gospel message, but a personal and unrestricted commitment to the service of Christ, a commitment which takes hold of the whole being and will henceforth govern the whole of the subject's life. But though this act of faith is great and decisive, it remains human and is disproportionately small in comparison with the supernatural life and the gift of the Holy Spirit (Gal. 3:14). There is no equivalence between the two. It is not, strictly speaking, faith which justifies, but God who justifies by the faith he finds in us, or rather, places in us, for faith is in itself

---

[14] Translator's own rendering.

a divine gift. Paul repeatedly and emphatically says so. Believing is a grace that comes from God (Phil. 1:29). Our opening to faith is the result of divine election (2 Thess. 2:13). No one can make an act of faith in the Lord Jesus Christ without being moved to do so by the Holy Spirit (1 Cor. 12:3). And it is God who apportions the measure of faith to each one (Rom. 12:3). Even more clearly, the apostle says: "Yes, it was grace that saved you, with faith for its instrument; it did not come from yourselves, it was God's gift, not from any action of yours, or there would be room for pride" (Eph. 2:8–9;[15] compare Rom. 11:6; 2 Tim. 1:9; John 6:44). We can now understand how the inheritance of Abraham is obtained through faith "and so by free gift" (Rom. 4:16). No one may glorify himself or claim that he has merited justice.[16] In granting justification through faith, both to the circumcised and the uncircumcised (Rom. 3:27–30), God sets a crown on his own gifts. Needless to say, he gives these gifts generously to all men of good will and he will judge every one according to the light that he will himself have apportioned to him (Rom. 2:6–11). It is clear, too, that good works, which are powerless to merit justification, are necessary and meritorious once justification is obtained. The believer is then under the rule of grace (Rom. 6:14). Would it not be profoundly immoral if the gift of ourselves to Christ were without influence on our lives, once we are justified? St. Paul over and over again exhorts his readers to the holy life, completely free from sin (Rom. 6:12–23, etc.), which is the necessary culmination of the change that has been operated in the soul: "God has created us

---

[15] In the author's version, the passage begins: "It is by the grace of Christ that you were saved", etc. Translator.

[16] Good works performed before justification can prepare the way for it, inclining God to grant it, though they cannot strictly merit justification. They are, moreover, very often accomplished with the help of actual graces.

in Christ Jesus, pledged to such good actions as he has prepared beforehand, to be the employment of our lives" (Eph. 2:10).

The last word, therefore, is that justification comes to us as a free gift from God's grace (Rom. 3:24), and that every man should humbly recognize the transcendence and generosity of divine bounty. The Mosaic law did not derogate from this unchanging design.

III. Moses and the Law

As an individual, Moses does not occupy a very large place in the epistles. The law was given through him (Gal. 3:19). The passage of the Red Sea and the cloud which protected Israel are figures of baptism and, in the same way, the water that gushed from the rock and the manna foreshadowed the Eucharist (1 Cor. 10:1–6). The veil which Moses assumed after his colloquies with God hid from the Israelites the brightness of his face, which they would have found unbearable, and it also prevented them from realizing that this brightness was only passing. If the ministry of Moses, for many one of condemnation since the effects of the law included the multiplication of sin, was the object of such a flash of glory, must not the ministry of justice, which is that of the new covenant, give rise to a veritable blaze of glory? The veil of Moses is the symbol, too, of the veil that hung over the hearts of the Jews when they read the scriptures. Their minds were clouded and they stopped short at the letter which kills, failing to penetrate to the spirit which quickens. But the veil falls away for those who turn to the Lord, distinguishing in holy writ the heralding of Christ and the preparation of the new covenant (2 Cor. 3:6–16). Admirable in many ways though the old economy was, it is infinitely surpassed by the new and the epistle to the Hebrews emphasizes on various occasions Christ's superiority (3:3–5; 8:5; 9:19–28), though without in any way reducing the importance of Moses as an individual and, indeed, praising his faith as shown in the events of the Exodus and in the celebration of the Passover (11:23–28).

St. Paul is much more concerned with the law than with the great prophet himself. The conversion of so many Gentiles to the gospel immediately raised the question of the permanence of the law and of its precepts and we have already noticed earlier[17] how much this troubled the infant Church. The apostle took a vigorous stand during his first journey to Jerusalem and at the time of the incident in Antioch involving Peter (Gal. 2), and again in the epistle to the Galatians and during the great council which settled the dispute in favour of the Gentiles. The Judaizing Christians had pursued him with their hostility as far as Corinth and perhaps as far as Rome, and they certainly again pursued him to Philippi (Phil. 3). This quarrel, the spiritual consequences of which might have been so serious, was one of the great trials of his life.

In his own case, the question had been settled, implicitly at least, right from the time of Christ's appearance to him, bringing about his conversion. Before this, for him, as for the whole of Israel, the law was God's pre-eminent gift, the summit of the revelation, the expression of his will, the centre of religion, and (we shall see in what sense) the source of justice. But this gift is eclipsed and replaced by a greater one which is that of Christ, whose resurrection proves that he brings the final revelation, the perfect expression of God's will, the true source of justice, sanctity and salvation.[18] There cannot conceivably be any looking back or even regret. The cherished advantages of belonging to the chosen people and of submission to the law are henceforth

---

[17] Chapter 4, pp. 60 et seq.

[18] See Démann, *Moïse et la Loi dans la pensée de s. Paul*, in *Moïse, l'homme de l'Alliance*, Desclée, 1955, 234–7.

devoid of value and the same goes for justification by the law. Paul looks for and desires only knowledge of Christ, justification obtained by faith in him and participation in his death and resurrection (Phil. 3:4–8). It is the same for every Christian, united by faith and baptism to the death of Christ. The Christian dies mystically with Christ to the whole of the old economy and thus to the law: "Well, brethren, you too have undergone death, as far as the law is concerned, in the person of Christ crucified, so that you now belong to another, to him who rose from the dead. We yield increase to God" (Rom. 7:4). The law, which required justice without itself providing what was necessary to achieve it, was an elementary and passing institution, a teacher leading to Christ, its role being due to finish once Christ appeared (Gal. 3:24–25; 4:2–3). Christ brought the end of the law, being at once its culmination and the goal towards which it tended (Rom. 10:4). In him the law found its fulfilment and its perfection (Matt. 5:17). And Paul cries magnificently, "Through the law, my old self has become dead to the law, so that I may live to God; with Christ I hang upon the cross" (Gal. 2:19). The vision of the risen Christ, his own experiences as an apostle, the effusion of the Holy Spirit, numerous wonders, and the transformation wrought in souls had all shown Paul that Jesus did in reality bring justification and salvation (Gal. 2:16), and he concludes: "Not I; it is Christ that lives in me... my real life is the faith I have in the Son of God, who loved me, and gave himself for me" (Gal. 2:20). Again, if the law were to be the essential element in justification, of what use was Christ's sacrifice? Was Christ's death to be needless? (Gal. 2:21).

The abolition of the law by Christ was also to be explained by the fact he took upon himself the curses invoked by the law against transgressors. Hung upon the cross and become, as it were, malediction personified (Gal. 3:10–13), he had put an end to the curses invoked by the law upon all men of whom he was the representative. He had suffered the sentence of death passed by the law on the gravest of crimes, having been condemned for an alleged blasphemy. Through him, therefore, the law had exhausted all its requirements and with them its maledictory power. Clearly, Christ reigning in heaven was no longer subject to this power. The same was true of the faithful united to the dead and resurrected Christ. The role of the law had thus been fulfilled.

That is not to say that its role was in vain. The strong words used by Paul, his attention henceforth directed to the future and forgetful of the past (Phil. 3:13), should not lead to any misconception about the nature of his thought.

In the moving plaint in the epistle to the Romans in which he depicts man faced with the requirement of the law and the allurements of sin, all battling for his assent, Paul declares, "The law, to be sure, is something holy; the ban is holy, and right, and good" (7:12). It proposes an ideal of religion and sanctity which is an enlightenment for mankind and also an appeal which the dispositions of the "inward man" (7:22) would delight to answer. It is, with other prerogatives, one of the Jewish people's titles to respect (Rom. 9:4). On the other hand, it was "brought in to make room for transgression" (Gal. 3:19; Rom. 5:20), has multiplied the faults of sinful man, called down divine anger (Rom. 4:15) and given full consciousness of sin (Rom. 3:20), through the falls it has occasioned. It should have led to life but has in fact stimulated concupiscence and led man to death. The attraction of the forbidden fruit, which led to the downfall of the first man, has shown itself with constant virulence in his descendants. Sin has taken the opportunity afforded by precept and, giving thus an extreme indication of its nature, has seduced man and brought him death. Man is, as it were, sold to sin and under the domination of the flesh. Sin lives in him, making him perform the evil that he would not do: "What I do is not what I wish to do, but something which I hate.... Praise-worthy intentions are always ready to hand, but I cannot find my way to the performance of them.... But I observe another disposition in my lower self, which wages war against the disposition of my conscience, and so I am handed over as a captive to that disposition towards sin which my lower self contains. Pitiable creature that I am, who is to set me free from a nature thus doomed to death?" (Rom. 7:15, 17, 23, 24).

The description of this terrible drama, from which no man is exempt, ends with a flash of brightness. "Nothing else than the grace of God, through Jesus Christ our Lord" (7:25). The terrible occasions of powerlessness, and the lamentable falls, avoidable by Christ's grace, could also be overcome, even under the old law, by divine help. Paul painted his despairing picture having in mind those all too numerous Jews who, in their pharisaical pride, laid claim to observe the law by their own strength and failed to do so. The needs of his argument led him to insist almost exclusively on this perversion of Judaism and to stress the deadlock into which it led, but he knew very well that there were holy people in Israel who obtained through their humble prayers the help necessary to observe the law as far as human frailty permitted. It was with the errors of the Pharisees in mind that he represented the law as having been added by God "to make room for transgression".

We need to understand the nature of this addition from which Abraham and those who imitated his faith benefited. It was not of the same kind as the promise and could not be substituted for it. A will drawn up in proper form cannot be cancelled or completed by any third party, but the law stands here in place of a third party. It came four hundred years after the promise and had contradictory characteristics. Admittedly, the law also had God for its author and was also his free gift, but God gave it the form of a bilateral contract, promulgated by angels through the intervention of Moses. The human side of this contract might therefore fail. The promise, on the other hand, was a unilateral and immutable divine initiative, fulfilled without recourse to any intermediary (Gal. 3:15–20). From this follows, as we have already shown, a second contrast. With the law there was a wage due in strict justice for work done. With the promise there was the free gift of justification through faith (Rom. 4:4–5). Again, the law was national in character, separating Israel from other peoples, particularly through the rabbinical traditions which had been superimposed on it and given an authority almost equal to that of the precepts of the Torah. This "hedge about the law", as it was called, had the advantage of preserving Israel from the contamination of idolatry. On the other hand, it also isolated Israel, becoming a factor of division. It placed a wall of hate between Jews and Gentiles which could be broken down only when Christ's sacrifice repealed the law and brought peace between those far and near, making it possible for all to approach the Father in the same Spirit (Eph. 2:11–18).

It follows clearly from this that the law was part of an entirely different system from the promise announcing to Abraham that all nations should be blessed in him (Gal. 3:8; Rom. 4:17). That is why St. Paul asserts so strongly that the law was not a substitute for the promise and that observance of the law could not justify, faith remaining the necessary condition for justification, after the time of Moses just as it had after Abraham (Gal. 3:10–14; Rom. 4:9–14; 10:2–4).

The law, therefore, could not justify and the same applies to all law as such, even to the law of the gospel, and to the dictates of conscience, which guide those who have no knowledge of positive law. These precepts, in fact, set out requirements but do not in themselves bring the necessary help to observe them. For that help, we must look to divine grace. The Mosaic law, too

83

often transgressed by the Jews (Rom. 2:17–24), could open the way to life only if there was also present a faith in the divine promises which led to mistrust in personal strength and recourse to prayer and which also inspired works. Now that Christ has come, the law and faith are separated. Faith is no longer tied to the observance of the law, from which the Christian is delivered by virtue of his mystical union with the death of the Redeemer. To regard the law as still in force and faith as insufficient is not only to imply denial of the efficacy of Christ's sacrifice, but to expose us to the sanctions of the law since, to keep the law under these conditions, we should in future be dependent on our own resources, God no longer having any reason to help us in conforming to an institution that has lost its validity. The Judaizing Christian, obstinately wedded to this view, would derive from his fidelity to the Mosaic law nothing more than a life rather better than that of the heathen, but not the true life which justice alone can confer (Gal. 3:10–14;[19] 6:2–5; Rom. 10:5, et seq.). For him, the yoke of the law would amount to slavery (Gal. 2:4; Rom. 7:6). Christians are not descendants of Agar, who represents the old dispensation, the dispensation of slavery, but children of Sara, the free woman, who represents the heavenly Jerusalem, children of the promise and not children according to the flesh (Gal. 4:21–31).

The law is thus not a codicil completing the promise, but a passing institution, a kind of parenthesis, useful in its own time and its own order, even though it served to multiply transgression and this had, at any rate, the advantage of bringing home to man his own powerlessness (Gal. 3:22). Christ nailed it to the cross (Col. 2:14) and from that time on the parenthesis was closed. The law had not in any way changed God's immutable plans for justification by faith, so often proclaimed in holy writ.

[19] This chapter 3 is difficult. We would refer the reader to our own commentary in the collection *Verbum Salutis*, 163–87.

There are thus three stages in the religious life of the world, starting with Abraham. From Abraham to Moses, there was justification by faith in the Messianic promises; from Moses to Christ, justification by faith in these same promises and, in addition, the need to observe the positive law of Sinai. From the time of Christ, there is justification by faith in him and at the same time through the observance of the law of the gospel. But in contradistinction to the ancient law, the law of Christ is intrinsically linked with the faith. It is the law of the faith (Rom. 3:27). We receive it from the hands of the Redeemer and after we have received the faith, God justifies us and gives us the gift of the Holy Spirit, carrying with it all the help required for a victory over the flesh and over our evil tendencies, and at the same time his divine presence makes of us the adopted children of the Father and brothers of Christ (Rom. 8:1–17, 29; Gal. 5:13–25; 4:6–7).[20] The Christian is no longer governed by imperfect doctrines, "the elements of the world" (Gal. 4:3 [Douai]), but he lives in the light of Christ (Eph. 5:8–14), sustained by the Spirit through whom his faith finds expression in love (Gal. 5:5–6). Those who believe in Jesus constitute the real Israel, God's true Israel (Gal. 6:16), which embraces all peoples. Circumcised and uncircumcised equally become new creatures in Christ (Gal. 6:15). There is no more Jew or Greek. All are one person in Jesus Christ and form the true posterity of Abraham (Gal. 3:28–29), assembled around the cross (Gal.

---

[20] The believer is not just called upon to show his respect for a body of legislation. He receives the gift of justice, a new life, a strength which enables him to conquer sin and to escape from its domination: "Make your bodily powers over to God, to be the instruments of right-doing. Sin will not be able to play the master over you any longer; you serve grace now, not the law" (Rom. 6:13–14). Cf. Cerfaux, *Lecture de l'épître aux Romains,* Casterman, 1947, 63. The law is no more than an illumination, though indeed a valuable one. Christ is at one and the same time a light and a force. Cf. Feuillet, RB, 1950, 375.

6:14), so that there is nothing but Christ in any of us (Col. 3:11). Adam, Abraham or Moses, all things point towards Christ and find their completion in him.[21]

---

[21] Further reading: Bonsirven, *Le Judaïsme palestinien*, II, 12–23; DT, *Péché originel*, Verriele, *Le surnaturel en nous et le péché originel*, Bloud, 1932, 168–80, 209–26; Kittel νόμος IV, 1057–73 (Gutbrod); SDB, *Judéo-chrétiens* (Colon).

6

CHRIST THE AUTHOR OF SALVATION.
THE REDEMPTION

> *"The glory of the great God, the glory of
> our Saviour Jesus Christ" (Titus 2:13).*

CHRIST'S central position in the doctrine of Paul is evident
throughout his epistles. As we have mentioned earlier,[1] Paul
repeatedly affirms that Christ is Saviour jointly with the Father,
and in this he follows Peter, whose preaching from Pentecost
onwards presented Christ as Saviour (Acts 4:12; compare
2 Peter 1:1, 11; 2:20; 3:2, 18) and author of the remission of
sins (Acts 2:33; 3:26; 5:31; 10:43).

This fundamental statement is corroborated by a number of
others in which Christ is shown as the source of all that goes to
make up salvation.

Christ is the author of eternal salvation for all who render
obedience to him (Heb. 9:5). The gospel of Christ is "an instrument of God's power, that brings salvation to all who believe
in it" (Rom. 1:16). The sacrifice of Jesus Christ preserves us
from divine anger (Rom. 5:9). All are saved by faith in our
Lord's pre-eminence and in his resurrection (Rom. 10:9, 13)
and this in spite of the scandal given to the world by the
preaching of his cross (1 Cor. 1:21). Our Lord is at once
both the head and the Saviour of the Church, which is his

---

[1] Cf. p. 59.

Mystical Body (Eph. 5:22). Through him, men gain remission of their sins and that justification that the law of Moses was powerless to obtain for them (Acts 13:38–39). In him we find redemption, reconciliation with God, and peace through his blood, shed on the cross (Col. 1:13, 20). Through faith in him, we are given the true justification in union with his resurrection (Rom. 3:21; Phil. 3:9–11). His blood purifies our consciences, setting them free from lifeless observances to serve the living God (Heb. 9:14).

St. Paul then completes his thought by presenting Christ more positively as the source of true life. Handed over to death for our sins, he is raised to life for our justification (Rom. 4:25). He becomes for us in a new way a "life-giving spirit" (1 Cor. 15:45). He gives the Holy Spirit abundantly to those who receive baptism in his name (Acts 19:1–6). He awakens and gives life to those who were spiritually dead (Eph. 5:14; Acts 26:23). It is through him that will come the resurrection of the body on the last day, just as through him now comes the resurrection of the soul (1 Cor. 15:20–23). By his appearance on earth, he has "annulled death" and "shed abroad the rays of life and immortality" (2 Tim. 1:10). When he returns in glory, he will judge men and will render to each according to his deeds (2 Thess. 1:7–10; 2 Cor. 5:10; 2 Tim. 4:1). In short, Christ is the principle of salvation (Heb. 2:10), the head, whose body is the Church (Col. 1:18), to which he communicates his life, the new Adam, principle of life and of grace, who repairs superabundantly the ravages caused by the fall of the first man and aggravated by his descendants (Rom. 5:14–21). One of the turns of phrase most frequently used by the apostle, "in Christ Jesus", recalls continually these fundamental truths.

The announcement of salvation by Christ provides an implicit affirmation of his divinity which is, moreover, several times made explicit. The titles given to Christ, Lord and Son of God,[2] are a significant testimony to the deeply impressive reality before which the human mind is confused and hesitant but which lies at the heart of St. Paul's teaching, as it did at the heart of primitive Christianity. The apostolic age considered the mystery of Christ in its various aspects without succeeding in exhausting all its richness (Eph. 3:8–19). The Saviour was looked upon as the Son of Man and the servant of Jahveh (Acts 7:55; 4:27) – as Lord, at once the Messianic King and Kyrios, equal to God – and as Son of God in the fullest sense of the word. It was recognized that he was Son of God not merely after the resurrection but from the moment when his earthly life began[3] (the tradition from which the synoptic gospels were later to issue was categoric on this point). It was also recognized that his mission in the world implied pre-existence and his divine sonship could not have had any beginning. He is the author of the new covenant as God had been of that of Sinai (2 Cor. 3:16–18). All these considerations are interlinked in the Acts and in the epistles[4] though in analysing them we are bound to seem to be dissociating them. This should not lead to any misunderstanding of their unity and importance. We should not be surprised either to find side by side explicit texts and less complete indications.[5]

[2] The juxtaposition of these various titles and the context in which they appear indicate clearly that the title "Son of God" is not intended metaphorically as it was in the case of the kings of Israel on the day each was enthroned (Ps. 2:7). Jesus is the very Son of God (Rom. 8:32).

[3] It was the resurrection alone that led to a full understanding of Christ's transcendent dignity and of the nature of his mission. Cf. Schmitt, 182–9.

[4] See Schmitt, 200–16.

[5] Compare, for example, 2 Cor. 8:9 with Phil. 2:5–11, and 1 Cor. 8:6 with Col. 1:15 et seq. During the apostolic period, development and progress took place in theological reflection under the guidance of the Holy Spirit. It is not surprising that points of doctrine such as the divine pre-existence of him who was crucified on Calvary and the deeper meaning of his redemptive work should have been understood and expressed

Inspired by the Holy Ghost and in conformity with the promises of the Saviour (John 14:25-26; 15:12-13), the infant Church gradually became more fully aware of the treasure it possessed. The saving action of Christ, intensely experienced by the faithful and confirmed by miracles of all kinds (Acts 2:43; 5:12; 1 Thess. 1:5; 2 Cor. 12:12, etc.), showed that he possessed both divine power and divine dignity. Unhesitatingly, and without arousing the least opposition, Paul wishes the readers of his letters, "grace and peace from God our Father and from the Lord Jesus Christ". He applies to Christ texts in the Old Testament referring to Jahveh, attesting in this way that for him, as for all the faithful, Jesus is as Stephen had seen him (Acts 7:56), glorified on the right hand of God and equal to God.[6]

I. The Pre-existing Christ

Christ's mission from the Father makes it evident that he existed before he appeared on earth:

> But when the fullness of the time was come, God sent his Son (Gal. 4:4 [Douai]).
>
> That which the law could not do... God has done, by sending us his own Son, in flesh like sinful flesh, to (defeat) sin (Rom. 8:3).[7]
>
> Christ Jesus came into the world to save sinners (1 Tim. 1:15).

explicitly only little by little and that the earliest formulations of these doctrines should have been incomplete. Nor is it surprising that the theology of St. John should be more precise than that of St. Paul.

[6] The statement that Christ is seated at God's right hand is characteristic (Rom. 8:34; Eph. 1:20; Col. 3:1; Heb. 1:4). It was already predicted in Psalm 110, to which Jesus himself referred in a discussion with the Pharisees (Mark 12:35-36) and it implies a certain equality with God which is confirmed by the context in which St. Paul places it.

[7] Translator's own rendering.

The expressions used by St. Paul imply previous existence, particularly ἐξαπέστειλεν, which occurs in the epistle to the Galatians and signifies "God has sent from beside himself". Not only was Christ announced by the prophets (Acts 13:32–33; Rom. 1:2; 3:21) but "he impoverished himself for your sakes, when he was so rich, so that you might become rich through his poverty" (2 Cor. 8:9) and he was already acting during the sojourn of the Israelites in the desert. He was the spiritual rock which accompanied them and dispensed the water miraculously drawn from the material rock (1 Cor. 10:4).

Even more striking, Christ's is for St. Paul "that first birth which precedes every act of creation" (Col. 1:15), the perfect image of the invisible God (Col. 1:15; 2 Cor. 4:4), "the radiance of his Father's splendour, and the full expression of his being" (Heb. 1:3). God's glory shines through his features and through him it is known to men and enlightens their hearts (2 Cor. 4:6). Through him, God is made visible and present on earth. He has all the divine attributes. He is the power and wisdom of God (1 Cor. 1:24; Col. 2:3). The intemperate speculations with which he had to contend in Asia Minor[8] led the apostle to teach that Christ is Creator just as is the divine Wisdom described in the later books of the Old Testament (Prov. 8:22–31; Wisd. 7:22, et seq.; Ecclus. 24:1, et seq.): "Only one Lord, Jesus Christ, the creator of all things. And our creator too" (1 Cor. 8:6). He created the world and supports all things by his enabling word (Heb. 11:2–3). They take their existence from him and could not subsist without him: "Yes, in him all created things took their being, heavenly and earthly, visible and invisible.... They

---

[8] Particularly Col. 2:4–23; Eph. 1:21. These speculations concerning angels amounted to a kind of anticipated Gnosticism which multiplied the mediators between God and man, were complicated by observances connected with the calendar and the use of foods and introduced ascetical practices influenced by Judaism. See SDB, *Gnose préchrétienne et biblique* 690–700 (Cerfaux).

were all created through him and in him; he takes precedency of all, and in him all subsist" (Col. 1:16–17).[9] He is infinitely superior to all those angelic powers that certain Christians in Colossae and Ephesus exalted unduly (Col. 1:16; Eph. 1:20–21). God had chosen and predestined in him from the foundation of the world those who were to be saints in his sight and to be his adopted children, brothers of his only begotten and beloved Son (Eph. 1:3, 4, 6; Rom. 8:29–30), the Son whose image they would reflect. From eternity Christ rules and vivifies all things. We can therefore hardly refuse him the title of God. Paul does not normally use it. Preoccupied as he is with the need to make the necessary distinction between persons and to avoid seeming to call into question the dogma of divine unity, he prefers the terms "Son of God" and "Lord", which are equally clear. An exception to this is, however, to be found in three celebrated passages. Writing to the Romans of the privileges of the Israelites, Paul concludes thus his catalogue: "Theirs is the human stock from which Christ came; Christ, who rules as God over all things, blessed for ever, Amen"[10] (Rom. 9:5). A little later, during a journey which was to end with his arrest in Jerusalem, he said in a farewell speech to the presbyters of Ephesus, who had been called to a meeting at Miletus: "Keep watch, then, over yourselves, and over God's Church, in which the Holy Spirit has made you bishops; you are to be the shepherds of that flock which he won for himself at the price of his own blood" (Acts 20:28).

[9] St. Paul is doubtless speaking here of the glorified Saviour, but his words nevertheless imply Christ's pre-existence, not, obviously, in his humanity, but as God. His divine prerogatives are shown by the resurrection which makes him completely divine. "Nunc per omnia Deus" as St. Ambrose puts it (PL XVI. 341). See below section 3 and Durrwell, 142–5. The expressions used by the apostle explicitly identify Christ as the eternal, creating Wisdom (Prov. 8:22–30; Wisd. 7:25–26).

[10] We do not accept the view of those who challenge the rendering of this passage and maintain that the doxology with which it ends refers to God the Father.

Finally, before his last captivity, he was to recommend Titus "to look forward, blessed in our hope, to the day when there will be a new dawn of glory, the glory of the great God, the glory of our Saviour Jesus Christ (Titus 2:13). These declarations form a crown to the other Christological passages and succeed in removing any doubt about Christ's supreme dignity. This God and eternal Son, the argument continues, made himself man to save us in the fullness of time. And he will come at the end of the world to exercise his divine prerogative as universal judge (2 Thess. 1:4–10; Rom. 14:9; 2 Cor. 5:10).

II. Christ Incarnate and Crucified

The reality of the human nature of Christ was not in question for St. Paul. The Saviour had been able to offer himself in expiation for the sins of men because God had endowed him with a body (Heb. 10:5–10). God sent him out and he "took birth from a woman, took birth as a subject of the law" (Gal. 4:4). "Descended, in respect of his human birth, from the line of David" (Rom. 1:3), "in flesh like sinful flesh" (Rom. 8:3). The appearance on earth of the Son of God endowed with a human nature shows forth in the flesh the "great mystery we worship" (1 Tim. 3:16) and the immense love of God who wishes to save the world. The incarnation appoints a sole mediator between God and men, "Jesus Christ, who is a man, like them" (1 Tim. 2:5). It is because he became part of humanity and was to represent it in his own person that Christ was able to redeem it. So completely is he a man that, as far as external appearance is concerned, he appears to have no more than "the nature of a slave", which he voluntarily assumed (Phil. 2:7). The constant reminder of the Passion and the proclamation of the resurrection clearly illustrate the reality of Christ's humanity

93

and its resemblance to our own. There is only one difference but it is capital. Christ is completely innocent, the Lamb without blemish, having "been through every trial, fashioned as we are, only sinless" (Heb. 4:15). Because Christ never knew sin, says St. Paul in a vivid passage, "God made him into sin for us, so that in him we might be turned into the holiness of God" (2 Cor. 5:21). God burdened him with the curse invoked by the law against transgressors (Gal. 3:13). He sent him into the world to sign the death-warrant of sin (Rom. 8:3), and it is in this sense that his death was to be "a death, once for all, to sin" (Rom. 6:10).

The cross of Christ dominates the Pauline teaching just as it lies at the centre of the gospel. The epistle to the Hebrews shows that right from the first moment of the incarnation, Christ looked forward to the baptism in blood of Calvary (10:5–10). In Galatia, Paul described the Passion in such moving terms that his hearers had, as it were, a picture of Christ crucified before their eyes (Gal. 3:1). When he was writing to the Corinthians, who were frivolous and eager for sterile debate, he decided that in their midst he should show knowledge only of Jesus Christ, and of him as crucified (1 Cor. 2:2). The first thing he wanted to do was to put them face to face with the cross of Christ. "To those who court their own ruin, the message of the cross is but folly; to us, who are on the way to salvation, it is the evidence of God's power" (1 Cor. 1:18). He considered that preaching the scandal and folly of the cross would be more effective than any arguments (1 Cor. 1:23; Gal. 5:12), and that what was necessary above all was to make known the superior wisdom of God who had chosen to redeem the world by a means which, although paradoxical in the highest degree, showed itself to those who meditated on it in the light of the Spirit as the crowning work of his love.

Assertions of the redemption by the cross stand out at various points in all the epistles. Jesus had died for our sakes (1 Thess. 5:9). God has made him an expiatory victim through his own blood (Rom. 3:25). In him, we find redemption, the remission of sins (Col. 1:14; Eph. 1:7). His blood, shed on the cross, wins back all things, whether on earth or in heaven, and reunites into a single body Jews and pagans, once irremediably separated by their enmity (Col. 1:20; Eph. 2:13–16). He is the true paschal lamb, sacrificed for us (1 Cor. 5:7). He is the High Priest who is to win us blessings that still lie in the future and who gains for us eternal redemption (Heb. 9:11–12). His blood is the seal of the new and eternal covenant, destined for all humanity and no longer restricted to a single people, as was the covenant of Sinai (Heb. 9:15–22). His sacrifice obtains remission for our sins and while the victims under the old dispensation had no true efficacy, his single offering suffices to wipe out sins (Heb. 9:13–14, 25–28; 10:1–3, 10–18).

This paradox of the redeeming cross which effects the salvation of the world in an abyss of humiliation and suffering is the greatest manifestation of divine love. It is the Father who has sent his Son and who has willed his sacrifice. He chose out from all eternity those who are to be saved by his blood (Eph. 1:4–7). He did not even spare his own Son but gave him up for us to death as an expiatory victim (Rom. 8:32; 3:24). The sacrifice of Calvary was consummated, thus fulfilling the scriptures (1 Cor. 15:3) in accordance with his will (Gal. 1:4). In Christ, God reconciled the world to himself (2 Cor. 5:19), not hesitating to make him into sin and into an accursed thing for our sakes (2 Cor. 5:21; Gal. 3:13). As a striking proof of his love for us, he has reconciled us to himself by the death of his Son, after sin had made us his enemies and rebels against his authority (Rom. 5:8–10). In his great work of clemency, his love has shown itself truly immense and the richness of his mercy without limit (Rom. 3:24; Eph. 2:4,7).

To the command and love of the Father, the Son replied with absolute obedience. The assuming of the status of a slave in a human nature subject to suffering and death and bereft of the glory with which it should have shone was in itself an inexpressible humiliation, an emptying of himself, as St. Paul says forcefully (Phil. 2:7). The cross brought both the humiliation and the obedience to their supreme point. From the moment he came into the world, Christ had started to offer himself as a sacrifice (Heb. 10:5–10). The offering continued throughout his life on earth and reached its culmination on Calvary. The dispositions in which Christ accepted his immolation and which are the bases of its value are recalled several times by the apostle. It was by obedience to the Father that Christ repaired the disobedience of the first man who had unleashed sin into the world (Rom. 5:19). The Redeemer, St. Paul boldly explains in the epistle to the Hebrews, had to suffer the bitter apprenticeship of the conditions the disobedience brought about. He had to make himself like his brothers in order to become a merciful high priest and had to go through suffering and trials in order to help those who are tried (Heb. 2:17–18). He sacrificed a life of happiness here below and endured the cross (Heb. 12:2). Son that he was, he learned in the school of suffering what it cost to obey, and having passed through the same trials as ourselves with the exception of sin, he was able effectively to feel for us in our weaknesses (Heb. 5:8; 4:15). He accomplished his sacrifice with immense love of the Father and of men, "that charity which Christ showed to us, when he gave himself up on our behalf" (Eph. 5:2). He gave his blood on behalf of his Church (Eph. 5:25) and for each one of its members, so that every Christian can repeat the moving words of Paul: "My real life is the faith I have in the Son of God, who loved me, and gave himself for me" (Gal. 2:20). While it effects the salvation of men, the purifying blood of Christ, which speaks with greater eloquence than that of Abel

96

(Heb. 12:24), is also a sacrifice having for God a sweet fragrance (Eph. 5:2). It brings him infinite glory (Eph. 1:14) acting as a pledge of the eternal covenant through which the Redeemer becomes "our Lord Jesus Christ... that great shepherd" (Heb. 13:20).

The voluntary character of the redemptive sacrifice implies that Christ offered himself for the salvation of the world at the moment when his executioners nailed him to the cross. He is thus, at one and the same time, priest and victim and his *priesthood* is the principal subject of the impressive fresco painted in the epistle to the Hebrews.

Christ, who was greater than the angels and Moses, was by the incarnation made representative of men in their dealings with God. Every high priest is, in fact, taken from among men and appointed to represent them for the offering of sacrifices in expiation of their sins (Heb. 5:1). Christ did not confer priesthood upon himself but received it from God, who proclaimed him High Priest for all eternity according to the order of Melchisedech, thus accomplishing the mysterious prophecy contained in Psalm 109. His priesthood is eternal. The fact that the genealogy of Melchisedech is not mentioned in the biblical account was an obscure indication of this (Heb. 5:6–10; 7:1–3). It is an unchanging priesthood, doubly guaranteed by God in the promise made to Abraham and in the solemn undertaking mentioned by the psalmist (Heb. 6:16–18; 7:20–22). This priesthood is distinct from that of Aaron, its superiority being as great as and greater than that which Melchisedech appeared to bear to Abraham whom he blessed and from whom he collected the tithe of the booty seized from the attackers (Heb. 7:4–10). Finally, Christ is a unique priest because he is eternal (Heb. 7:23–24) and, by his sufferings, he has been made perfect and has been given the power to help those who suffer (Heb. 2:10, 18).

Such was the high priest that suited our need, holy and guiltless and undefiled, not reckoned among us sinners, lifted high above all the heavens; one who has no need to do as those other priests did, offering a twofold sacrifice day by day, first for his own sins, then for those of the people. What he has done he has done once for all; and the offering was himself. (Heb. 7:26–27).

In his blood is concluded the new and final covenant announced in former days by Jeremias (Jer. 31:31–34; Heb. 8:8–12). He has not offered the blood of animals, a sacrifice incapable of remitting sins, its ineffectiveness in this regard being shown by its repetition (Heb. 10:1–4). He has offered his own blood, a perfect offering that does not need renewal. To present this precious blood, he did not enter into the Holy of Holies, a sanctuary made by man's hands, as the Jewish high priest did each year on the Day of Atonement, but went to heaven itself where he is eternally living, interceding on our behalf (Heb. 9:11–14; 7:24; 10:11–18) and applying to us the merits of his sacrifice. Thus his priesthood continues in heaven. His resurrection brings the fulfilment of his priestly consecration, inaugurated when he was made man.

When Paul contemplates the redemptive mystery he cannot refrain from remarking that a great price was paid to ransom us (1 Cor. 6:20; 7:23). But what exactly do we mean by the term buying back or redemption, applied to the voluntary sacrifice of Christ?

Redemption, $\alpha\pi o\lambda\upsilon\tau\rho\omega\sigma\iota\varsigma$, means the buying back of a captive by means of ransom (1 Tim. 2:6). It follows clearly enough that the captive is the guilty human race and the ransom, the price of deliverance, is the precious blood of the Saviour. But we must not push the comparison too far. There is no need to ask ourselves to whom the ransom has been paid that frees us from the slavery of sin. It has clearly not been paid to sin which has no existence apart from sinners. Nor has it been paid to the devil,

as some of the Fathers thought – as though the devil had rights
to enforce over us through being the instigator of sin. It remains
true, however, that God had the right to demand satisfaction
from guilty humanity. He might certainly have granted men a
straight-forward amnesty, being satisfied with their sincere
repentance, but in doing so would he not have allowed it to be
thought that sin was of no consequence to him or that he considered it to be an only moderately serious matter? The guilty
had earned punishment and the punishments inflicted before the
coming of Christ – such as the flood, the ruin of Sodom and
Gomorrah, and the Babylonian captivity – made only partial
satisfaction and were powerless to restore order. The extermi-
nation of sinners had fixed them in a state of eternal death and
was thus not in any sense a remedy, except in so far as it inspired
fear among those who survived. Forgiveness through the annual
sacrifice of the Day of Atonement was merely indirect and obtained by anticipation, heralding and assuming as it did the
atonement effected by Christ. The sacrifice of bulls and goats
which it involved was clearly incapable of remitting sins (Heb.
10:1–4, 11). God showed forbearance and was content to leave
sins in a way unpunished so long as he was not insisting upon
an adequate payment of the debt contracted by sinners in their
revolt against him (Rom. 3:25). It would seem that he owed
it to himself to require this satisfaction, not only to throw into
relief the seriousness of sin and the disorder it occasioned, but
also to bring home to man the need for a complete renunciation
of evil and a conversion in the full sense of the word. Satisfaction
for the offence against God had been made by the sacrifice of
Christ, offered with unsurpassable obedience and love. His immolation had an infinite value because he was the only begotten
Son of God and, possessing divine life in all its fullness, he
could communicate it to us in union with his resurrection (Rom.
4:25) through which God was to show the efficacy of his sacrifice.

The agonizing death of Christ was to be a source of life and that is the striking feature meriting repetition, whereas, we must once more emphasize, the putting to death of sinners did not justify them but, on the contrary, rendered their state of sinfulness final and irrevocable. In Christ's case, death was an act of obedience and total renunciation and not, as it is for us, the final stage in sin's domination. It brought him to glory and earned for him, as a recompense for humiliation, the resurrection that is the source of salvation for mankind.[11] "We can see... Jesus, crowned, now, with glory and honour because of the death he underwent; in God's gracious design, he was to taste death, and taste it on behalf of all" (Heb. 2:9). It was doubtless in this sense that during his agony he prayed in a loud voice and with tears to the Father who could save him from death. His prayer was answered because of his devotion in the sense that, raised to life and glorified, "he wins eternal salvation for all those who render obedience to him" (Heb. 5:7–9).

It seems therefore true to say that Christ has suffered in our place the punishment we merited, becoming for us an accursed thing and being made into sin (Gal. 3:13; 2 Cor. 5:21). If we restricted ourselves, however, to this aspect of the redemptive work, we should not escape the repugnant substitution of an innocent victim for the guilty. St. Paul's thought includes this point of view but extends beyond it. Christ has taken our sins upon himself in order to free us from them in so far as he is our representative and links us to himself as we were linked to Adam. He resumes and contains the whole of humanity, as it were, in himself. The victim who makes expiation is thus not entirely separate from the guilty. With the victim, they compose a corporate body and it is, in a certain sense, humanity that expiates and obtains forgiveness in the person of the greatest and

[11] Durrwell, 72 et seq.

most holy of its members. Through one man's obedience, we become acceptable to God, just as we became guilty through the disobedience of the first man (Rom. 5:19). The dominant theme is solidarity. Humanity's debt is extinguished and sins are remitted by the death of Jesus on the cross and the solidarity persisting still in the resurrection makes us sharers in his life, here and now in our souls, and on the last day it makes us sharers through the glorification of our bodies.

Nevertheless, our co-operation is needed if we are to share in the fruits of his sacrifice. Jesus did not die to dispense us from the need to die and make satisfaction, but in order to obtain forgiveness for us and to reconcile us to God. The Father appointed him as an expiatory victim, a means of propitiation infinitely more efficacious than the sprinkling of the blood of victims offered on the propitiatory of the Ark of the Covenant (Rom. 3:24). But we shall not share in his merits except through faith; through the unstinting gift of ourselves and through reception of baptism, which requires from us a complete conversion to the true, living God (1 Thess. 1:9) in the renunciation of sin and the striving after a new kind of existence in union with his death and resurrection (Rom. 6:3–11). The example of Christ crucified will also help us to follow in his footsteps, while his Passion shows us how odious sin is in the sight of God.

Thus, there has not been the simple substitution of an innocent man for the guilty, but partial substitution through the solidarity of the sinners with the Redeemer. It is in this way that sinful humanity enters once more into favour with God. Uniting itself with Christ crucified, it can henceforth obtain forgiveness, acquire God's favour and merit eternal life, achievements that would have been impossible had humanity been reduced to dependence on its own resources and had the sacrifice of the true paschal Lamb not come to save it (1 Cor. 5:7). With the last sigh of Jesus on Calvary[12] all was thus in principle consummated. But in practice – and the conception is of great moral value, worthy of God and of mankind – every Christian must crucify himself with Christ if he is to profit by the fruits of the redemption (Gal. 2:19; 5:24). He must associate himself mystically with Christ's death, and live for God in union with Christ (Rom. 6:11). That is, he must put into effect the words of St. Paul which are so full of fervent gratitude: "My real life is the faith I have in the Son of God, who loved me, and gave himself for me" (Gal. 2:20).[13]

III. Christ Glorified

The task of redemption could not possibly have been completed on the cross. The drama of Calvary had apparently ended in complete failure and while Jesus remained in the tomb, conquered by death, he appeared powerless against sin, the dominion of which was demonstrated by death. Without the resurrection his death seemed like that of any other man, meriting glorification neither for himself nor for us.[14] He could then have been con-

[12] In so far, that is, as redemptive merit is concerned. But the resurrection was necessary for the merits of the redemption to be applied to us. See the following section.

[13] See Prat, II, 226, 240. Some theologians insist more than we have done on the substitution of Christ for sinners and on the punitive and expiatory aspect of his sacrifice. From this point of view, Christ suffered death because it was the punishment due for our sins. He endured all his sufferings for us and in our place and these sufferings are credited to our account. See the carefully argued treatment of this subject by Médebielle in SDB, *Expiation*, 255–9; *Enseignement de s. Paul*, I, 63–110, 168–95; DT, *Rédemption* (Rivière), 1969–75; Kittel, ἀπολύτρωσις IV, 354–9 (Büchsel).

[14] See Durrwell, 74–5. The sacrifices of the Mosaic law were definitely a making over of the victims to God. The consuming by fire and the offering of blood in the Holy of Holies on the Day of Atonement sym-

sidered only as a false prophet and an impostor, having given his resurrection as the chief sign of his divine mission. (Matt. 12:39–40; 16:4), and the apostolic preaching, of which the resurrection was an essential part, would have amounted to false witness (1 Cor. 15:15). Paul did not hesitate to write with particular vehemence: "If Christ has not risen, then our preaching is groundless, and your faith, too, is groundless. Worse still, we are convicted of giving false testimony about God.... All your faith is a delusion; you are back in your sins" (1 Cor. 15:14, 15, 17). But he immediately turns away from such a terrifying prospect: "But no, Christ has risen from the dead, the first-fruits of all those who have fallen asleep" (1 Cor. 15:20). And, basing himself no doubt on an early creed, he enumerates the principal apparitions of the Saviour, including the one with which he was himself favoured:

> He "...as the scriptures had foretold, rose again on the third day. That he was seen by Cephas, then by the eleven apostles, and afterwards by more than five hundred of the brethren at once, most of whom are alive at this day, though some have gone to their rest. Then he was seen by James, then by all the apostles; and last of all, I too saw him, like the last child, that comes to birth unexpectedly" (1 Cor. 15:5–8).

An extraordinary impression of substance and certainty is conveyed by this text and Paul concludes with assurance: "That is our preaching, mine or theirs as you will; that is the faith which has come to you" (1 Cor. 15:11). Later, when he was appearing

bolized divine acceptance. But the acceptance was certain and complete only in the case of Christ who, after having offered himself, penetrated into the presence of God in the sanctuary of heaven, his glorification showing that the shedding of his blood was pleasing to God. This is what the epistle to the Hebrews intends to convey when it asserts that Christ reached his full achievement and was made perfect (2:10; 5:9; 7:28; 10:14), and that the spotless victim, having returned to God, has opened up for us a way of approach to him (4:16; 10:19–22). See Durrwell, 90–2.

before the Procurator, Festus, and King Agrippa, he was to declare, not without a touch of humour, talking of the Passion and the resurrection: "It was not in some secret corner that all this happened" (Acts 26:26). The events from which our salvation stems were all duly recorded. Right from the morrow of Pentecost, the other apostles placed the Easter message in the forefront of their teaching and Paul followed their example.

But, considered as a basic element in the faith, the significance of Christ's resurrection is not restricted to its evident apologetic value. With the ascension, which comes as a crown, it is an essential part of the redemptive work, inseparable from the Passion. It has a soteriological value, frequently brought out by the apostle. One of the weightiest expressions of this is to be found in Rom. 4:25, in which he speaks of Christ as having been handed over to death for our sins, and raised to life for our justification.

St. Paul does not mean by this that the resurrection has merited the gift of grace for us. Clearly only the Passion was meritorious. But the resurrection is inseparable from it, being the second phase of an indivisible act, and the redemption is the fruit of this complete act with its double aspect. The apostle relates the negative aspect to the Passion since Christ endured death because of our sins and to obtain for us their forgiveness. The positive effects in relation to salvation follow from the resurrection, which they have not as their meritorious cause but, to use the language of the schoolmen, as exemplary and efficient cause.[15] It is the

[15] By his death, Christ merited especially his own resurrection and glorification, which were the subject of repeated demands to his Father (John 3:14; 12:28; 13:31; 17:1–5). But he also attracts all men to himself (John 12:32). He returned to the Father to prepare a home for them (John 14:2–3; 17:24) and to unite them in the most intimate way, even while here below, by the gift of the Holy Spirit and by transmitting his own life (John 14:19–20; 15:4–5; 17:21–23). By meriting resurrection for himself, he merited it for us with all that resurrection implies: death to the flesh of sin, superabundance of supernatural life, and the

risen Christ who transforms believers into his own image. Full of life and henceforth beyond the power of death, having already accepted it in an ineffable disposition of obedience, he justifies us, communicating his life to us (Rom. 6:8–9). Christ, dead and resurrected, purifies and sanctifies us: these are the two inseparable aspects of the transformation of the redeemed, just as the resurrection was required by the Passion,[16] the glorification of Christ being the reward for his sacrifice "Propter quod et Deus exaltavit illum" (Phil. 2:9), even while it was a necessity of his divine nature.[17] Christ, who died on account of our sins,

glorification to come. His resurrection had our salvation as its object; it was for us that he wished to die and rise again. See Durrwell, 75–7; 92.

[16] Christ's soul was glorified, invisibly as far as we are concerned, immediately after the Passion, and his body was visibly glorified by the resurrection.

[17] The splendour of the Godhead should have shone forth in his humanity as it did at the transfiguration. This is probably the sense in which we are to understand the opening of the epistle to the Romans (1:3–4), although certain shades of meaning in this passage are the subject of argument. (Is it, for instance, the power of the Son of God who is risen that is referred to, or the power of the Father who raises him?). The Son of God is, "in respect of his human birth, from the line of David" in the fashion of our guilty nature (Rom. 8:3). That is to say, he was capable of suffering and mortal but free from sin (2 Cor. 5:21) and his incarnation has as its aim the abolition of the reign of sin. He was thus in a certain way marked with the sin he had just expiated, but that state could not be final and Christ was raised to life by the Father "in respect of the sanctified spirit", in accordance with the requirements of his supereminent holiness, of the great holiness of his spiritual nature, and of his divine sonship, veiled by the flesh. He was thus placed in the rank of Son of God (compare Acts 13:33–34; Heb. 1:5), not, obviously, in himself, but in his capacity as Messiah and ruler of nations, in the majesty demanded by his status as Son of God that was to be expressed in the divine name of Kyrios, Lord (used in this passage and in Phil. 2:11). After having appeared as terrestrial man, exception made for sin, Christ was henceforward to appear as the celestial man and "life-giving spirit" in his almighty sanctifying power (1 Cor. 15:45). See Boismard, Revue Biblique 1953, 5–17; Durrwell, 70–1; 122–4.

makes us die to sin. His own life is for God and he gives us the gift of a life in him that is also for God (Rom. 6:10–11). We are reconciled to God through his death and find salvation in his life (Rom. 5:10). "In life and in death, we belong to the Lord. That was why Christ died and lived again" (Rom. 14:9). But justification was accomplished by a unique act and in dependence upon the resurrection. Simplifying the situation somewhat, we might say that the Passion merited justification – which is at once death to sin and the gift of life – and that the resurrection confers justification on us. But let us say once more, death and resurrection are inseparable in Christ and in the Christian. We can see immediately the moral approach that these great truths impose. The Christian who is forgiven and justified must in future live the life of one who is crucified and has been raised again, in a persevering effort of death to sin and of renewed life (Rom. 6:5–8). We can understand, too, why the resurrection is always mentioned in conjunction with the Passion. Strictly speaking, it is not a question of two separate events, but of a single mystery with a two-fold aspect. The liturgy, like scripture, is always careful never to separate the resurrection and the Passion.[18]

The Father showed in this way that he accepted his Son's sacrifice and the resurrection is his work. Paul speaks of it with the deepest admiration, remarking: "What surpassing virtue there is in his dealings with us, who believe. Measure it by that mighty exercise of power which he showed when he raised Christ from the dead, and bade him sit on his right hand above the heavens" (Eph. 1:19–20). At the same time as he raised him by his power,

---

[18] Christ "by dying hath overcome our death, and by rising again hath restored our life" (Preface for Easter). Compare the collects for Palm Sunday and the Thursday in Holy Week and the antiphon *Crucem tuam* in the Good Friday liturgy. The sacrifice of the Mass is offered in memory of the Passion, the resurrection and the ascension (the prayer *Unde et memores* after the consecration).

he raised him by his glory (Rom. 6:4). The apostle regards these expressions as practically equivalent to each other (2 Thess. 1:9; Col. 1:11). In his estimation, the power designates the Spirit with whom, moreover, it is constantly associated in the same passage, both in the Old Testament, the gospels and the Acts (Luke 4:14, 18; 24:29; Acts 1:8; 10:38). Thus it is that the apostle writes: "May he (the Father)... strengthen you through his Spirit with a power that reaches your innermost being" (Eph. 3:16). He makes it sufficiently clear that the resurrection of the Saviour was also the work of the Spirit when he says: "And if the Spirit of him who raised up Jesus from the dead dwells in you, he who raised up Jesus Christ from the dead will give life to your perishable bodies too, for the sake of his Spirit who dwells in you" (Rom. 8:11). Elsewhere, he later speaks more explicitly of the "great mystery we worship. Revelation made in human nature, justification won in the realm of the Spirit... taken up into glory" (1 Tim. 3:16). What can this mean except that the mystery, which is here none other than Jesus Christ himself, after having been shown in the weakness of the flesh, has come to be seen perfectly just and eminently holy, thanks to the Spirit which dwelt in him and which has taken possession of his flesh in order to glorify it?[19] He writes of Christ in the same sense to the Corinthians, remarking that "weakness brought him to the cross, but the power of God brought him life" (2 Cor. 13:4).[20]

Christ, risen and raised to heaven, sees his own primacy as first born before every act of creation (Col. 1:15), and as creature honoured with the precedence of "the first birth out of death; thus in every way the primacy was to become his" (Col. 1:18). He is raised infinitely higher than the angels, seated at the right hand of God the Father in heaven, high above all princedoms,

[19] See Spicq's commentary on this passage.
[20] Compare: 1 Peter 3:18 and see Durrwell, 115–121.

powers, virtues and dominations, and every name that is known, not in this world only, but in the world to come (Eph. 1:21). His dominion is universal and he not only possesses the "plenitude of Deity" (Col. 2:9), but is also the principle of the Cosmos, of the created universe. All completeness dwells in him; and he wins back to God all things celestial and all men (Col. 1:19–20). He brings his gifts to men (Eph. 4:7–16) and becomes the head whose body is the Church, acquired through his blood (Col. 1:18). The Father "has put everything under his dominion, and made him the head to which the whole Church is joined, so that the Church is his body, the completion of him who everywhere and in all things is complete" (Eph. 1:22–23).

Thus, the risen Christ is not merely transformed by the Spirit in his human nature but becomes a "life-giving spirit" (1 Cor. 15:45). His body is henceforth a spiritual one, filled to overflowing with the Spirit. He is the celestial man, possessing all the power and fullness of divinity and he fulfils his spiritual activity without any of the limitations hitherto imposed upon him by his flesh, which was "in the fashion of our guilty nature" (Rom. 8:3). That is why the dispensation of the Spirit could not precede Christ's glorification. The Spirit could shine forth fully from his sacred humanity only when it was no longer in the fashion of our guilty nature.[21] It is in the same sense that the fourth gospel vigorously underlines how the gift of the Holy Spirit was limited until the glorification of the Saviour: "the Spirit which had not yet been given to men" (7:39). Our Saviour himself declared that the sending of the Spirit depended on his own return to the Father (16:7). Monsignor Cerfaux even goes so far as to say that logically the resurrection is the first thing. Christ had to die in order to be the first of the risen and

---

[21] From being a living soul, Christ becomes a "life-giving spirit", his body becomes a spiritual body, freed from the weaknesses and restrictions inherent in matter (see Durrwell, 218–9).

thus inaugurate the new creation, but before this could happen it was necessary for the old creation, contaminated by sin, to be destroyed and from this followed the need for Christ's death to destroy everything that was opposed to God and, for the Christian, the need to die to sin[22] in order to live according to the Spirit in Christ, in fulfilment of God's eternal plan: "And now, exalted at God's right hand, he has claimed from his Father his promise to bestow the Holy Spirit; and he has poured out that Spirit, as you can see and hear for yourselves" (Acts 2:33).[23]

The statements in the epistle to the Hebrews on the exercise of *Christ's priesthood* from the time of the resurrection should be interpreted in the same sense.

Christ is clearly priest and victim from the first moment of the incarnation: 10:5-10; 2:14; etc. But the epistle dwells more readily on the eternal character of his priesthood (7:3, 24, 28) and consequently on its exercise in his glorified state. He is the excellent and perfect High Priest because he passed with his blood not merely into a sanctuary made by human hands, but into heaven (4:14; 9:24; 7:26). He was thus appointed a minister "in the sanctuary, in that true tabernacle" (8:2), living on still to make intercession on our behalf (7:25). As our escort, he has entered already "a high priest, now, eternally with the priesthood of Melchisedech" (6:20). He is "crowned, now, with glory and honour because of the death he underwent" (2:9) and his

---

[22] Cerfaux, *Christ in the Theology of Saint Paul*, 126-7, 158.

[23] It goes without saying that St. Paul does not confuse Christ with the Spirit, in spite of expressions such as that in 2 Cor. 3:17-18, which may seem ambiguous. But he associates Christ and the Spirit in the sanctification of the redeemed. The Spirit is communicated thanks to the redemption accomplished by Christ. They join in a common work, hence the partial equivalence of the expressions "in Christ" and "in the Spirit". The Spirit dwells in us to unite us to Christ. It is extremely important to realize that the whole Pauline theology is Trinitarian, based on the distinction and the divinity of the Persons, even though the matter is not expressed quite in this form.

glorification shows that he indeed died on behalf of all (ibid.). He sits at the right hand of God, waiting until his enemies are reduced to impotence and made a footstool under his feet (10:12–14). The resurrection was the starting point of a new stage in his priesthood (5:9–10). It was an essential part of that priesthood, being the continuation of the offering of his Passion, together with the exercise of his intercession, of his mediation. If he had remained on earth he would not have been a priest, since he was not a descendant of Aaron (8:4–5). In heaven, he is eternally a priest: he remains a victim because he continues to offer himself, and his glorification shows also the enduring nature of the Father's acceptance of his sacrifice, which was inaugurated at the resurrection. The blood of Jesus has all the time "better things to say than Abel's had" (12:24). As Durrwell says, "The offering of his death is made eternal in the divinizing acceptance which crowns it".[24] It is in this sense that we can follow the French school in speaking of a celestial sacrifice of Christ. True, Christ was already the Son of God and High Priest during his earthly life but he is so even more completely in heaven. His priesthood is no longer meritorious, but it is perpetuated and becomes fully efficacious. Through the risen Jesus, we are brought closer to the Father and can approach him with confidence (4:16; 10:19; 12:22–24). We are purified from "lifeless observances" (9:14).

The salvation of men is thus dependent entirely on the Son of God, incarnate, crucified and glorified. The role of Christ's humanity is fundamental and permanent. It had been the instrument of the redemption. It is as man that Christ has merited our salvation. But the role of his sanctified humanity continues in his glorified state. It is entirely penetrated by the Spirit which it spreads forth over us, applying the fruits of the redemptive

[24] Durrwell, 174.

sacrifice. Redeemed man is intimately united to Christ's glorified body and we shall see later the light thrown by this outlook on the doctrine of the Mystical Body and of the Eucharist. The sacred body of the Saviour is indeed the Temple of the new law, the place where God and man meet, as our Lord mysteriously indicated at the time of his first sojourn in Jerusalem (John 2:19–22).

When St. Paul speaks of Christ, he makes little distinction between our Saviour's successive states and, as it were, says everything at once. In his intuitive approach, he does not indicate explicitly the distinctions that theology had later to make, but there can be no doubt that, for him, Christ is a unique person who eternally pre-exists, who created the world and saved it by his Passion and resurrection. The apostle's teaching implies a complete doctrine of the incarnation, as we shall see in a celebrated passage which we have deliberately kept until now.

In his letter to the Philippians, in an exhortation to charity one towards the other, we find an exceptionally full doctrinal exposition, the rhythm of which suggests a liturgical hymn, adapted or composed by the apostle:

"For let this mind be in you, which was also in Christ Jesus: who being in the form of God, thought it not robbery to be equal with God: but emptied himself, taking the form of a servant, being made in the likeness of men, and in habit found as a man. He humbled himself, becoming obedient unto death, even to the death of the cross. For which cause, God also hath exalted him and hath given him a name which is above all names: that in the name of Jesus every knee should bow, of those that are in heaven, on earth, and under the earth: and that every tongue should confess that the Lord Jesus Christ is in the glory of God the Father (Phil. 2:5–11 [Douai]).

Christ, whose pre-existence is indirectly affirmed, was of divine rank and, in consequence, had from the very moment of his entry into the world, the right to a glorified human nature such as he

111

has possessed since the resurrection. But he did not see, in the rank of Godhead, a prize to be coveted,[25] that is to say, of course, not the divine nature of which he could obviously not empty himself, but the divine honours going with it, in which he ought to have shared in his human nature. He gave up this manifestation of divine glory and voluntarily emptied himself, in contrast with the first man who had tried to make himself equal to God. The vigorous expression "dispossession" or *kenosis* emphasizes the extent of the renunciation that Christ accepted. Instead of assuming in his human nature a rank consonant with his divinity, he took the status of a slave or servant, that is to say a human nature like our own and subject to all its limitations, including suffering and death.[26] He is the servant of Jahveh foretold by Isaias (53). Nevertheless, his emptying did not consist in the fact of the incarnation. The dispossession was, no doubt, a condition of it but did not constitute it, because the incarnation

[25] The precise meaning of the word ἁρπαγμός is disputed. The active sense is "robbery" or "usurpation": Christ did not regard the equality with God which was his as a theft or a robbery. But it seems better to take it in the passive sense of "prey" or "booty" of which Christ voluntarily stripped himself. The question is not one of claim but of renunciation. (The passage rendered in Knox "His nature is, from the first divine, and yet he did not see, in the rank of Godhead, a prize to be coveted" is rendered in the Douai, "who being in the form of God, thought it not robbery to be equal with God" — a version closer to the author's — Translator.)

[26] A distinction is clearly made between permanent existence in the divine dignity (ὑπάρχων in the present participle) and the condition of servant assumed at a particular moment of time (γενόμενος in verse 8, reinforced by the aorists ἡγήσατο and ἐκένωσεν). Two other successive states are equally in opposition, one with the other. They are μορφή which signifies the divine rank which cannot be divested and supposes divine nature but is distinct from it, and the condition of servant which is a human, non-privileged state, together with all the exterior accompaniments (σχήματι). Christ did not abandon the divine μορφή, but did give up exterior equality with God. ἴσα Θεῷ, which was something capable of abandonment. Cf. SDB, *Kénose*, 8–38 (Henry).

112

persists and the glorified Christ can obviously not be considered as stripped or emptied. Also, in spite of the contrary view held by many of the Fathers, we consider it more likely that St. Paul is dealing here with Christ's renunciation of treatment as an equal with God, his renunciation of a showing forth of the divinity in majesty, power and glory, of an exercise of divine attributes. Christ assumed the status of a servant though he was by right Son of God and Lord. He thus appeared outwardly as a man and seemed to be man only. In the servile condition constituted by obedience, he humbled himself even more, not merely as a servant but in obedience unto death and unto the death on the cross. It would have been quite impossible to obey more perfectly and to humble himself more completely.

In return, God exalted him sovereignly by the resurrection and the ascension and gave him the Name that is greater than any other name – he gave him, that is to say, the supreme dignity: the servant had become the universal Lord, re-established in the glory that he possessed as Son of God before he took on human nature that shines forth henceforward in his risen humanity. "In Christ the whole plenitude of Deity is embodied, and dwells in him" (Col. 2:9). The whole universe and particularly those beings that are endowed with intelligence must acknowledge his overlordship because, by the Passion, the descent into hell[27] and the ascension, he took possession of the whole of the universe in a new way as redeemer (compare Col. 2:19; Eph. 1:22; 4:10) and this universal homage has as its aim the greater glory of God the Father.

The name henceforth given to Jesus is "that name which is greater than any other name", the unutterable name which, in the final analysis, can be none other than that of Jahveh, but whose concrete translation is the title of Lord, the Kyrios of the

---

[27] Like all those who die, Christ had to descend to *Sheol*.

Septuagint, which translates the Adonai of the Hebrew bible, the name reserved to God.[28] By the resurrection he becomes Lord in the eyes of men, possessing the full Messianic overlordship conferred on his humanity in so far as it is united to the divinity. Peter proclaimed this on Pentecost morning: "Let it be known, then, beyond doubt, to all the house of Israel, that God has made him Master and Christ, this Jesus whom you crucified" (Acts 2:36). And Paul said it many times after him (1 Cor. 8:6; 12:3; Rom. 1:4), but never, doubtless, with more solemnity than in the passage in the epistle to the Philippians. He was not unaware that the title of Lord, a term of respect, was given to emperors and to false gods (1 Cor. 8:5). But the use he made of it excluded any ambiguity. He gives it also to the Father (1 Cor. 3:5) and fills out the sense with connected expressions, which he applies equally to the Father and the Son. Examples are the invocation of the name of the Lord (1 Cor. 1:3; Rom. 10:13; 2 Tim. 2:22), fear of the Lord (2 Cor. 5:11; Eph. 5:21), the grace of the Lord (Gal. 6:18; Rom. 16:20), the day and Parousia of the Lord (1 Thess. 5:23; 2 Thess. 2:1–2), faith in the Lord as shown by belief in his resurrection: "Thou canst find salvation, if thou wilt use thy lips to confess that Jesus is the Lord, and thy heart to believe that God has raised him up from the dead" (Rom. 10:9). He is "Lord both of the dead and of the living" (Rom. 14:9), the Lord of glory (1 Cor. 2:8 [Douai]; 2 Cor. 3:18; compare Eph. 1:17); the glory of God shining forth in the face of Christ Jesus (2 Cor. 4:4, 6). We see this glory at present like a confused reflection in a mirror, waiting till we shall see it face to face (1 Cor. 13:12). The title "Son of God", less frequently used than that of "Lord" and preferred to it in the epistle to the Hebrews (1:1–13), is no less significant: Christ is the pre-

---

[28] That is why St. Paul does not hesitate to apply to Christ the passages in the Old Testament relating to Jahveh. Even here, the terms he uses are partly borrowed from Isaias, 45:23, a passage dealing with Jahveh.

existing Son of God (Gal. 4:4; Rom. 8:3). He is the only be-gotten and well-loved Son, the true likeness of God (Col. 1:13, 15), "the radiance of his Father's splendour, and the full ex-pression of his being" (Heb. 1:3). In a word, he is God's own Son (Rom. 8:32), like the Father in the identity of the same nature received from him.

No one will deny that this constitutes a great mystery, but there could hardly fail to be a mystery in the assumption by the eternal Son of human nature. This mystery, foreseen by the prophets, underlying the gospels and epistles alike, demands our faith unless we are to reject the inspired texts as valueless and refuse to admit the divine testimony expressed by Christ's holi-ness, his miracles, his resurrection, and the action of the Holy Ghost in the Church. The timidity and denials of the theologies described as independent make them incapable of accounting for the faith of the apostles and of primitive Christianity. For Paul, as for the Eleven (1 Cor. 15:11), it is one individual, a single person, who pre-exists from all eternity, who took on a human nature like our own, suffered on the cross and has been glorified at the right hand of God. This essential truth is gradually brought out more and more explicitly in a respectful meditation. It is made clearer by apostolic effort and by the enlightenment of the Holy Spirit. The ancient Christian creeds expressed it in more elaborate terms and served until the time when the Christological heresies were to provoke the definitions of Nicea, Ephesus and Chalcedon. It is in one sense more satisfying for the mind, and no doubt clearer, to recognize the existence in Jesus Christ of the two natures, divine and human, in the one person of the Son of God and to proclaim him consubstantial with the Father.[29] But was not the early Christian community proclaiming the same

[29] Speaking of the definitions of the councils concerning the incar-nation, Father de Grandmaison wrote: "These definitions are sacred for us. They preserve our hopes. But their light shows the reef. It does not

faith when it delighted in calling him who was crucified on Calvary, "Jesus Christ our Lord", and repeated after Paul this fragment of a hymn, overflowing with zeal and love:

> It is a great mystery we worship. Revelation made in human nature, justification won in the realm of the Spirit; a vision seen by angels, a mystery preached to the Gentiles; Christ in this world, accepted by faith, Christ, on high, taken up into glory (1 Tim. 3:16).[30]

---

attract like the glow of a friendly hearth. They are made of a hard metal ... armour rather than sustenance. For spiritual nourishment and warmth the Christian will always prefer the inspired words, full of sap, that are to be garnered in the scriptures" (*Jésus-Christ*, Beauchesne, 1928, 11 and 216).

[30] It is worth noting that the doctrine of the incarnation and the resurrection is incompatible with a dualism that would regard matter as evil. All that God created is very good (Gen. 1:31). The redeeming and sanctifying role of Christ's humanity establishes the same point in an even more striking way. His "spiritual" body (the word does not imply immaterial) is the focal point of the redeemed world. It is in his image that our bodies will be transformed on the last day (Phil. 3:21) with perhaps a repercussion on the material world itself (Rom. 8:19–22). The institution of the sacraments also infinitely exalts matter by using it for the transmission of supernatural life.

Further reading: Cerfaux, *Christ*, 375–97; *Recueil Lucien Cerfaux*, Gembloux, Duculot, 1954, I, 3–186; II, 425–54; Bonsirven, *Évangile de Paul*, 64–9; Spicq, *Épître aux Hébreux*, I, 291–301; Bonsirven, *Épître aux Hébreux*, 36–48; SDB, *Kyrios*, 221–8 (Cerfaux); Kittel, *κύριος* III, 1083–95 (Foerster).

PART TWO

PARTICIPATION IN SALVATION
INDIVIDUAL ASPECT

CHRIST, man and God, is the author of salvation. All men are saved by his sacrifice and vivified by his resurrection. This result existed by right from the moment of the last breath drawn by the Saviour and, from his glorification onwards, he has spread the fruits of it among men. In earlier chapters, we have attempted to give some inkling of the nature of these fruits. It is important, however, to show also in what salvation consists and what is required of men in order to attain it.

All men are called to salvation,[1] the heathen as well as the Israelites. This is a mystery at one time hidden, or at least only incompletely revealed, and St. Paul received the special mission of making it known (Eph. 3:2–12). He gives general expression to the idea: "Christ among you, your hope of glory" (Col. 1:27) and completes the thought by insisting on the abolition of all distinction between Jews and Greeks. "There is nothing but Christ in any of us" (Col. 3:11). Not only are barriers broken down and differences wiped out, whether they arise from race, social condition or sex, but, through their participation in salvation, all men join in the deepest unity. "You are all one person in Jesus Christ" (Gal. 3:28). The central idea expressed thus is of a sanctifying and unifying presence of Christ through the communication of his life. The individual and collective aspects are closely linked and we shall distinguish them only to make the account clearer, without forgetting that they are, in fact, inseparable and complementary.

[1] See chapter 4 above.

7

THE NEW MAN. JUSTIFICATION

God "imparts holiness to those who take their stand upon faith in Jesus Christ" (Rom. 3:26).

IF it be true, as St. Irenaeus asserted, that Christ "brought complete renewal in giving himself"[1] there is no room for surprise that St. Paul should present a share in salvation as a renewal which reaches to the very depths of our being. The Christian is a new man, built on the ruins of the old or sinful man. This is a fundamental theme, acting as a corollary to the theme of salvation and to that of Christ the new Adam who came to make superabundant reparation for the ravages caused by the fall of the first man. All died in Adam, but all will live in Christ, "the life-giving spirit" (1 Cor. 15:22, 45). By Adam's disobedience all became guilty, but by Christ's obedience all will be made acceptable to God (Rom. 5:19). The effect of a share in salvation is to crucify our former nature and annihilate the living power of our guilt (Rom. 6:6). This means man in so far as he is like the fallen Adam, and the body to the extent that it is given over to sin. But death invades life, and our former nature makes way for our new nature, similar to that of Adam before the fall. A radical change is thus effected in two inseparable phases:

[1] "Omnem novitatem attulit seipsum afferens." *Adv. haer.* 1.4, c. 34, n. 1; PG, VII, 1083.

You must be quit of the old self, and the habits that went with it; you must be clothed in the new self, that is being refitted all the time for closer knowledge, so that the image of the God who created it is its pattern (Col. 3:9–10).

You must be quit, now, of the old self whose way of life you remember, the self that wasted its aim on false dreams. There must be a renewal in the inner life of your minds; you must be clothed in the new self, which is created in God's image, justified and sanctified through the truth (Eph. 4:22–24).

To put the matter precisely, the new self is none other than Christ whom we put on in baptism (Gal. 3:27) in a complete submission to his divine influence. The change is so radical as to result in a divine creation in Christ Jesus (Eph. 2:10) – in other words, a new creature (Gal. 6:15). It would be impossible to conceive a more striking expression of the idea. At all events, what was old has passed away and something new has appeared (2 Cor. 5:17). There has been a regeneration, and a renewal of our nature in the Holy Spirit (Titus 3:5), the ultimate effect of which is to form Christ in the Christian by a process of spiritual birth (Gal. 4:19).[2] It is not a question of a static condition, perfect from the start, but of a state that the life of the neophyte must confirm and complete in an uninterrupted spiritual progress, calling forth "such good actions as he has prepared beforehand, to be the employment of our lives" (Eph. 2:10).

St. Paul delights in celebrating this renewal, which is the beginning of salvation and which fills him with admiration. Those who believe in Christ have turned away from idolatry to the worship of a living God, a God who really exists (1 Thess. 1:9); from darkness to light (1 Thess. 5:4–5; Rom. 13:12; Eph. 5:8; etc.); from the principle of sin and death to that of the spirit of life (Rom. 8:2); from the service of the law to that of grace

---

[2] Compare the rebirth announced by Christ to Nicodemus (John 3:3–5). St. Paul's predilection for such expressions as "new self", "new creature" and "renewal" is symptomatic.

and of justice (Rom. 6:14, 18, 19); from the bondage of anger to that of love (Rom. 5:8-9). They have rid themselves of the leaven which remains over, so that they may be a new mixture (1 Cor. 5:7). A breath of Spring has transformed the world, the era of life and of peace has been inaugurated by Christ (Rom. 8:6). The ultimate effects of conforming to the new Adam will become apparent on the day of the resurrection (Rom. 8:11). Christ's victory is the guarantee of our own and justifies a fundamental optimism that should not be shaken by the drama of the internal dissensions and the tragic character of the Church's struggles.

Paul once more uses various metaphors to describe the new state of the Christian. The debt of sin has been remitted to him and his sin forgiven (Col. 1:14). He has been ransomed – and at a great price (1 Cor. 6:20; 7:23) – by the outpouring of the blood of Jesus (Rom. 3:24). He has thus been reconciled to God (Rom. 5:10-11; 2 Cor. 5:18-19; Col. 1:22) and no judgement now stands against him (Rom. 8:1). From being God's enemy, he has become a son by adoption (Gal. 4:5; Rom. 8:15; Eph. 1:5). To resume, then, he is justified – and this is the expression most frequently used – by the completely free granting of divine justice (Rom. 3:24; 1:17). This not only puts an end to the state of sinfulness but also has the positive effect of sanctification.

Justification is thus, at one and the same time, destruction of sin and communication of a new life. The first aspect is adequately shown in the passages in which the apostle deals with the stripping and crucifixion of the old self, forgiveness of sins and reconciliation to God, but there is no forgiveness that is not accompanied by the transmission of new life, that is without positive justification or sanctification, without the formation of the new self. The texts already quoted all indicate in some degree this two-fold aspect. There are others even more characteristic:

Christ Jesus, whom God gave us to be all our wisdom, our justification, our sanctification, and our atonement (1 Cor. 1:30).
Now you have been washed clean, now you have been sanctified,
now you have been justified in the name of the Lord Jesus, by
the Spirit of the God we serve (1 Cor. 6:11).

We shall show further on how it follows clearly enough from
the gift of the Holy Spirit, from the life of Christ in us, and
from the adoption of sons, that it is a question on all sides of
interior realities and that justification is not, as Luther would
have it, a simple imputation of divine justice, or a reconciliation
still leaving a state of sin. This interior character is, moreover,
implied by the antithesis between our solidarity in Adam and our
solidarity in Christ. In Adam, all are made sinners and in Christ,
all are made just. The fault of the first man merits condemnation
for all. Christ's act of justice merits for them the justification
which gives life. Sin was amplified, but grace has been more
amply bestowed than ever (Rom. 5:18–20). The second state,
which corrects the clearly interior stain of the first, must have the
same characteristics. It is in the same sense that we are to understand affirmations that God made Christ into sin for us, so that in
him we might be turned into the holiness of God (2 Cor. 5:21),
that justification saves us from God's displeasure (Rom. 5:9) and
makes us heirs, with the hope of eternal life set before us
(Tit. 3:7), and that, by Christ's sacrifice, God shows that he is
himself holy and imparts holiness to those who take their stand
upon faith in Jesus (Rom. 3:26). To regard justification as
nothing more than an ineffective declaration or a purely formal
imputation is to adopt a view diametrically opposed to St. Paul's.[3]
How can we understand except as an interior reality that Christ
was "handed over to death for our sins, and raised to life for our

[3] For a Semite particularly, the word of God has a creative effect. If
God declares a man just he renders him truly so.

justification" (Rom. 4:25)? Paul again shows that this is what he means when he contrasts the justification of the Christian with the purely legal justice resulting from the observance of the Mosaic law.[4] The converted heathen obtained the true justice that comes from faith because, following the example of the apostle, they did not seek a justice depending upon themselves, the result of fulfilling legal requirements, but justice coming from God and founded on faith in Christ (Rom. 9:30; Phil. 3:9).

In order to indicate this essential truth, St. Paul sometimes uses the expression "justification"and at others that of "the justice of God". The latter term is used to describe justice both as a divine attribute and as a gift transmitted to men, "the just and merciful action of God who obtained satisfaction for sins through the sacrifice of the cross and who dispenses justice and new life to men, through the mediation of Christ".[5] God shows that he is himself just and that he justifies those who have faith in Jesus (Rom. 3:26). Clearly, God considers just those whom he has rendered just, and implicitly declares them to be so. But he does not, strictly speaking, pronounce a judgement. The judgement is reserved for the day of the appearance before the judgement seat of Christ (Rom. 2:16; 14:10; 2 Cor. 5:10). Then it is that God will finally declare just those who are just, having remained faithful to the end.[6]

Justification is a fixed state but one that can be lost and which thus does not allow us to doze in careless spiritual apathy. The moral exhortations contained in the epistles are a constant

[4] We will not return here to the question of the law's inability to justify, already dealt with in chapter 5, section III.

[5] Huby, *Épître aux Romains*, 66. In the act of justifying, God therefore operates as a merciful Father, faithful to his promises, rather than as a judge.

[6] Further reading: Tobac, *Le problème de la Justification dans s. Paul*, Louvain, Van Linthout, 1908; SDB, *Grâce* (Bonnetain), 1270–8; *Enseignement de s. Paul*, I, 219–32; Kittel, δικαιοσύνη, I, 204–14; δικαιόω, I, 219–23 (Schrenk).

invitation to effort. Once justified, we must be at peace with God (Rom. 5:1), shedding our old nature more and more fully. We must free ourselves from sin in order to make ourselves over to God (Rom. 6:11–14), multiplying those good works which God has prepared beforehand to be the employment of our lives (Eph. 2:10). But, when St. Paul speaks of justification, he is thinking particularly of initial justification or the passage from the state of sin to that of justice, which requires the fulfilment of a two-fold condition: faith in Jesus Christ and reception of baptism.

8

THE WAY TO JUSTIFICATION:
FAITH AND BAPTISM

*God "saved us, with the cleansing power
which gives us new birth, and restores
our nature through the Holy Spirit"
(Titus 3:5).*

THE study of St. Paul's conversion and of justification in the
light of the story of Abraham[1] has shown us what faith means
for the apostle and how it leads to justification independently
of the works of the Mosaic law. We need to go more deeply
into certain points which we have so far only touched upon in
passing and also to add more details.

The epistle to the Hebrews (11:1) gives what has become
a classic definition of faith:

What is faith? It is that which gives substance to our hopes,
which convinces us of things we cannot see.

The second part of this definition repeats and goes beyond the
first. Faith convinces us of the existence of invisible things,
whether present realities or future blessings, the possession of
which is promised to us but is not yet realized, at least completely.[2]

---

[1] See chapter 1 and chapter 5, section II, above.
[2] See Spicq, in I. In this world, we possess only the first-fruits of the
Spirit: 2 Cor. 1:22; 5:5; Eph. 1:14.

It gives us the certainty of possessing these good things one day. This, as the epistle insists a little further on, was the case with Abraham (11:11–12; compare Rom. 4:18–21), when he believed on the word of God that he would become the father of a numerous posterity. But in a more general way, faith is the proof of those things that are not seen. It shows the existence of the supernatural realities which are beyond the reach of our senses.

The immediate source of Christian faith is the witness of the preachers of the gospel. But the preaching of the apostles was in reality the word of Christ and, ultimately, the word of God: "See how faith comes from hearing; and hearing through Christ's word" (Rom. 10:17). Paul congratulates the Thessalonians on having received the divine word that he preached to them and with having accepted it "for what it is, God's message, not man's" (1 Thess. 2:13). This being its character, the apostles would have to be regarded as guilty of false witness regarding God himself, were they to preach false doctrine (1 Cor. 15:15). The faith is a tradition, a παράδοσις, an unchanging deposit (1 Cor. 11:2, 23; 15:1–2; 1 Tim. 6:20; 2 Tim. 1:14; etc.) transmitted by the apostles and, in a word, by "the Church of the living God, the pillar and foundation upon which the truth rests" (1 Tim. 3:15). But this guarantee of infallible doctrine is based in the last analysis on the fact that it is on divine authority.

The object of this divine witness is to transmit the content of the gospel message which is, above all, that of Christ, Son of God and Redeemer, and also to pass on the message of the existence of a God who rewards – belief in this latter point is indispensable, even for those who know nothing of Christ (Heb. 11:6). Thinking no doubt of his own conversion, the apostle readily sums up this message in an expression of the paschal mystery: "Thou canst find salvation, if thou wilt use thy lips to confess that Jesus is the Lord, and thy heart to believe that God has raised him up from the dead" (Rom. 10:9; compare: 1 Cor. 15:2 et seq.; 2 Cor. 4:13–14; Col. 2:12; Eph. 1:19–20; 1 Thess. 4:14). This succinct confession of faith has the advantage of linking the Christian faith with that of Abraham, which was its precursor and, as it were, a preliminary sketch; for the patriarch believed in God "who can raise the dead to life, and send his call to that which has no being" (Rom. 4:17). It enunciates, too, the central point of revelation: God's redemptive action in the dead and risen Christ, Saviour and Lord. Christ is both the author and the object of faith.

In itself, the divine witness transmitted by the apostles remains hidden and obscure in spite of the miracles and Christ's resurrection, which authenticate it. We have to accept the mysteries of divine life, of Christ and of the redemption on the authority of the word. We walk here below with faith and not with a clear view to guide our steps (2 Cor. 5:7). We know the object of our faith only imperfectly, as though seen in a mirror, and as an enigma. The vision face to face is reserved for eternal life (1 Cor. 13:12). But it is, nevertheless, an infinitely precious light that shines in our hearts "in order that there should shine forth from them the knowledge of the glory of God [that radiates] from the face of Christ" [3] (2 Cor. 4:6). St. Paul calls upon the faithful to progress unceasingly in that wisdom in which the world sees nothing but folly (1 Cor. 1:22–25), in order that they may become spiritually mature (1 Cor. 3:1–2) and live in a manner worthy of the Lord (Col. 1:9–10). It follows from this that for the Christian, as for the apostle, faith is not simply the assent of the intelligence to the word of God and of Christ but is a total gift, a complete change of direction, which makes thought prisoner in order to bring man entirely into the obedience of Christ (2 Cor. 10:5). In this way, not only

[3] Translator's own rendering.

does the believer give up the autonomy of his own thinking[4] but he deliberately abandons the idea that he is himself a centre. He is ready to put on Christ, allowing himself to be penetrated with Christ's life (Gal. 3:27; 2:20). In the light of his knowledge of Christ, he deliberately chooses to look upon as refuse what he was once wont to consider enviable privileges, to give up his own justice in favour of that which comes from God and

---

[4] Intellectual humility, which is a constituent of faith, is clearly brought out in the famous passage in which St. Paul contrasts the false wisdom of the world with *Christian wisdom:* 1 Cor. 1:17 to 3:16. The apostle vigorously criticizes the frivolity and what we would today call the rationalism of the Greek mind which amused itself with mere sophistries having no real influence on life and which rejected all revelation, accepting only the enlightenment that came from natural reason. He attacks at the same time the attenuated rationalism of the Jews who, while accepting the revelation of Moses, rejected Christian revelation which was its continuation and completion and particularly rejected the mystery of the cross. "Here are the Jews asking for signs and wonders, here are the Greeks intent on their philosophy; but what we preach is Christ crucified; to the Jews, a discouragement, to the Gentiles, mere folly; but to us who have been called, Jew and Gentile alike, Christ the power of God, Christ the wisdom of God" (1 Cor. 1:23–25).

Proud reason having shown itself incapable of recognizing God in his works (1 Cor. 1:21 and Rom. 1:19–23), God has scorned its shortsighted wisdom and turned instead to an apparently senseless expedient, the paradox of Christ crucified, the efficacy of which it accepted as the supreme wisdom. Paul, the wiser for his set-back in Athens (Acts 17:32–34), did not bother in Corinth to use the methods dictated by human wisdom and was not willing at first to preach anything but Christ crucified and risen (1 Cor. 2:1–5). To present Christ crucified and persuade people to read the Gospel will normally prove more effective than arguments and proofs which later come in useful to strengthen faith but will always presuppose the submission of reason to the divine witness which is beyond reason. Paul does not therefore condemn reason itself but only its abuse and its refusal to accept supernatural enlightenment.

Far from excluding the operation of man's intelligence and reasoning, the gospel offers to the human mind the most profound themes for meditation in the shape of the divine mysteries and the plan of salvation. This supreme wisdom is revealed by the Holy Spirit who finds out the

is founded in the faith of Christ (Phil. 3:7–9). Embracing the highest form of liberty, he is ready to make himself God's slave (2 Cor. 10:7; Rom. 6:17–19). In short, he is willing to become a new creature (Gal. 6:15). Understood in this way, faith extends to every aspect of life. It can be described as a paschal action because, with baptism to which it leads, it unites to the death and resurrection of Christ. Does not becoming a new creature in fact mean crucifying the flesh with its passions (Gal. 5:24) and offering oneself as a sacrifice with the Saviour (Rom. 15:16; Phil. 2:17)? But death with Christ enables us to share in his life and guarantees salvation (Rom. 10:9–11).[5]

This indispensable co-operation, whereby man places himself unreservedly in the hands of God is itself a divine gift. Everything in justification is unearned so that man has no cause to glorify himself.[6] No act of faith in Jesus Christ can be made without an intervention of the Holy Spirit (1 Cor. 12:3). If we are saved through faith, it is by the grace and gift of God (Eph. 2:8–9), it is not due to works (Rom. 11:6). Thus, strictly speaking, it is not faith that justifies but God who justifies by means of faith. Faith would be of no avail, and indeed would not be possible at all, but for God's merciful bounty and Christ's

---

very depths of God's nature, revealing the redemptive design and providing preachers with the means of communicating a knowledge of it in language best suited to the purpose, in such a way that they have an understanding of the Word and of its expression which is the very mind of Christ (1 Cor. 2:6–16). This is the starting point both of rational and of mystical theology. Paul earnestly hopes that those to whom he is writing will become adult in faith, capable of understanding and penetrating Christian wisdom (1 Cor. 3:1–4). Reason is thus not set aside but purified and exalted by the admirable object that is proposed for its exercise. See Allo, *Première épître aux Corinthiens*, 112–5; de Finance, *La Sophia chez s. Paul*, RSR 1935, 385–417, *Enseignement de s. Paul*, II, 160–8; Bonsirven, *L'Évangile de Paul*, 29–34; Dupont, *Gnosis*, Gabalda, 1949.

[5] See Durrwell, 387–9.

[6] See chapter 4 and chapter 5, section II.

sacrifice (Rom. 3:21–26).[7] The believer enters into the way of salvation, sustained on every side by God's generous gifts (Rom. 1:16), and saved in this way in principle, he will be saved in fact if he remains faithful (1 Cor. 15:1–2).

After having come to the faith, he must persevere and progress in it, in a word, live by the faith: "The justice of God is obtained through faith and itself increases faith" (Rom. 1:17).[8] The epistles continually repeat that no one will enter the kingdom of Christ and of God, and, in consequence, that no one will be saved, unless he observes all the requirements of Christian morality (Rom. 2:6–10; 6:11–12, 17–22; 8:5–9, 12–13; Gal. 5:21; Eph. 5:5; etc.). St. Paul sees the faith as something consistent, inspiring the whole life of the believer, as it inspired his own life. It must be animated by charity (Gal. 5:6; Eph. 3:17). The lyric quality of the first epistle to the Corinthians (13) in the passage dealing with the superiority and necessity of this, the greatest of all virtues, leaves no need for further quotations.

"I may speak with every tongue that men and angels use; yet, if I lack charity, I am no better than echoing bronze, or the clash of cymbals. I may have powers of prophecy, no secret hidden from me, no knowledge too deep for me; I may have utter faith, so that I can move mountains, yet if I lack charity, I count for nothing. I may give away all that I have, to feed the poor; I may give myself up to be burnt at the stake; if I lack charity, it goes for nothing. Charity is patient, is kind; charity feels no envy; charity is never perverse or proud, never insolent; does not claim its rights, cannot be provoked, does not brood over an injury, takes no pleasure in wrongdoing, but rejoices at the victory of

[7] The need for faith is so great that the epistle to the Hebrews (6:4–6; 10:26–29) declares the sin of apostasy or renunciation of the faith to be irreparable and of itself without remedy. Only a moral miracle of grace can rescue the apostate from his state which has put him outside the stream of salvation.

[8] Translator's own rendering.

truth; sustains, believes, hopes, endures, to the last" (1 Cor. 13:1–8).[9]

So great is the importance of charity that Paul calls it "the bond which makes us perfect" (Col. 3:14) and refers to it as the fulfilment of the law, contained in the special commandment to love our neighbour (Rom. 13:8–10; Gal. 5:14), a commandment we must follow the example of Christ crucified in observing (Eph. 5:2), rooting ourselves in charity and basing ourselves on it (Eph. 3:18).[10]

Faith also includes hope, for it is in part a waiting for good things to come, eternal life, celestial glory, and the graces necessary to accede to them. It is not for nothing that, right from the beginning of his epistles, St. Paul brackets together the three theological virtues: "Put on our breastplate, the breastplate of faith and love, our helmet, which is the hope of salvation" (1 Thess. 5:8; compare Gal. 5:5–6; Col. 1:4–5).[11] The works that we find here mentioned once more are not those of the Mosaic law but those of the Christian way of life and they are necessary in order to put off completely the old man, to persevere

[9] An exhaustive commentary on this passage will be found in Spicq, *Agapé dans le Nouveau Testament*, Book II (Études Bibliques), Gabalda, 1959. See also Kittel, I, ἀγάπη, 49–52 (Stauffer).

[10] See *Enseignement de saint Paul*, II, 126–32; Spicq, *Agapé*, I, 208–316.

[11] For a commentary on other Christian virtues such as liberality, humility, meekness and the requirement to work and on the evangelical counsels, see *Enseignement de saint Paul*, II, 133–9. Observance of the requirements of Christian morality makes the believer a balanced and admirable individual. "All that rings true, all that commands reverence, and all that makes for right; all that is pure, all that is lovely, all that is gracious in the telling; virtue and merit, wherever virtue and merit are found – let this be the argument of your thoughts. The lessons I taught you, the traditions I handed on to you, all you have heard and seen of my way of living – let this be your rule of conduct. Then the God of peace will be with you" (Phil. 4:8–9). This seems to us to provide an exceedingly attractive charter of Christian humanism.

in the state of justice and to raise ourselves to sanctity. It is in this sense that St. James's epistle (2:14–24) speaks of the need for works with faith, even in the case of Abraham. In doing so, St. James does not contradict St. Paul because he is referring to works accomplished after the preliminary justification. The co-operation that is demanded of man right from his first act of faith continues to be necessary until his last breath, but it is possible and meritorious only through the graces of the risen Christ and with the help of the Spirit received in baptism (Rom. 6; 8:1–13; etc.). Thus, from the first moment until its final con-summation, justice remains the communicated justice of God and a divine gift.

Some texts already quoted might lead us to suppose that St. Paul attributes justification to faith alone but he does not in fact speak of justification by faith except to contrast it with the works of the law. In his mind, faith presupposes a desire for baptism and should lead the person concerned to ask for it,[12] so that justification is both by faith and baptism. Even in his discussions with the Judaists, he occasionally mentions them together:

> Through faith in Jesus Christ you are all now God's sons. All you who have been baptized in Christ's name have put on the person of Christ (Gal. 3:26–27).

[12] St. Paul does not deal with the situation in which baptism has been deferred or is impossible, but it follows from his teaching that faith saves before baptism if it is perfect and includes a desire for baptism with an acceptance of the demands that baptism makes. The catechumen who fulfils these conditions is therefore saved but he must make an exterior profession of his faith and ask for the sacrament. When a whole family was baptized (Cornelius: Acts 10:47–48); Lydia, and the gaoler at Philippi, Acts 16:14–15; 29–34; Crispus: Acts 18:8, etc.), all its members do not seem to have been questioned about their faith, at least at the beginning. They were assumed to have the same dis-positions as the head of the family. For the children, the faith of the Church was a substitute and this has always been admitted to be the case since.

And in another passage:

> You, by baptism, have been united with his burial, united, too, with his resurrection, through your faith in that exercise of power by which God raised him from the dead (Col. 2:12; compare Eph. 4:5; Heb. 10:22).

He was himself baptized by Ananias, immediately after his conversion (Acts 9:18). Before that, from the time of Pentecost onwards, and again after the conversion of St. Paul, the first thing called for from converts by the apostles was baptism, coupled with faith and regret for sin (Acts 2:38, 41; 8:12–13, 36–38; 10:48; 19:5; etc.).

St. Paul's teaching on baptism is particularly rich and varied.

The salvation merited by Christ on the cross has a collective quality. It is the salvation of the new people, of the Church. Christ "gave himself for us, to ransom us from all our guilt, a people set apart for himself, ambitious of noble deeds" (Titus 2:14). He effected this salvation by his own reception of the sorrowful baptism of blood which he had foretold to the apostles (Mark 10:38; Luke 12:50) – a baptism which was completed by his resurrection and by the reception in his human nature of the overflowing of the Spirit which he was to communicate to the faithful.[13] The baptism of the cross constitutes at the same time the baptism of the Church:

> "Husbands show love to your wives as Christ showed love to the Church, and gave himself up for it in order to sanctify it by purifying it through bathing in water and through the words (which accompanies the bathing). Thus he would summon into his own presence a Church in all its beauty, without stain, wrinkle, or disfigurement but holy and immaculate" (Eph. 5:25–27).[14]

[13] By calling his death a baptism, Jesus prepared the way for the apostle's teaching.

[14] Translator's own rendering.

THE WAY TO JUSTIFICATION: FAITH AND BAPTISM

The Church is thus established and, in principle, baptized by the sacrifice and glorification of Christ. The allusion here to the sacrament is quite clear. In practice, everyone will receive baptism at the time the Church considers appropriate. The individual aspect completes the collective. Baptism constitutes an immersion in water combined with a form of words which explains its significance. A further text shows that it effects a regeneration, a new birth, which comprises justification, and therefore forgiveness of sins, and an abundant outpouring of the Spirit:

> God "saved us; and it was not thanks to anything we had done for our own justification. In accordance with his own merciful design he saved us, with the cleansing power which gives us new birth, and restores our nature through the Holy Spirit, shed on us in abundant measure through our Saviour, Jesus Christ. So, justified by his grace, we were to become heirs, with the hope of eternal life set before us" (Titus 3:5–7. Compare John 3:3 et seq.).

Thus, by baptism we come entirely gratuitously into the era of salvation, our entry depending solely on God's mercy.[15]

The aspect of purification and renewal is also to be found in another passage in which he appears to be referring to baptism. Paul reminds the Corinthians of their former vices which excluded entry into the kingdom of God, and adds: "That is what some of you once were; but now you have been washed clean, now you have been sanctified, now you have been justified in the name of the Lord Jesus, by the Spirit of the God we serve" (1 Cor. 6:11). The transformation is complete, and this is again shown by the apostle's parallel between circumcision and baptism:

[15] This is the commencement of salvation which awaits its eternal consummation. In the final analysis, it is Christ who baptizes, thus constituting the Church and introducing humanity into it in order that humanity may enter into communion with himself and with the Father (Eph. 2:18). But Christ acts through the Church and it is in the Church that we make contact with him.

"You have been circumcised with a circumcision that was not man's handiwork. It was effected, not by despoiling the natural body, but by Christ's circumcision" (Col. 2:11). Elsewhere (Rom. 2:25–29), he contrasts circumcision according to the flesh with true circumcision, which is that of the heart, according to the spirit and not the letter. Not that there can be any full parallel between the two: circumcision introduced the old covenant, as baptism introduced the new covenant, of which it was the harbinger. But it is baptism alone that strips the natural body of its passions and human weakness, by associating it with the death and resurrection of Christ.

Baptism is not only a rite of purification and renovation, but also constitutes an illumination. This point is not made quite explicit, but it may legitimately be deduced from a number of assertions. Christians are those who have received, once for all, their enlightenment and who have partaken of the Holy Spirit (Heb. 6:4; 10:32). They were once all darkness and now in the Lord they had become all light and must act in conformity (Eph. 5:8; compare 1 Thess. 5:8). But it is not a question of an illumination acting merely on the intelligence. The nature of faith as St. Paul sees it is enough to establish the point. Baptism is, in addition, a seal, and one which transforms, imprinted in the soul by the gift of the Holy Spirit: "It is God who gives both us and you our certainty in Christ; it is he who has anointed us, just as it is he who has put his seal on us, and given us the foretaste of his Spirit in our hearts" (2 Cor. 1:21–22; compare Eph. 1:13–14; 4:30).[16]

The fundamental thought in Paul is the one referred to above, linking the baptized with the death, burial and resurrection of

[16] Some take this passage to refer to the sacrament of confirmation, as do 1 Cor. 12:13 and Titus 3:4–7, but this interpretation is challenged. It is in any case certain that the first outpouring of the Spirit evokes the more complete outpouring in confirmation, clearly indicated in Acts 8:16.

Christ. He sets it out in a well known passage which provides the Lenten and Easter liturgy with frequent inspiration:

> You know well enough that we who were taken up into Christ by baptism have been taken up, all of us, into his death. In our baptism, we have been buried with him, died like him, that so, just as Christ was raised up by his Father's power from the dead, we too might live and move in a new kind of existence. We have to be closely fitted into the pattern of his resurrection, as we have been into the pattern of his death; we have to be sure of this, that our former nature has been crucified with him, and the living power of our guilt annihilated, so that we are the slaves of guilt no longer. Guilt makes no more claim on a man who is dead. And if we have died with Christ, we have faith to believe that we shall share his life. We know that Christ, now he has risen from the dead, cannot die any more; death has no more power over him; the death he died was a death, once for all, to sin; the life he now lives is a life that looks towards God. And you, too, must think of yourselves as dead to sin, and alive with a life that looks towards God, through Christ Jesus our Lord. You must not, then, allow sin to tyrannize over your perishable bodies...; make yourselves over to God, as men who have been dead and come to life again (Rom. 6:3–13).

Christian baptism unites the catechumen to the bloody and glorifying baptism of Christ which, by anticipation, procured for all believers pardon for their sins and glorification. By the reception of baptism the recipient is plunged into the death and burial of Christ at the same time as he is immersed in the water, and is linked with his resurrection on emerging from the baptismal font. The two actions are in reality one and are inseparable for the catechumen as they were for Christ. By them, the catechumen becomes one plant with Christ. Christ is dead once for all to sin and on account of sin and he has left behind in the tomb the infirmities of the flesh, consequent on sin. He lives henceforth for God, immortal, his action free from all limitations of space and time and enjoying the fullness of the Spirit, a "life-giving spirit" (1 Cor. 15:45). This is so not only of Christ as an individual but in the sense that he communicates the Spirit to a regenerated world. In the baptized person, the former nature is crucified with Christ, and evil tendencies are in principle fatally stricken. The neophyte is provided with the means to make this death effective and to avoid being any longer the slave of sin: Is not death essentially a final and irrevocable state? Similarly, the baptized is resurrected with Christ and, like him, should no longer live except for God, in a complete shunning of sin and in the perfect service of God.[17] Elsewhere, we shall find the apostle asserting that the spiritual resurrection will be completed on the last day by the bodily resurrection, so that the glorious destiny of the Christian completely resembles that of Christ.[18] But even now his life is heavenly and divine.

It must not be forgotten that redemption, of which baptism applies the fruits, derives its efficacy in the first instance from the power and glory of the Father and that the faith, of which the catechumen must make a solemn profession before being regenerated, is primarily faith in the power of God who has raised Christ to life (Col. 2:12; Rom. 6:4). And Pauline teaching will be found tirelessly reminding us that baptism is no kind of

[17] Baptism thus comprises communion in the redemptive sacrifice, in union with the sacrificed and risen Body — and also, according to other texts, in the communication of the Spirit, with which the Father filled the body of the Saviour when accepting his sacrifice. See Durrwell, 369.

[18] A participation in the death and resurrection of Christ is also the fruit of the other sacraments — of confirmation which completes baptism, of penance, which is a kind of second baptism, of the Eucharist, of course, of extreme unction, which cleanses the remains of sin, and of the sacraments of orders and of marriage which relate to the Passion (*Imitamini quod tractatis* of the Pontifical, and Eph. 5:25). The same also applies to extrasacramental graces. The whole of Christian life is death to sin and life for God in Christ. Death is not inflicted for its own sake. It is the condition and measure of life. It is a victorious and triumphant death like that of the Saviour (see John 10:17–18; 12:32).

magic rite that remains without effect on the life of the one who submits himself to it.[19] The union it brings about with Christ has not just a kind of legal validity but it makes the recipient like Christ so that a new man is born (Eph. 4:24). Even so, recourse to a ritual form is necessary. St. Paul's mysticism is not simply a mysticism of faith, and the sacramental rites are in harmony with the realism that is so patent in the incarnation and the redemption.

The baptized person, as we have already briefly indicated, is not incorporated in Christ crucified and glorified merely as an individual but is brought into his body with all Christians. Before writing his epistle to the Ephesians, in which he was to present the Church as the bride acquired by Christ through the shedding of his blood (5:25–27), St. Paul had taught the Corinthians that our bodies, having become members of Christ, must be preserved in complete purity (1 Cor. 6:15–18).

A little further on, in a passage linking baptism with incorporation in the body of Christ, he added:

> A man's body is all one, though it has a number of different organs; and all this multitude of organs goes to make up one body; so it is with Christ. We too, all of us, have been baptized into a single body by the power of a single Spirit, Jews and Greeks, slaves and free men alike; we have all been given drink at a single source, the one Spirit (1 Cor. 12:12–13).[20]

[19] The apostle warns the Corinthians against evil desires and against the danger of once more falling into idolatry. They should meditate on the example of Israel. Those who passed through the Red Sea and were given by Moses a baptism that was figurative of true baptism had nevertheless shown themselves faithless and their bodies were strewn in the desert (1 Cor. 10:1–13).

[20] In the Old Testament, water is often a symbol of Messianic graces (Isa. 12:3; 55:1; Jer. 2:13; Ecclus. 15:3; and the gift of the Spirit is compared to a vivifying water (Isa. 32:15; Joel 3:1 et seq.; Ezech. 17:7; 32:6; 36:25; Zach. 12:10. Compare John 4:4–5; 7:37–39; 19:34). See La source d'eau vive, Ligue de l'Évangile, 1955.

The Church is here likened, not just to a society or corporate body, but, it seems, to Christ's own individual, risen body which, by baptism, acquires for itself additional members through the outpouring of the Spirit.[21] His glorified body, receptacle of the fullness of divine life, is thus mystically identified with humanity, which receives that life from it. Men are gathered together in a single family, of which the Spirit of charity constitutes the soul. Baptized in Christ, all have taken on Christ and are so completely obedient to his divine action that every distinction is wiped out. All are henceforth but one person in Christ Jesus (Gal. 3:27–28; compare Col. 3:9–11). The wall of hate that separated Jews and Gentiles has been thrown down through the blood of Christ. All are united in a single body, reconciled with God. They are brought into his house, the house of which Christ is the cornerstone. Built on Christ and the apostles, they become God's dwelling place, through the action of the Spirit (Eph. 2:11–22).

The baptized person is incorporated into Christ's glorified body and sanctified by the gift of the Spirit.[22] He is transformed once for all and his baptism will never be repeated. St. Paul says as much in a fine passage dealing with the Trinity, in which he indicates once more the role of the three divine Persons in the work of redemption and salvation:

> You are one body, with a single Spirit; each of you, when he was called, called in the same hope; with the same Lord, the same faith, the same baptism; with the same God, the same Father, all of us, who is above all beings, pervades all things, and lives in all of us (Eph. 4:4–5).[23]

[21] This point will be dealt with again in the third part of this book.

[22] Thus, there is in baptism, as throughout the whole economy of grace, a common action of Christ and of the Spirit. See Durrwell, 368–9.

[23] Compare the Nicene Creed: *Confiteor unum baptisma in remissionem peccatorum.*

140

THE WAY TO JUSTIFICATION: FAITH AND BAPTISM

It can be seen from what we have said that baptism and faith imply each the other. Faith enlightens and already justifies. Baptism incorporates into the Christian community and into the body of Christ. Baptism provides an entry into the visible Church and gives faith its full extension by virtue of the public and solemn proclamation of the sacrament which accompanies reception and by the action of the sacrament throughout life. Baptism and faith are divinely ratified by the gift of the Holy Ghost, which makes the person baptized an adopted child of God, destined for resurrection. Baptism reminds the neophyte that it is God who has made him die to sin in union with the death of Christ and that God will complete his own work. It provides certainty of entry into the kingdom and of a share in the new life. As it makes the catechumen capable of receiving the other sacraments and able to share in the worship of the Church, baptism constitutes an invitation to spiritual growth in order to attain the future kingdom. Through it, there is a marvellous sharing in the redemption, which is static from the point of view of spiritual regeneration, and dynamic considered as a gift of supernatural life, vivifying and strengthening the soul.[24] If the newly baptized submits himself to divine action, the influence of Christ's resurrection will be unceasingly at work in him until the day he enters into glory.

[24] The passages in Acts 19:6; 1 Cor. 12:13, and Heb. 6:2 may refer to confirmation, but the interpretation is the subject of debate. For a further consideration of baptism see the review *Lumière et Vie,* March and May, 1956; Spicq, *Épître aux Hébreux,* II, 336–9; Prat, II, 291–300; DT, *Justification,* 2063–67; SDB, *Baptême* (d'Alès et Coppens), 865–72; 895–902; Lemonnyer, *Notre baptême d'après s. Paul,* Desclée, 1935; Cerfaux, *The Church in the Theology of S. Paul,* 131–41; SDB, *Justice, Justification* (Cerfaux), 1471–96; Kittel, βάπτω I, 534–43 (Oepke).

9

UNION WITH CHRIST

"Rather, not I; it is Christ that lives in me" (Gal. 2:20).

By faith and baptism the Christian enters into an intimate union, a κοινωνία with Christ: "The God, who has called you into the fellowship of his Son, Jesus Christ our Lord, is faithful to his promise" (1 Cor. 1:9). The union includes participation in his sufferings (Phil. 3:10),[1] while waiting to share in Christ's glory (Rom. 8:17) and it finds its nourishment, that is to say its permanent character and its growth, in the communion in the body and blood of Christ (1 Cor. 10:16). It is not a question of a passing transformation, but of a common sharing in life that ought never to be interrupted by sin, of a mystical union expressed in a number of forms that manifest its depth.

It seems, in the first place, as though the Christian no longer has any stake in himself. Paul proclaims himself the servant and slave of Christ (Gal. 1:10; Rom. 1:1) and he implies that the faithful are in the same case as himself (Phil. 1:1; Eph. 6:6; Col. 4:12). In another passage, made even more striking by its brevity, he asserts that they are Christ's (1 Cor. 3:23). It is their duty, therefore, to crucify the flesh (Gal. 5:24), to give themselves completely to the Lord, without making any proud claims to be more perfect than other men (2 Cor. 10:7), to act in such

---

[1] In this way the Christian imitates Christ in his condition as a slave, which he voluntarily assumed for the salvation of the world (Phil. 2:7).

a way that the Spirit of Christ dwells in them (Rom. 8:9). The belonging to Christ is so complete and final that death is not able to put an end to it. "In life and in death, we belong to the Lord" (Rom. 14:8). In this text, we can perceive an unconquerable trust, which shows how thoroughly Pauline mysticism is shot through with joy at abandonment in Christ, in spite of the severe and necessary demands it makes.

The apostle shows an even more marked predilection for two interrelated expressions. He speaks of Christ in the Christian and the Christian in Christ.

Paul experienced participation in the life of Christ to a privileged degree. He expresses this perfectly in the epistle to the Galatians: "Rather, not I; it is Christ that lives in me" (2:20). Going into greater detail, he also declares that the sufferings and comfort of Christ abound in him (2 Cor. 1:5), that the truth of Christ lives in him (2 Cor. 11:10), and that Christ speaks through him, making the faithful aware of Christ's own strength (2 Cor. 13:3), to the extent that the apostle's weakness needs fortifying (2 Cor. 12:9). So much is his life Christ that he looks upon death as a gain because it will render the union with Christ indissoluble (Phil. 1:21). He is anxious to experience the power of Christ's resurrection with growing effectiveness, and in order to do so, accepts a share in his sufferings and conformity with him in death (Phil. 3:10). This is a profoundly encouraging realism which applies, it need hardly be said, to everybody alike. All are predestined to be moulded into the image of the only Son, who will thus become the eldest born among many brethren (Rom. 8:29). Christ lives in them (Rom. 8:10). He dwells in them through faith and roots them in charity (Eph. 3:17). The aim of all Paul's apostolic endeavours is to engender the faithful in Christ and to make them grow to such stature that Christ is formed in them (1 Cor. 4:15; Eph. 4:13; Gal. 4:19), by an admirable exercise of spiritual paternity.

It goes without saying that this task requires the complete renunciation mentioned in the gospel (Matt. 16:24; Luke 9:23; 14:33), a complete surrender of proprietorship, fulfilled in generous love, which will enable Christ to live in us (1 Cor. 16:22), and is a return for the ineffable love of Christ, who loved us and gave himself for us in a sacrifice breathing out fragrance to God (Gal. 2:20; Eph. 5:2). And the Lord will sometimes permit a delightful appreciation of his mysterious presence (2 Cor. 13:5; compare Rom. 8:10).

Just as Christ is in us, we are also in him. *In Christo Jesu* is an expression which St. Paul loves above all others and which is to be found more than a hundred times in his epistles.

In some cases it bears only a weak interpretation, meaning simply in harmony with the principles or the Christian spirit (1 Cor. 3:1; 2 Cor. 12:2; Rom. 16:9). In most cases, however, it is to be understood in the full sense. To be in Christ Jesus signifies to be intimately united with him and to live with his life. The Christian is the Son of God by faith in Christ Jesus (Gal. 3:26), baptized and living for God in Christ Jesus (Rom. 6:3, 11), created by God in him, pledged to good actions (Eph. 2:10), sharing in the redemption in Christ Jesus (Rom. 3:24) and filled in him with God's ineffable peace (Phil. 4:7). His life is aimed at the perfect possession of the divine gifts, "life everlasting in Christ Jesus our Lord" (Rom. 6:23 [Douai]). Briefly – we could easily multiply the quotations – the Christian is in any case "in Christ" (2 Cor. 5:17). What does this signify?

Certainly not that Christ would provide, so to speak, the space in which our lives were to be lived out, and it would be a mistake to press so far the simile of putting on Christ (Gal. 3:27). The apostle indeed shows that this is not his idea, by adding immediately: "You are all one person in Jesus Christ" (Gal. 3:28). Christ becomes our vital principle, identifying himself with our own being: "Not I; it is Christ that lives in me"

(Gal. 2:20). Christ is our life (Col. 3:4). These magnificent phrases imply a transmission of Christ's life and do not in any way suggest a kind of pantheistical fading away of our personalities. St. Paul points out, too, that we do not cease to live according to the flesh when we live according to the faith in the Son of God (ibid.). The distinction is, then, clearly sustained, but, the point having been made, the apostle is free to affirm that Christ identifies with himself the new creature, the new "I" resulting from faith and baptism. He superimposes, as it were, his own personality on ours but, far from annihilating us, removes only our imperfections and afflictions. We are mysteriously taken up in the glorified Christ in an intimate community of being and of life.[2]

Enumerating and setting out the consequences of this general statement, St. Paul describes Christian life as conformity with Christ and participation in his mysteries, his various "states", as we like to put it, repeating an expression dear to the great theologians of the French school. This participation begins with baptism, which unites us to the death, burial, and resurrection of Christ (Rom. 6:1–11). It ought to continue throughout life by means of a spiritual effort that is bold and persevering.

> Our sins had made dead men of us, and he, in giving life to Christ, gave life to us too; ... raised us up too, enthroned us too, in the heavens, with Christ Jesus and in him (Eph. 2:5–6).

[2] See Durrwell, 251–3. We shall again be faced with the same question in considering the Church as the body of Christ. The reciprocal dwelling of Christ in the Christian and of the Christian in Christ is compared in the gospel to the reciprocal immanence of the Father and the Son: John 14:19–20; 17:21, 23. We readily talk in this connection of identification or of a life of identification in Christ. It is useful to note that the identification is not complete. It does not take place "in the heights of the divinity but in that corporeal humanity in which he went through death and the resurrection and was filled with the treasures of salvation" (Durrwell, 255). This corporeal humanity is identified with the Saviour without equalling him (ibid., 253 and 257).

We are to share his life, because we have shared his death; if we endure, we shall reign with him (2 Tim. 2:11–12).

Risen, then, with Christ, you must lift your thoughts above, where Christ now sits at the right hand of God... you have undergone death, and your life is hidden away now with Christ in God. Christ is your life, and when he is made manifest you too will be made manifest in glory with him (Col. 3:1, 3, 4).

These texts, which are among the most beautiful in the epistles,[3] setting before us an exalting ideal of life in union with Christ, nevertheless create a difficulty. How can we die and be raised with Christ? Do we have to suppose that there is an impossible going back in time to the moment in history when the Passion and the resurrection took place? The answer is doubtless that the union in Christ is not only at baptism, but constitutes in a permanent way communion in the dead and risen Christ because, in the glorified Christ, death is, as it were, made eternally actual. The risen Christ has none of the weaknesses of the flesh. The flesh, the resemblance with our guilty nature, is dead in him and he lives no longer except by the Spirit. Death therefore remains in him, not as something that is gradually developing, but in its final form, not in the separation of body and soul, which could only be something passing, but in a new and glorified existence which supposes the elimination of life according to the flesh. Christ is thus permanently fixed in the redemptive act, in a sacrifice, a prolonged "death to sin". Our union with him can reach and associate itself with that act, both in baptism and throughout life.[4] It can readily be seen that this incorporation in the glorified Christ is not something static, but

---

[3] They are full of the neologisms invented by the apostle, the famous compounds in συν: to die with, to be buried with, to reign with, to be enthroned in the heavens with, etc. The complete list is to be found in Prat, II, 21.

[4] See Durrwell, 177–8; 262–8.

is a dynamic identification, constantly in action. St. Paul clearly shows that he looks upon it in this way when he invites the baptized to make continual progress and when he calls upon the faithful to aim at "full knowledge of the Son of God and at the state of perfect man" (Eph. 4:13),[5] and invites them to grow up in every way through the exercise of charity in him who is the head, the Christ (Eph. 4:15). He recognizes that he has not himself attained perfection and that he must continue the race in order to achieve the reward of the heavenly summons in Christ (Phil. 3:12, 14).

No one will deny that this spiritual dynamism in union with Christ[6] is an almost dazzling ideal, difficult to achieve in practice. But, none the less, it is not optional, for it is the very essence of the Christian life. Realization of the ideal is, however, greatly helped by St. Paul's graphic presentation. To kill the old man and crucify the flesh and its lusts will always be hard things for human nature to accomplish and their need is ceaselessly proclaimed in the apostolic preaching. But the Christian is not faced with a number of severe precepts nor enmeshed in a series of "don'ts" that restrict his full development. Death is imposed upon him only as a liberation from sin and from evil inclinations and in order that life may blossom forth. The Christian dies with Christ to death and to sin (Rom. 6:10) only to live with a higher life, in God and for God (Rom. 6:10–11).[7] The special point is that the striving for perfection takes place in the intimacy and love of the Son of the living God, through the working-out of the spiritual possibilities placed in the soul by baptism, so as to achieve an ever closer union with the dead and risen Christ. Carrying the cross with Christ transforms and simplifies the

[5] Translator's own rendering.

[6] It is the very dynamism of the divine Pneuma (Rom. 8:11), "the virtue of his resurrection" (Phil. 3:10), which seems manifest, not only in the miraculous charismata, but in the spiritual progress of the faithful.

[7] See Durrwell, 269–70.

spiritual battle, giving it an interior quality and a warmth that makes the fight attractive in itself, all the more so since, at the end of it, lies the prospect of a share in the life of the risen Christ. We suffer with Christ in order to be glorified with him (Rom. 8:17). We deliver ourselves up to death on his account in order that his life should be shown forth in mortal flesh. From the apostolic point of view, death has power over the preacher of the gospel only in order to enable life to exercise its power on those he is evangelizing (2 Cor. 4:11–12). We should be bold, therefore, in lifting up our thoughts on high, to where Christ sits at the right hand of God (Col. 3:1).

We see here the starting point of Christian morality and the reason why it is so strict. For the neophyte it is, in short, a matter of respecting the seal of baptism: he will do so by making more and more effective the death to sin and life resurrected in union with Christ glorified. This unchanging doctrinal foundation stamps Christian life with a mark of solidity and grandeur which increases its appeal and makes its practice the more easy. The reminder of his dignity and of his duties constitutes for the baptized person the most effective means of bringing his life into conformity and pushing aside temptation, facing him as it does with an inspiring ideal which, instead of imposing sterile obligations, calls forth all he has in him that is noble, elevated and pure. In Christ Jesus! The phrase expresses the whole of Christian life in its most profound aspect. The Christian life also, of course, consists in the imitation of Christ, and St. Paul does not omit to say so (1 Cor. 11:1). But that is an extrinsic point of view, emphasizing the distance which always separates us from the model. For some spiritual families at least, the thought of the union with Christ provides the greater inspiration by stressing the partial achievement of the Christian ideal in a union that is already effective and insisting on the mysterious action of Christ's presence rather than on puny human effort, though there is no question of hiding the need for this effort. The question is one of different spiritual temperaments and also of different schools. What must not be forgotten is that the final state is one of union in Christ and thus a sharing of life and not merely imitation, and that even in this life, "reflecting as in a mirror the glory of the Lord, we are transformed into this ever more resplendent likeness" (2 Cor. 3:18).[8]

[8] Translator's own rendering. See *Enseignement de s. Paul,* II, 104–7; Morice, *La vie mystique de s. Paul,* 2 vol., Téqui, 1932; Mersch, *Morale et corps mystique,* de Brouwer, 1941.

10

GRACE. THE HOLY GHOST

"It was grace that saved you" (Eph. 2:8).

THE word grace, χάρις, is one of those dear to St. Paul who uses it to describe supernatural gifts. It is such a happy choice that theologians have retained it unchanged, giving it the same meaning as in the epistles. The term χάπισμα, charisma, is also to be met with on occasion, either in the same sense or to denote the extraordinary gifts of the Holy Ghost, which are designed for the common good of the Church rather than the sanctification of the recipient and are often miraculous.

The word grace, which is equivalent in many respects to salvation, justification and sanctification, has the advantage of emphasizing that we are concerned with a gift. It underlines the absolute gratuity of spiritual life. The redemption is grace *par excellence* (Rom. 3:24; 5:15), the source of salvation for all men alike (Titus 2:11). Grace is the powerful gift that abounds still more where sin abounded and which reigns through justice to bring eternal life (Rom. 5:20–21). As a fruit of the preaching of the gospel (Col. 1:6), it is of such richness that it brings us salvation (Eph. 2:8), redemption, and the remission of sins through the blood of Christ (Eph. 1:7; Heb. 2:9). It constitutes the new economy, the new dispensation, one which liberates from sin and is very different from the dispensation of the law with which St. Paul contrasts it (Rom. 6:14; Gal. 2:21; 5:4). It is the affirmation and the beginning of the supreme gift, of the consummation of salvation which is eternal life in Christ our Lord (Rom. 6:23).

Like all the great Pauline themes, the notion of grace is complex. As it appears in man, it seems like a new quality, moulding the soul inwardly. It is distinct from justification, understood in the strict sense as the passage from a state of sin to one of justice. It is a new mode of being which follows upon justification. In other words, it constitutes the "new creature". But this privileged state can be lost by falling once more into sin (1 Cor. 10:12; Rom. 6:12–14; 1 Tim. 1:19). Theology labels it final justification to distinguish it from initial justification, which is the act itself whereby the sinner is justified. It also refers to it as sanctifying grace, because it is the source of holiness. It is the fruit especially characteristic of the redemptive sacrifice. That is why the apostle cannot find a better introduction to his letters than to express the hope that his readers will obtain grace with the resulting peace of soul that comes from God the Father and the Lord Jesus Christ. Like the redemptive act from which it springs, grace is completely gratuitous and merciful, and it supernaturalizes the whole of Christian life, from the first call to faith onwards. Paul has a very vivid realization of this. He likes to repeat that God set him apart from his mother's womb, persecutor that he was, and called him by his grace (Gal. 1:15; 1 Cor. 15:10; 1 Tim. 1:13–16). In the same way, the faithful have been called by the Father to the grace of Christ (Gal. 1:6). And he insists on the gratuitousness of the divine gift: "It was grace that saved you, with faith for its instrument; it did not come from yourselves" (Eph. 2:8). "Has he not saved us, and called us to a vocation of holiness? It was not because of anything we had done; we owe it to his own design, to the grace lavished on us..." (2 Tim. 1:9).

Sanctifying grace, the habitual state of holiness and of peace with God, is accompanied by the transient supernatural aids that are equally gratuitous and necessary and that theologians refer to as actual graces. No act of faith can be accomplished except through the movement of the Holy Ghost (1 Cor. 12:3). The Father alone can enlighten the eyes of the heart so as to enable it to know the grandeurs of Christian hope and of the eternal heritage (Eph. 1:17–18). Grace is necessary at the beginning of the apostolate and for the effective preaching of the gospel (Eph. 3:7–8), but it is no less so for the whole exercise of the apostolic ministry and for the building of the Church (1 Cor. 3:10). If St. Paul was able to accomplish more than all the others who laboured to spread the gospel, the credit, in truth, goes not to him but to the grace of God working with him (1 Cor. 15:10). It is God alone who gives increase to what the apostles have planted and watered (1 Cor. 3:5). Man is unable through his own resources to keep the divine law and everybody knows the moving passage in the epistle to the Romans (7:7–25) in which Paul says that man is fleshly, sold to sin, and powerless because of the sin that dwells in him to accomplish the good to which, nevertheless, the interior man aspires; powerless, that is, to fulfil the highest aspirations of the soul.... Who has not experienced these terrible struggles from which, without grace, it would be impossible to emerge victorious? But grace is freely offered. God in his goodness produces in us the will to do, and the accomplishment of that will (Phil. 2:13) and our ability to perform supernatural works comes from him (2 Cor. 3:5).[1]

The fabric of graces from which God mercifully makes the web of our lives clearly does not dispense us from the need to accept the advances he makes. God wishes to respect our freedom and will exercise no constraint on unsubmissive instruments. Thus it is that the epistles are full of invitations to faithfulness

[1] This passage relates to the apostolic labours. Applying it more generally, theologians have legitimately deduced the need for grace in the fulfilment of all supernatural actions.

and effort. No one will be called upon to undergo trials beyond his powers (1 Cor. 10:13). Grace is offered abundantly but we must greatly fear receiving it in vain (2 Cor. 6:1) and it is in this sense that we have to work for our salvation "in anxious fear" (Phil. 2:12). The stake is a serious one and humiliating experiences demonstrate that the possibility of defection is always present. It is necessary to have a thorough training, which St. Paul compares with that of an athlete (1 Cor. 9:24–27) and of a soldier (Eph. 6:11–17). The antitheses, of which he lists so many in describing the antagonistic powers which fight to capture our wills, illustrate the same need. Our free will remains intact and each one of us will have to appear before the judgement seat of Christ to receive the reward for our good and evil actions (2 Cor. 5:10). Each "will receive his own wages, in proportion to his own work" (1 Cor. 3:9). It follows that good actions, accomplished under the stimulus of grace, are meritorious and give claim to a reward that Paul legitimately hopes to receive himself and hopes will be accorded to all those who have lovingly awaited the showing forth of the Lord, crown of justice (2 Tim. 4:9). But it remains true that the just Judge will thus crown his own gifts. It is everywhere a question of grace and we might say that Pauline teaching is centred on grace.[2] Grace and merit, mysteriously and harmoniously linked, both have as their final end eternal life, which is the gift of the heavenly heritage, man's supreme happiness, and God's great glory. "So may the name of our Lord Jesus Christ be glorified in you" (2 Thess. 1:12; compare Eph. 1:14).

The transformation effected in the soul by grace is referred to by Paul as "spirit" and he describes it as being in a special way the work of the Holy Spirit, the third person of the Trinity.

[2] Bonnetain, in SDB, *Grâce,* 1001.

The sanctifying and transforming action of the Spirit began with the resurrection and Pentecost – at least in its full and final form – and has never ceased. Peter and Stephen were filled with the Holy Ghost when they announced Christ to the Jews (Acts 4:8; 7:55). It was under the orders of the Holy Ghost that St. Peter received the men sent by Cornelius (Acts 10:19) and also under his orders that the prophets and doctors of Antioch sent forth Paul and Barnabas (Acts 13:2) and that the council of Jerusalem promulgated the famous decree exempting converts from paganism from the precepts of the Mosaic law (Acts 15:28). In the same way, Paul was subject in his apostolic labours to the movements of the Spirit (Acts 16:6–7; 20:23) and the description of the Acts of the Apostles as the gospel of the Holy Ghost is not an exaggeration.

The action of the Holy Ghost predominates in the epistles and is constantly mentioned, but the idea conveyed by the word "spirit" is complex and has many different aspects.

From this point of view, Rom. 8:9–10 merits quotation:

> But you live the life of the spirit, not the life of nature; that is, if the Spirit of God dwells in you. A man cannot belong to Christ unless he has the Spirit of Christ. But if Christ lives in you, then although the body be a dead thing in virtue of our guilt, the spirit is a living thing, by virtue of our justification.[3]

Paul here has in mind in succession: The spirit opposed to the flesh, considered as a new principle, acting and influencing.

The person of the Holy Spirit, residing in man, both the Spirit of God and the Spirit of Christ, whose presence in the soul is necessary if the soul is to belong to Christ.

[3] The French text of the last part of this quotation has: ". . . though your body is (in truth) destined to die, your spirit lives by virtue of justice." Translator.

154

Man's own spirit, that is the higher part of the soul, informed and vivified by the Holy Spirit.

In other passages, we shall find the word "spirit" used in the sense of intellectual soul (1 Cor. 2:11), of perverse spirit of the world, contrasted with the spirit of God (1 Cor. 2:12), and of spirit as opposed to the letter in the interpretation of scripture (2 Cor. 3:6).

These different acceptations of the word should be carefully distinguished, where that is possible, for there are cases where St. Paul seems to be considering at one and the same time the Spirit, the divine person and the Spirit as communicated to man. But in such instances, he is dealing with realities so closely connected that the lack of precision arising from the richness of the thought does not make for obscurity.

The Spirit is primarily and essentially a gift. His outpouring is the fruit of the redemptive sacrifice: "We too, all of us, have been baptized into a single body by the power of a single Spirit, Jews and Greeks, slaves and free men alike; we have all been given drink at a single source, the one Spirit" (1 Cor. 12:13). He is the dispenser of all spiritual gifts which he distributes as he wills to each severally (1 Cor. 12:6–11). He has also been called the soul of the Mystical Body in so far as he is the element interior to the Mystical Body whereby Christ unites the faithful with himself. His action is infinitely varied and can be considered from many points of view, which should nevertheless not lead us to overlook the fundamental unity of this divine activity.

In accordance with the promises of the Saviour (John 14:25–26; 16:12–15), the Spirit is the source of *enlightenment*. He finds out everything, right to the depths of the divine nature, makes known the gifts received from him and communicates the very thought of Christ (1 Cor. 10:14–16). He conveys an understanding of the deeper meaning of scripture by showing that the

155

Old Testament was a preparation for the new covenant and that
its end was Christ (Rom. 10:4) and he inspired the prophecies
that foretold his own pouring out into souls (Ezech. 36:26–28;
37:14; Joel 3:1–5, etc.). The letter kills whereas the spirit brings
life (2 Cor. 3:6): the Spirit is opposed to the letter, or rather
surpasses it, eliminating the veil that stood between the heart of
Israel and the true interpretation of scripture so long as it refused
to cleave to Christ (2 Cor. 4:13–17). Spirit of Wisdom, he
illuminates the eyes of the heart, making God known, showing
forth the riches of hope and of the glorious Christian heritage
and the sovereign power used by the Father in the resurrection
of Christ (Eph. 1:17–20). He shows to the apostles and the
prophets the fullness of the redemptive plan and the gospel's call
to the heathen (Eph. 3:5–7). This role of enlightenment is particularly striking where the charismata are concerned, especially in
the case of the prophets whose words are inspired by the Spirit:

> One learns to speak with wisdom, by the power of the Spirit,
> another to speak with knowledge, with the same Spirit for his
> rule; …one can prophesy, one can test the spirit of the prophets;
> one can speak in different tongues, another can interpret the
> tongues (1 Cor. 12:8, 10).[4]

Paul has a strong sense of having received in abundance the
light given by the Spirit, particularly in the matter of the universality of the call to faith (Eph. 3:2–3, 8–9). For himself and
for the whole Church, this constitutes an untold benefit.

The gift of understanding is completed by that of fortitude.
To appreciate this we have only to note the change wrought in
the apostles by the miraculous outpouring of Pentecost and the
courage with which they henceforth proclaimed Christ. The Spirit
guides those who are sons of God and his action makes manifest
the authenticity of their sonship (Rom. 8:14–16), helps them

---

[4] Instead of "one can test the spirit of the prophets" the author has
"to another, the discerning of spirits". Translator.

to call God Father and to act accordingly (Rom. 8:15, 26; Gal. 4:6). He is power in a pre-eminent degree, the power that raised Christ to life and will one day raise us as well (Rom. 8:11), the power showing itself in the results of apostolic preaching (1 Cor. 3:4; 1 Thess. 1:5) and in the miracles accompanying it (Gal. 3:5). He is the power strengthening the faithful and giving growth to the inner man (Eph. 3:16). He is not a spirit that shrinks from danger but is one of power, love and wisdom (2 Tim. 1:7).

Finally, the essential characteristic of the Spirit is *love:* by his coming, the love of God is poured out in our hearts (Rom. 5:5). The numerous charismata which he liberally spread throughout the infant Church were, moreover, intended for the consolation and edification of the faithful. They were a work of love (1 Cor. 14:2–5). And Paul preferred the gift of prophecy to that of speaking in divers tongues, because the latter, not being understood, lacked the power of edification possessed by the former – a power which brought enlightenment to all who heard (1 Cor. 14, passim).

These varied operations of the Spirit show that he is, in the highest degree, a *principle of life.* He is the agent of resurrection for Christ and for the Christian and, in spite of the inevitable occurrence of bodily death, he does not cease to vivify our spirit by the justice and sanctity that his presence brings (Rom. 8:10–11). This life, imperfect here below, will blossom forth later in eternal life (Gal. 6:8; Rom. 6:22). Full possession will take the place of the first-fruits (2 Cor. 1:22; 5:5; Rom. 8:23; Eph. 1:14). And from the time at which St. Paul is speaking onwards, the Spirit is infusing into men's hearts a life that is truly divine.

The Spirit is, indeed, a *Spirit of adoption,* making of us the adopted children of the Father and brothers of Christ. He is both the Spirit of God and the Spirit of Christ (Rom. 8:9). He is sent into our hearts by the Father and makes us like the Son. We thus become children of God, not according to nature, for it is only too evident that we are born sinners and children of wrath, but by an adoption which, unlike human adoption, is not a legal fiction, but effects a profound transformation, a true assimilation with Christ, who is made the elder brother of an immense family (Rom. 8:29). Our attitude towards God should, therefore, be the same as that of Christ, and when we call him our Father, it is not so much we who pray as the Spirit who prays in us (Gal. 4:6; Rom. 8:15–16): "The Spirit himself thus assures our spirit, that we are children of God" (Rom. 8:16). The time has passed for a spirit of fear and servitude. The Christian spirit is that of the adoption of sons which, like all adoption, implies the right to an inheritance: the Christian becomes the heir of God and co-heir with Christ, with whom he is invited to suffer, only to be eventually glorified with him (Gal. 4:7; Rom. 8:17). The Spirit is at one and the same time the agent of our adoption and the proof of its reality.[5] The intimate conviction his presence gives us that we are children of God and the call to act as such are the signs of the truly Christian spirit which gives our relations with God a filial intimacy and confidence. This is a great wonder which we shall never be able either to understand sufficiently or express adequately in our lives. It is something which affects the whole bearing of our existence, since it not only means being in a relation of sonship with God but also behaving towards our fellow men as brothers in Jesus Christ. The essential commandment of charity towards God and our neighbour is brought to perfection and to the limit of its demands upon us in the communication of the Spirit of love.[6]

[5] Between the gift of the Spirit and the adoption lies a kind of mutual causality. The priority of the gift over the adoption exists merely in the logical order. We must avoid being too subtle.

[6] We can see here the extent to which Pauline morality, like the

The Christian must therefore turn his back on the ways of the flesh with a new thoroughness and live according to the Spirit (Gal. 5:25). The flesh is opposed to God and those who live according to it cannot please him (Rom. 8:7–8). The incompatibility between the flesh and the spirit is absolute. "The flesh tends towards death, the spirit towards life and peace" (Rom. 8:6).[7]

Paul depicts eloquently the contrast between the desires of the flesh and of the spirit, between the abominable works of the flesh, which bar the way to the Kingdom of God, and the excellent fruit of the spirit, which is charity, joy and peace (Gal. 5:17–23). He brings the Christian face to face with the decisive choice: "Since we live by the Spirit, let the Spirit be our rule of life.... A man will reap what he sows; if nature is his seed-ground, nature will give him a perishable harvest, if his seed-ground is the spirit, it will give him a harvest of eternal life" (Gal. 5:25; 6:7–8). The dilemma is impossible to escape. We must crucify the flesh with its passions and its lusts (Gal. 5:24). But it is precisely the gift of the Holy Spirit that makes it possible to conquer the flesh, to thrust aside its temptations, to practise charity and all the other virtues and to accomplish the good works that God expects of us, in filial obedience to the Father and in bringing our lives into conformity with Christ. The law of the Spirit of life frees us in Christ from subjugation to the law of sin and death (Rom. 8:2). "But you live the life of the spirit, not the life of nature; that is, if the Spirit of God dwells in you" (Rom. 8:9). The Christian has become "the spiritual man" (Gal. 6:1; 1 Cor. 2:14–16) and in a magnificent ellipsis in which he contrasts the shameful union of fornication with the

morality preached in the gospel, is interior and mystical, based on the relations of the Christian with the divine Persons. It all comes back to living as a child of the heavenly Father, as a brother of Christ, and in the temple of the Spirit.

[7] Translator's own rendering.

holy union with Christ, Paul goes so far as to say: "The man who unites himself to the Lord becomes one spirit with him" (1 Cor. 6:17). The divine principle giving him life enables him to comply with the divine precepts that are beyond the strength of natural man and also beyond that of the Jew when he pretends to fulfil the law without recourse to prayer (Rom. 7:14–23; 8:3). Under the guidance of the Spirit, the Christian will practise the essential virtue of charity, the superiority of which over all charismata is proclaimed by the apostle (1 Cor. 13; compare Rom. 13:8–10). The Christian will perform the many good works prepared by God and for which God has given the necessary graces (Eph. 2:10), and he will thus merit eternal life by his co-operation with these graces (2 Cor. 5:10; Rom. 2:6–7).

At the end of the vista of salvation, we again find the action of the Spirit. The risen Christ already possesses the fullness of the Spirit in order to communicate it to us. He is a "life-giving spirit" (1 Cor. 15:45). On the last day, the power of the Spirit, producing its supreme effect, will raise our bodies, making them like that of the glorified Christ. He will make of them spiritual bodies, incorruptible, immortal, and filled with power (1 Cor. 15:42–44, 53), fulfilling the prophecy of Ezechiel (36:1–14) in a fuller sense than the prophet himself could have envisaged. There will not merely be resurrection of the body and the gathering together of the new people of God, but also the vivification and glorification by the Spirit of the bodies which had in this life been his temple (1 Cor. 6:19). The Spirit is *glory* and the principle of glory as well as power. Paul often links the Pneuma and glory and even identifies them with each other in so far as they are communicated to man (Col. 1:11; Eph. 3:16; 1 Cor. 15:43–45). What he describes as the glory of God is the sanctity which is lacking in sinners (Rom. 3:23). The glory of the Lord, which transforms us even in this life in a more and more striking way, comes to us from Christ who is entirely penetrated with the Spirit (2 Cor. 3:17; 4:6) and it is the Spirit, of whom we already possess the first-fruits, who induces us to ask God for complete adoption through the redemption and glorification of our bodies (Rom. 8:23–27).

The multifarious action of the Spirit is the source of the duties the Christian acquires in his regard. Sealed by the Spirit with an indelible sign on the day of his baptism (Eph. 1:13), ceaselessly refreshed and vivified by him (1 Cor. 12:13), and having become his temple (1 Cor. 6:19), the Christian must hear his voice, never stifling it (1 Thess. 5:19). He must never do anything to hamper the action of the Spirit, being consecrated to the Spirit and no longer belonging to himself. That is why he must obey the Spirit's promptings with a fervour that is careful to cause no displeasure. "Do not distress God's holy Spirit, whose seal you bear until the day of your redemption comes" (Eph. 4:30). We can see to what heights of perfection we are thus called. The obedience to the Spirit required by the regeneration he has operated in us (Titus 3:5–7) ought to be spontaneous and joyful and to owe more to the impulse of conscience than to any constraint. Even though it can be referred to as servitude and slavery to God (Rom. 6:16–18), it is in reality the supreme liberation that snatches us from the slavery of sin and death in order to lead us to holiness and eternal life (Rom. 6:20–23). In the faithful Christian, the Spirit brings about a complete supernatural education, ranging from the simple act of faith, which is impossible without his action (1 Cor. 12:3), and prayer inspired by him in all its forms (Eph. 5:18–20), to the life lived in the spirit of the adoption of sons, by those who henceforth belong to God's family (Eph. 2:19), with all that this new state implies – the struggle against the flesh and its lusts, the judging of all things in a Christian spirit (Eph. 4:23), and a constant striving after holiness (1 Thess. 4:7–8). The believer thus makes of himself an offering that God finds worthy of acceptance

(Rom. 15:16) and lives in a state of higher liberty, compounded not of licence but of the enduring exercise of charity (Gal. 5:13). Charity, in which is summed up the whole of Christian morality, is in the highest degree the fruit of the Spirit (Gal. 5:22; Rom. 15:30; Col. 1:8; Phil. 2:1). Hope, vivified by his enlightenment, gives an ever deepening knowledge of the divine gifts (1 Cor. 2:9–12), increases charity, and leads the believer to become an imitator of God, and of Christ who has loved us and delivered himself up for us (Eph. 5:1–2). Life is magnificently renewed under the new dispensation of the spirit which replaces the old dispensation of the letter (Rom. 7:6). Perfection is certainly not attained at a single stroke. It must be the object of patient effort (Phil. 3:12–16). And without this effort, the believer would remain a child in Christ, still partly retaining his old nature (1 Cor. 3:1–4) and incapable of reaching maturity and a full spiritual stature (Eph. 4:13–15). The more we strive sincerely for perfection, the more we become like Christ, through him who is the Spirit of Christ and supremely responsible for unity within the body of Christ (Eph. 4:4).

The nature and action of the Holy Spirit, as they are described by St. Paul, imply his divinity. His work of inspiration and regeneration is entirely divine. Through him is obtained the gift of life which comes from Christ and blossoms forth in eternal life (Rom. 8:10; 6:22), for he is the Spirit of Christ. Through him, also, comes the adoption that makes us children of God and co-heirs with Christ (Rom. 8:14–17). Through him, finally, will come the resurrection (Rom. 8:11). The numerous Trinitarian texts in the epistles show clearly the divine nature of the three persons, all being equal in dignity and all equally active in ensuring the salvation of believers and the dispensation of graces. It is sufficient to quote a few passages:

You are one body, with a single Spirit; each of you, when he was called, called in the same hope; with the same Lord, the same faith, the same baptism; with the same God, the same Father, all of us, who is above all beings, pervades all things, and lives in all of us (Eph. 4:4–5).

And yet there are different kinds of gifts, though it is the same Spirit who gives them, just as there are different kinds of service, though it is the same Lord we serve, and different manifestations of power, though it is the same God who manifests his power everywhere in all of us (1 Cor. 12:4–6).

May he, out of the rich treasury of his glory, strengthen you through his Spirit with a power that reaches your innermost being. May Christ find a dwelling-place, through faith, in your hearts; may your lives be rooted in love, founded on love... the love of Christ, to know what passes knowledge (Eph. 3:16–17, 19; compare Titus 3:4–6; 1 Cor. 6).

We can see, then, that the Spirit is God just as the Father and the Son are God, though St. Paul does not call him by this name. He is the Spirit of God and the Spirit of the Son, or of Christ. Thus, he proceeds from one and the other. He is sent by the Father (Gal. 4:6) and it is through Christ that the Father spreads him forth among us.[8] Theologians conclude from Rom. 5:5 that the procession of the Spirit is through love because it is through him that the love of God is spread in our hearts.

It follows from all we have said that the Spirit is not an anonymous and abstract force but a person, even though his manifestation in the world is obviously more mysterious than that of the incarnate Son. He dwells in men's hearts (Rom. 8:9, 11). The faithful, body and soul, provide a temple in which he resides (1 Cor. 3:16; 6:19), and they must obey him as a guide and master (Gal. 5:16, 18, 25; Rom. 8:14). He has spoken

---

[8] The sending of the Holy Spirit by the Son is indicated more explicitly by St. John than by St. Paul (John 14:15; 16:26; 15:7).

in the past through the scriptures (Heb. 3:7; 10:15). He was sent to complete Christ's work (Gal. 4:6). He presides over the work of the apostles and over the government of the Church (Acts 13:9; 16:6–7; 20:22, 23, 28). He predicts what is to come (Acts 21:11; 1 Tim. 4:1), and distributes supernatural gifts as he wills (1 Cor. 12:11).

The Spirit and the Son are so closely linked in the gift of grace that the apostle seems to attribute it indifferently to one and the other. The words "in Christ" and "in the Spirit" seem to be treated as equivalent. He goes so far as to say that the risen Christ is Spirit (2 Cor. 3:17–18), and at first sight this seems to be a confusion and causes a feeling of discomfort. But there is, in fact, no confusion involved. The whole Pauline teaching distinguishes Christ from the Spirit, who was sent by Christ as well as by the Father. The statement that Christ is the Spirit is simply an elliptical form meaning that he is entirely penetrated in soul and body by the Spirit and that he possesses the Spirit fully, in the same sense as there is elsewhere reference to a "life-giving spirit" (1 Cor. 15:45) and in which the risen bodies of the faithful are described in advance as "spiritual" bodies (1 Cor. 15:44). This joint operation of the Holy Spirit and of Christ affects only the sanctification of souls which, arising as it does from their common action, can be attributed to one or the other. We can see that the identification of the two is merely in relation to their action. The Spirit is imparted thanks to the redemption accomplished by Christ – and from this there arises a material though not formal confusion in the mode of expression – but it is clear that Christ, incarnate and redeeming, is always distinguished from the Spirit.[9] The Christian is in Christ Jesus thanks to the merits of Christ. But the union with Christ is

---

[9] "The Spirit is present through the communication of himself; Christ is present in his activity and by anticipation of his Parousia" (Cerfaux, *Christ*, p. 293). Cf. Prümm, *Die Katholische Auslegung von II. Cor. III,*

effected in the gift of the Spirit from which comes the adoption of sons by the Father. Christ, vivifying spirit, entirely penetrated by the divine force of the Spirit, communicates it to the faithful. In other words, they live by the Spirit, sent by the risen Son and by the Father, who work together in a like manner with the gift of the Spirit and adopt the faithful by the action of sending the Spirit to them.

The action of Christ and the action of the Spirit are thus not completely equivalent. The Spirit dwells in his fullness in Christ and dwells in us, who are the body of Christ. We are identified by grace with Christ and not with the Spirit, the role of the Third Person being, not to work for himself, but to ensure that we belong to Christ, giving us to Christ and making us part of his glorified body (1 Cor. 12:13). There is no body of the Holy Spirit. Christ lives in us by the action of the Spirit, imparting to us the divine life which identifies us mystically with himself by giving to us, jointly with the Father, the Spirit that his own risen humanity possesses superabundantly (Titus 3:6). Life is thus transmitted to us at one and the same time both by Christ and by the Spirit, but in a different respect and in union with the risen body of Christ. Such is probably the meaning of 1 Cor. 6:17: "The man who unites himself to the Lord becomes one spirit with him." The Spirit who, at Easter-tide, came into the human nature of the Saviour brings about our salvation by uniting our humanity with that of the risen Redeemer, and thanks to the merits of the Redeemer. The Spirit is given to us in order to assimilate us into the glorified humanity of Christ. It is by possessing the Spirit that we belong to Christ (Rom. 8:9) and henceforth are one person with Christ (Gal. 3:26–28). It is Christ who lives in us, rather than we who live ourselves (Gal. 2:20).[10]

17a *in den letzten vier Jahrzehnten, nach ihren Hauptrichtungen;* Bibl. 1950, 316–45, 459–82; 1951, 1–24.

But, that being the case, it must be recognized that the life of grace constitutes a participation in the life of God himself, or, to be more specific, in the life of the Trinity. The Christian who is justified and sanctified is the adopted child of the heavenly Father (Gal. 4:5–7; Rom. 8:15–17), and the temple of God (1 Cor. 3:16), the brother of Christ (Rom. 8:29), the temple of the Spirit (1 Cor. 6:19; Rom. 8:9) who acts in him (Rom. 8:14). It is through the Spirit that this marvellous union is effected. St. Paul wishes the Corinthians: "The grace of our Lord Jesus Christ, and the love of God, and the imparting of the Holy Spirit" (2 Cor. 13:13). It is through Christ that, "far off or near, united *in the same Spirit,* we have access through him to the Father" (Eph. 2:18). It is the presence of the Spirit, the Spirit of the Father and the Son, that brings about our adoption and proves its reality (Gal. 4:6). There is, therefore, the particular action of the Holy Spirit, giving rise to new relationships with the divine persons and the presence in the soul of these three persons (the texts we have just quoted clearly show this). The persons are, moreover, inseparable. The change brought about in the soul in this way was to be later described by St. Peter (2 Peter 1:4) as participation in the divine nature, common to the three persons. St. Paul is saying in effect the same thing when he shows the Christian as assimilated to God by knowledge and love (1 Cor. 2:10; Rom. 5:5), in a way that remains imperfect, but will blossom forth one day in perfect knowledge, in the vision of God face to face and in a charity that will not pass (1 Cor. 13:12, 8). Nevertheless, it is by the Spirit that we can penetrate to the very depths of God's nature and that his love is spread in our hearts. We can see that the whole of the New Testament looks towards the gift of the Spirit as towards the supreme good and the greatest fruit of the redeeming blood.

[10] See Durrwell, 256–61.

How, then, are we to look upon the special role of the Spirit in the union with the Trinity as a whole?

This is a complex and delicate theological problem that has given rise to a number of studies. The difficulty seems to be reduced if we remember that the primacy of the action of the Holy Spirit lies merely in the logical order. In the unique act whereby God gives himself to us and in the unique state of grace resulting from this gift, it is by the Spirit that man is privileged to resemble the Son and is intimately linked with his glorified humanity, entering into a filial relationship with the Father. We find here the verification of the scriptural texts declaring the real relationship that exists between the justified Christian and the three persons, while at the same time the unity is preserved of the justifying act whereby God raises us even to himself, both by participation in his unique nature and by the new relationship with the three persons. It is God, one and triune, who changes us into his own image.[11]

We can see from this the incomparable dignity of the Christian, admitted as he is to membership of God's family, in the intimacy of the divine persons, and to a participation in their common nature. At the same time, St. Paul gives an inkling of the mysterious relationship that constitutes the three persons. When he speaks of the Son as the radiance of divine splendour (Heb. 1:3), as the image of God (2 Cor. 3:18; 4:4; Col. 1:15) and the wisdom of God (1 Cor. 1:24, 30), he makes it sufficiently clear that the eternal generation of the Son consists in a communication that must be considered spiritual in nature. He looks forward, therefore, to St. John's doctrine of the Logos, all the

[11] See Fraigneau-Julien, *Nouvelle Revue Théologique*, 1955, 356–7. There is thus a special activity of the Holy Spirit in the gift of grace and not simply the reference to one person of a work common to all three, as happens in the case where creation is attributed to the Father, though it is the work of the Trinity as a whole.

167

more so since in Col. 1:25–28 he links Christ with God's word in such a way as almost to identify the two.[12] The Holy Spirit, sent by the Father and by the Son and referred to indifferently as Spirit of God and Spirit of the Son (Gal. 4:4, 6; Titus 3:5–6), clearly proceeds from both. Again, the statement that charity is spread in men's hearts by the Spirit (Rom. 5:5; compare 15:30) is an indication of the doctrine of the procession of the Spirit through love, developed later, particularly by St. Augustine.[13] God is not "a sterile monad, isolated in his majesty".[14] He is superlatively alive and is knowledge and love existing substantially and personally and he deigns to impart his life to s. Paul declares this Trinitarian doctrine unhesitatingly, without any rhetorical safeguards, for he knows that it follows the teachings of the Saviour and cannot call into question the dogma of the divine oneness.[15]

[12] See DT, *Fils de Dieu*, 2401–3, *Processions divines*, 656.
[13] See DT, *Processions divines*, 657–61.
[14] Lagrange, *Le Judaïsme avant Jésus-Christ;* (Études Bibliques), 590.
[15] See *Enseignement de saint Paul*, I, 125–30.

PART THREE

PARTICIPATION IN SALVATION
COLLECTIVE ASPECT

11

COLLECTIVE AND INDIVIDUAL SALVATION

"You are all one person in Jesus Christ"
(Gal. 3:28).

BY showing the human race interdependent with the first man in sin and, in an infinitely more efficacious way, interdependent with Christ for salvation and eternal life, the doctrine of the two Adams indicates clearly that the search for salvation cannot be an individual matter (1 Cor. 15:45–49; Rom. 5:12–21). In the same way that the human race is affected by the fall both collectively and individually, those who are saved make up a new humanity of which all the members are henceforth one in Christ (Gal. 3:28), intimately linked with the Saviour and linked also with one another in a relationship so close that it eliminates all differences arising from birth, social condition and sex. The two men at the head as it were of the columns lead in their wake innumerable armies but, in the case of Christ even more than in that of Adam, the individuals who compose the army act upon each other. As members of Christ, they are, at the same time, members of each other (Rom. 12:5). There is "no such thing as a separate and individualistic holiness".[1]

"For Paul, whatever is social must be applied to the individual, while each Christian is essentially a member of a group",[2] a member of the community of Christian people. The members

[1] Mersch, *Morale et corps mystique,* I, 109: compare 110–7.
[2] Cerfaux, *The Church in the Theology of St. Paul,* 148, n. 8.

of Christ are in a state of constant interaction and would not be able to achieve salvation or damnation alone. This supernatural solidarity is illustrated in many aspects of the apostle's message. Paul thus reflects the supreme prayer of the Saviour who asked that the faithful of every generation might be united in him and in the Father (John 17:20–22), and he also reflects the essential precept of the gospel law: "This is my commandment, that you should love one another as I have loved you" (John 15:12).[3] The great mystery of which Paul was made the prophet through revelation and through a special mission (Eph. 3:2–9) is the participation of the Gentiles in the Messianic promises and in the "unfathomable riches of Christ" by the same right as the children of Abraham. The Gentiles were formerly without Christ, outlaws from the commonwealth of Israel, strangers to every dispensation of the promise, with nothing to hope for, with the world about them and no God (Eph. 2:12). Everything is henceforth changed and those who are far off have been brought near in the blood of Christ. The Saviour has thrown down the barrier of hate that separated them from the Jews. All have now access to the Father in the same Spirit. The two reconciled antagonists make up the one new creature and one body. The Gentiles are fellow citizens with the saints, brought into God's household (Eph. 2:14–19). "Through the gospel preaching the Gentiles are to win the same inheritance, to be made part of the same body, to share the same divine promise, in Christ Jesus" (Eph. 3:6). They have in them Christ, their hope of glory (Col. 1:27). And when he contemplates this

---

[3] The collective and individual approaches are both essential. The importance attached at the present time to the social aspect should not distract us from the personalism inherent in Christianity and should also not obscure the fact that the religious problem is presented to each individual, who must solve it personally. See Bouyer, *Du protestantisme à l'Église*, Cerf, 1954, 121.

mystery of the universal call to salvation, which was once hidden and is now revealed (Col. 1:25–27; Eph. 3), Paul breaks forth into cries of admiration: "It is a great mystery we worship. Revelation made in human nature, justification won in the realm of the Spirit; a vision seen by angels, a mystery preached to the Gentiles; Christ in this world, accepted by faith, Christ, on high, taken up into glory" (1 Tim. 3:16). The solemn affirmation of the universal call to salvation in its collective aspects should never be overlooked.[4] It is through the instrumentality of the community of the Church that the regenerated faithful have made available to them the means of salvation.

They are, in fact, saved through the new covenant, through making themselves members of a new people, through entering the new household of God, which is the Church, and becoming members of Christ – for these are but varied ways of expressing a single collective reality.

The covenant that God concluded with his people at Sinai was limited and provisional. It affected only Israel to the exclusion of the Gentiles, but the prophets had announced that a new and eternal covenant would replace it one day, an alliance which would be more interior than the first and would have as its effect complete pardon for sin and a fuller knowledge of God, thanks to the Holy Spirit, penetrating and renewing hearts (Jer. 31:31–34; Ezech. 36:25–28; Isa. 55:3; 59:21; 61:8). They predicted, too, that all peoples would come to Jerusalem to adore the true God (Isa. 2:2–3; Mich. 4:1–3; Jer. 16:19–21; Isa. 45:14, 20–25; Soph. 3:9–10; Zach. 6:15; 8:20–23; 14:9, 16) and would have a share in the new covenant (Isa. 55:3–5), thanks to the intervention of the mysterious Servant of Jahveh, filled with his Spirit, the light of nations (Isa. 42:1; 49:6) and expiatory victim for the sins of the people (Isa. 53:4 et seq.). We find these

[4] See pp. 103–4 above.

prophecies fulfilled in Jesus. In him, the new alliance of the spirit replaces that of the letter (2 Cor. 3:6). It is concluded in his blood, infinitely more efficacious than the blood of victims in which the covenant was sealed (Heb. 9:15–22) and this blood of the new covenant, which speaks with more eloquence than that of Abel (Heb. 12:24), is proposed as a food in the mysterious Eucharist which commemorates the redemptive sacrifice and applies its fruits: "This cup, he said, is the new testament, in my blood" (1 Cor. 11:25).[5]

Thanks to the merits of the blood of Jesus and through faith in him, Christians share in the blessings received by Abraham, the believer, blessings which were destined to go beyond the interlude of the Mosaic law and be extended to all the nations of the earth (Gal. 3:8–9, 14; Rom. 3:16–17, 24–25). It is Christians who make up the true posterity of Abraham, the posterity according to the spirit and not according to the flesh (Rom. 9:6–8), descending not from Agar, the bondwoman, but from Sara, the free woman (Gal. 4:21–31). They are the new people, God's true Israel (Gal. 6:16). As a people, they were constituted in principle at Calvary and are constituted in practice as new believers come along to accept the gospel message and have themselves baptized in the name of Jesus.

The collective aspect here predominates. We find it again in various comparisons with similar meaning, of which most are so simple they hardly require comment.

Speaking of the effects of his preaching in Corinth, St. Paul declares that the faithful are God's field. The apostle had planted and after him had come his disciple, Apollo, who had watered, but it was God alone who had given the increase (1 Cor. 3:6–9). Those who are baptized have become the same plant as Christ by death to sin, in union with his Passion (Rom. 6:5).

---

[5] See Cerfaux, *The Church in the Theology of St. Paul*, 49.

They grow up together like shoots from a single stock, depending on Christ and growing in him in union with his resurrection. They make up a family and a household. The Gentile converts are no longer foreigners or passing guests. On an equal footing with the Judeo-Christians, they form part of the household of God (Eph. 2:19). Besides being a family, the members of which are interdependent, this house is a building in which Christ Jesus fills the role of foundation and corner-stone (1 Cor. 3:9–11; Eph. 2:20–22), a function essential to the strength of the structure. The apostolic labourers build on this foundation and will be judged according to the quality of the materials they use, that is according to the value of their work. They themselves, as apostles and prophets of the New Testament, are also dependent on Christ, the foundation of the spiritual structure which "being framed together, groweth up into an holy temple in the Lord" (Eph. 2:21 [Douai]). All the faithful enter into the construction of this building and, on receiving the gift of the Spirit, become the dwelling place of God. The mortar of this dwelling place is the very charity of Christ and the conjugal union is only a weak image of the union of Christ and the Church: "Husbands show love to your wives, as Christ showed love to the Church and gave himself up for it in order to sanctify it. Yes, these words are a high mystery, and I am applying them here to Christ and his Church" (Eph. 5:25–26, 32).[6] We shall have occasion to mention the Church once more in speaking of the body of Christ. For the moment, it is sufficient to notice how far, in all these comparisons, external elements (field, plant, family, building) are linked with interior aspects of the supernatural life (spiritual growth, union in Christ, participation in the Spirit, charity), and how the individual point of view is joined with the collective. The complexity of these great realities should

---

[6] Translator's own rendering.

never be lost sight of.

The same richness is to be found in the charismata. St. Paul uses this word signifying gifts to indicate divine favours and a variety of personal graces. It also signifies – and it is in this restricted sense that theologians use it – the graces accorded by the Holy Spirit to serve the general good of the Church rather than to provide for the sanctification of the recipients themselves (1 Cor. 1:7; 12:4, 9, 28, 30, 31; Rom. 12:6).

Four lists of charismata are to be found in the epistles, none of which is claimed to be complete: 1 Cor. 12:8–10 and 28–30; Rom. 12:6–9; Eph. 4:11.[7] All these charismata are of divine origin and in a fine passage the apostle attributes them to the three divine persons, insisting at the same time, as he did when he spoke of grace, on the special action of the Holy Ghost.

> And yet there are different kinds of gifts, though it is the same Spirit who gives them, just as there are different kinds of service, though it is the same Lord we serve, and different manifestations of power, though it is the same God who manifests his power everywhere in all of us. The revelation of the Spirit is imparted to each, to make the best advantage of it....[8] But all this is the work of one and the same Spirit, who distributes his gifts as he will to each severally (1 Cor. 12:4–7, 11).

Some of these charismata are miraculous: faith capable of moving mountains (1 Cor. 12:9; 13:2), the gift of healing and the gift of miracles, the gift of tongues, and the gift of interpreting languages. These were freely granted by God to the early Church and for this reason they have been well called the wedding presents of Christ and the Church. They have never completely disappeared except the gift of tongues. The other

---

[7] See Prat, *Théologie de saint Paul*, I, 498–503; *Enseignement de saint Paul*, II, 86; Kittel, γλῶσσα, I, 721–6 (Büchsell).

[8] The author has "for the general advantage". Translator.

charismata are those of teaching: prophets, doctors, evangelists; the charismata appropriate to government: pastors (who can perhaps be regarded as identical with doctors), those called upon to preside over assemblies, ministers. Finally, there are the charismata of corporal mercy. These gifts are doubtless more frequent than some people realize in the long history of the Church, and members of the hierarchy have often been favoured with them, a fact which should not surprise us. But, however that may be, it is remarkable that St. Paul never mentions them except when he is speaking of the Mystical Body, and then always in relation to the general good of the Church. This is particularly evident where he is dealing with the gift of tongues.

We do not know much about the nature of this charisma which must have disappeared early. It had given rise to abuses in the community at Corinth. The faithful took particular delight in it because of its extraordinary character, but its use gave rise to a certain disorder in the Christian gatherings. This was, indeed, so great as to be reflected in the description given in the first epistle to the Corinthians, chapter 14. The recipient of the gift of tongues entered into a sort of ecstasy and praised God in a way which seemed more or less inarticulate and incoherent, even though expressing himself in his mother tongue.[9] His hearers recognized vaguely that the inspired person was praying and praising God, but did not understand him. The action of the Holy Ghost was undeniable, but the utility of the gift was not very great unless another charismatic was present capable of interpreting clearly the thought of the one endowed with the gift of tongues. The risk of an unhealthy emotionalism was

[9] We are here basing ourselves on Allo, *Première aux Corinthiens*, Gabalda, 1943, 374–84. Prat (I, 153–5) considers that the charismatic spoke a foreign language. Other authorities worth consulting are SDB, *Charismes;* Catholicisme, *Charismes;* Kittel, I, at the word γλῶσσα (Behm).

177

undeniable, particularly in the case of converts previously initiated in the pagan mysteries, and the apostle did not want Christian gatherings to be taken by unbelievers as meetings of lunatics. He therefore drew up a wise set of rules, accompanying them with remarks which showed a sense of humour at the expense of those who were fond of exceptional phenomena. Edification was what chiefly mattered. Paul himself spoke in tongues more than anyone but preferred, in the gatherings, to say five words with his intelligence rather than ten thousand in tongues. Indeed, the one who prophesied, that is who spoke in an intelligible fashion under the influence of the divine spirit, exhorted, consoled and edified the Church, whereas the one who spoke in tongues edified only himself. That was why St. Paul says that only two or three inspired people at the most were to be allowed to speak in tongues, in turn, and on condition that there was somebody present to interpret them. If an interpreter was not available, the inspired person was enjoined to keep silent, speaking only to himself and to God. As for the prophets, they were all to be allowed to speak, but each in turn, in such a way as to give useful instruction and encouragement to their hearers. Finally, women were told to remain quiet in the gatherings, keeping their questions for their husbands when they returned home. Everything must be conducted with dignity and good order and in submission to the hierarchy. The gifts of the Spirit and the individual graces were in no way hampered by these regulations, but their manifestation was subordinated to the edification of the Church. A religion of authority and religion of the spirit were thus harmoniously brought together. Moreover, the charismata were to last only for a time. The vision face to face of eternal life would make them of no further use (1 Cor. 13:8–9). Charity[10] alone, which summed up the whole of the gospel and of Christian life, would remain (Gal. 5:6; Rom. 13:8; Col. 3:14;

[10] In a certain sense. See chapter 16, p. 237.

etc.). Even in this world it is far more necessary and excellent than even the most enviable of charismata. St. Paul says as much in the eloquent hymn (1 Cor. 13) in which he asserts the superiority of charity over the most marvellous gifts: "I may speak with every tongue that men and angels use; yet, if I lack charity, I am no better than echoing bronze, or the clash of cymbals.... I count for nothing" (13:1, 3).

The *Leitmotiv* is thus the common good, the edification of the Church, mutual charity. The charismata of teaching and government have all the same object. This is seen clearly in the accounts given in the Acts, in which preaching and apostolic authority take precedence at the birth of the new Israel. The same thought runs through the whole of the epistles and, to deal with it, we might feel called upon to re-read them completely. It will suffice, however, to recall that the great mystery of the universal call to salvation is known to the heavenly powers themselves only through the Church (Eph. 3:9–10) and no one can come to faith and salvation except by the apostolic preaching:

> Every one who calls upon the name of the Lord will be saved. Only, how are they to call upon him till they have learned to believe in him? And how are they to believe in him, until they listen to him? And how can they listen, without a preacher to listen to? And how can there be preachers, unless preachers are sent on their errand?... (See how faith comes from hearing; and hearing through Christ's word)... (Rom. 10:13–15, 17).

The position is such that a false teacher, whether he be man, or even an angel coming from heaven, who announced a different gospel would merit an anathema (Gal. 1:8–9). Paul and the other apostles alone had the mission of preaching the word of Christ in its fullness and preaching the glorious richness of the great mystery (Col. 1:25, 27). To know this and make it a rule of life, it was necessary to hear the apostles and join the communities founded by them. We are repeatedly brought back to a consideration of the body of Christ and of the Church.

12

THE BODY OF CHRIST[1]

> *"And you are Christ's body, organs of it depending upon each other"*(1 Cor. 12:27).

THE vision on the road to Damascus had shown Saul right from his conversion˚ how closely the faithful were united to Christ: "Why dost thou persecute me?... I am Jesus, whom Saul persecutes" (Acts 9 : 4-5). The apostle quickly recognized that these words must be understood in the strictest sense and not simply as an expression of the great interest the risen Christ had in his disciples. Jesus communicated his life to them to such a degree that each one could say what Paul was to write later: "And yet I am alive; or rather, not I; it is Christ that lives in me" (Gal. 2 : 19) and he also added that, having put on Christ in baptism, they were henceforth one person in him (Gal. 3 : 27-28). The rest of the context indicates, however, that their individuality was not affected by this, that it was not a kind of absorption in which their own personality would be submerged. When the apostle declares that all are now one person,[2] he wishes simply to proclaim the deep union and the close interdependence that are the consequence of a sharing in the life and divine sonship of Christ. But more

---

[1] This chapter and chapter 14 owe much to Father Benoit's *Corps, tête et plérôme dans les épîtres de la captivité,* RB, 1956, 5-44.

[2] The word "one" is masculine not neuter in the Greek texts. The reference is, therefore, to a single person, a single new man.

precise details were needed to supplement this general view and they took shape in St. Paul's mind when he came to write the first epistle to the Corinthians.

Already, in his correspondence with Thessalonica, when dealing with the worries of the faithful about the second coming, St. Paul assured them that a consequence of Christ's resurrection would be the resurrection of the dead on the last day and the reunion of all with Christ (1 Thess. 4 : 16-17). Christian unity, apparent from the time of the vision on the road to Damascus, was so assured that death could not break it and that it would reach fulfilment in eternal life. Paul was to reaffirm this unity on several occasions in his letters to Corinth.

Upset by the appearance of cliques which were disrupting the young community, he cried out: "What, has Christ been divided up?" (1 Cor. 1 : 13), thus identifying the Saviour with the Christians to whom he is writing and of whom he had just said that God had called them "into the fellowship of his Son" (1 : 9). Further on, speaking of meat sacrificed to idols, the eating of which he considered licit in certain circumstances (10 : 23-30), he declares that is necessary to abstain if there is fear of scandalizing a brother who is less enlightened on the matter, and adds: "When you thus sin against your brethren, by injuring their doubtful consciences, you sin against Christ" (8 : 12). It is as though one heard an echo of the words of our Saviour, at the last judgement: All that will have been done or refused to the least among his brethren will have been done or refused to himself (Matt. 25 : 40, 45). The indissoluble link between Christ and the faithful is so fundamental that it sets the tone for the admonishments made to them and the rules of conduct prescribed for them.

The idea is further developed by means of the comparison with the body.

The Corinthians, whose immorality was, unhappily, celebrated, did not all come on conversion to a full practice of Christian purity. Paul reminded them of their union with Christ in order to dissuade them from fornication: "Have you never been told that your bodies belong to the Body of Christ? And am I to take what belongs to Christ and make it one with a harlot? God forbid. Or did you never hear that the man who unites himself to a harlot becomes one body with her? . . . Whereas the man who unites himself to the Lord becomes one spirit with him" (6 : 15-17). This is admirably expressed and the argument is convincing. Christians are members of the body of Christ. They must live holy lives and avoid from now on breaking their union with the Lord, who transmits to them his life and the fullness of the Spirit.

Later, speaking of charismata, St. Paul uses a new allegory, based on the ancient fable, to show the supernatural interdependence of Christians (12 : 14-26). In the human body, there are several members, head, feet, eyes, ears and hands. None of these members can deny belonging to the body, but nor can it maintain that it is the whole of the body or say that it has no need of the other members. All the members are necessary and the least worthy are treated with the most respect and honour:

> Thus God has established a harmony in the body, giving special honour to that which needed it most. There was to be no want of unity in the body; all the different parts of it were to make each other's welfare their common care. If one part is suffering, all the rest suffer with it; if one part is treated with honour, all the rest find pleasure in it (1 Cor. 12:24–26).

The application of the teaching is given immediately after: "And you are Christ's body, organs of it depending on each other" (12 : 27). And the apostle enumerates the different

183

functions established by God in the Church — apostles, prophets, doctors, etc.

The question arises whether the interdependence thus described is simply comparable with that uniting a society or closely knit corporate body. At first sight, we might be tempted to believe that it was. In the past, this has been the opinion of many commentators and even recently that of Father Allo in his commentary on the first epistle to the Corinthians, but if we look at the matter more closely this interpretation seems to underestimate the apostle's thought. We must take all the texts into account and many indicate clearly that he is speaking of the individual body of Christ:

> A man's body is all one, though it has a number of different organs; and all this multitude of organs goes to make up one body: so it is with Christ (1 Cor. 12:12).

> Just so, we, though many in number, form one body in Christ, and each acts as the counterpart of another (Rom. 12:5).

Nowhere in the epistles is the term "Christ" used to signify a moral entity, which would include both Christ personally and the body of the faithful who are united with him. Christ is always Christ as an individual. We must therefore understand the body of Christ as his physical body, to which we are closely joined and which, being a spiritual and life-giving body (1 Cor. 15 : 45), transmits life to us. The providential order instituted by the incarnation remains unchanged and the blessed humanity of Jesus, the instrument of the redemption, is also the means by which the fruits of his sacrifice are applied to us. This way of looking at things is in harmony with the thought of the bible, which, taking man's unity as its starting point, does not differentiate between the body and the spirit. The body must not be dissociated from the soul. Sin and sal-

vation concern the whole man and this implies resurrection
in order that salvation shall be complete and that there shall
be true immortality.[3] We are far here from the Greek outlook
which regarded the body as a prison for the soul and, in consequence, objected to the idea of resurrection. But this approach no doubt influences us without our noticing it when we
concentrate too exclusively on the salvation of the soul.

Paul starts from the conviction that salvation is realized
through the union of the body with the dead and resurrected
body of Christ, through the profession of faith in him and
through the reception of baptism (Rom. 6:3-11), and, in
another way, through the Eucharist (1 Cor. 10:17). In the
references to Christ, as in the references to ourselves, it is always a question of the physical body and of man as a sentient
being.[4] The body of Christ, formerly crucified and now glorified, inseparable from the person of Christ, unites to itself all
the faithful. They become members of Christ in baptism by
means of their bodies. The physical union of Christians to the
individual body of the risen Christ brings about participation
in Christ's life in a mystical union, or, in other words, a real

[3] The reply of Christ to the Pharisees concerning the resurrection
(Matt. 22:31-32 and similar texts) is in the same sense.
[4] Cf. Benoit, 13. In Pauline terminology, we must therefore make
a careful distinction between the body and the flesh. The flesh, when
it is referred to in contrast with the spirit (Gal. 5:16-25; Rom. 8:
3-13), refers to all those evil tendencies that dispose man to sin. It is
synonymous with the old man (Rom. 6:6; Col. 3:9; Eph. 4:22) and
must be done to death. The body remains destined to death because
of sin but will rise again (Rom. 8:10-11). In other passages, flesh
is synonymous with body (Rom. 1:3; 3:20; 9:3; 1 Cor. 1:29;
5:5; etc.). More often than not, man is looked upon as composing a
unity with his body. This is sometimes so much the case that the word
body is used to signify person and becomes equivalent to the personal
pronoun, signifying man as a whole. The bodies of the faithful – that
is to say, the faithful themselves – are members of Christ: 1 Cor. 6:13;
cf. Eph. 5:28.

and mysterious union. It is in this way that the Mystical Body of Christ is built. The expression itself is not to be found in St. Paul but it is a familiar one with theologians and has been authenticated by the encyclical of Pope Pius XII in 1943 as a way of expressing, if we may put it thus, the extension Christ gives to himself through uniting himself with his members (cf. Eph. 1 : 23). It is a way of conveying the great reality lying behind the expressions "new man" (Eph. 4 : 24; Col. 3. 10), "the new creature" in Christ (Gal. 6 : 15; 2 Cor. 5 : 17), Christ "all and in all" (Col. 3 : 11 [Douai]). However mysterious it may be, this realism seems necessary to do full justice to the thought and expressions of St. Paul. It throws retrospective light on the passage we have already quoted – 1 Cor. 6 : 15-17 – on fornication. The context – a comparison with a guilty union of bodies – shows that the single spirit formed by the Christian with the Lord is not the spirit as opposed to the body, but the spirit from which the spiritual body of the risen Christ overflows (1 Cor. 15 : 44-49).[5]

These repeated references to the real body of Christ lead us to think that the allegory contained in 1 Cor. 12 : 14-26, which does not go beyond the idea of a social group of which the members are interdependent, is merely an illustration of one aspect of the doctrine, St. Paul's main idea being that of a physical union of the body of the Christian to the indi-

---

[5] See Durrwell, 208-9. The encyclical *Mystici Corporis* does not speak of union to the physical body of Christ but states that the union of the faithful in Christ is much more than a moral one because the presence and action of the Holy Spirit (compare 1 Cor. 12 : 13) in the members of the Mystical Body bring about a much more perfect unity than that of a physical or social body. The Pope leaves theologians free in their attempts to explain this unity, provided that anything savouring of pantheism is rejected and also any idea that Christians share the divine attributes. See the English translation of the encyclical published by the Catholic Truth Society (pp. 38-48).

vidual body of Christ, as a means of salvation.[6] Some have proposed calling the union sacramental, but the expression might lead to misunderstanding, except in the case of the Eucharist.

In the epistles to the Colossians and the Ephesians, which he wrote during his captivity, we find a new point. Christ is presented as the head of his body which is his Church (Col. 1 : 18; Eph. 1 : 22-23). In these passages, Paul answers a kind of anticipation of the gnostic doctrines, which exaggerated devotion to the angels, whom there was a tendency to regard as mediators between God and man to such an extent that the importance attached to Christ's mediation was reduced (Col. 2 : 6-23). The apostle vigorously attacked this false philosophy and the traditions of purely human origin that were added to it and were, moreover, claimed to be based on a higher doctrine or *gnosis,* reserved for initiates. The allusions St. Paul here makes to the matter lead us to believe that these errors

---

[6] St. Paul links with his teaching on the doctrine of the Mystical Body – and this should surprise no one – what he has to say of the reciprocal duties of married couples (1 Cor. 11 : 3; Eph. 5 : 21-33), of parents and children (Eph. 6 : 1-4; Col. 3 : 20-21), and of masters and slaves (Col. 3 : 22-24; Eph. 6 : 5-9; the epistle to Philemon in its entirety). Wives should be submissive to their husbands as to the Lord, children should obey their parents in the Lord, and slaves obey their masters as they would Christ. See *Enseignement de saint Paul,* II, 111-8. Christians are members one of another at the same time as they are members of Christ (Eph. 4 : 25; 1 Cor. 12 : 12, et seq., and 27). This, it seems, entitles us to conclude that they are incorporated in Christ, not only from the personal standpoint, but also to the extent that he communicates life to the other members of his body, intimately uniting them to himself. "While it is true that each one receives individually the grace that sanctifies him, it is not true that he receives it entirely separately; for whatever we receive, we receive by incorporation in Christ, which is the same thing as incorporation in all the members of Christ" (Mersch, *Morale et corps mystique,* 115). Thus each benefits from the efforts of his brethren and it becomes profoundly true in this sense to say that each soul that raises itself raises the world. The great law of charity is given a stronger and deeper meaning.

amalgamated Judaic prejudices with Eastern speculations which, considering God's transcendence to be incompatible with direct action in the world, multiplied the intermediaries between God and creation (principalities, powers, and so on: Col. 1 : 16; 2 : 10, 15). They were also influenced by a dualist philosophy which looked upon matter as evil.[7] It becomes less surprising to meet such dark imaginings in the tormented environment of Phrygia when we reflect that two centuries later it was there that the extravagances of the Montanist heresy were to make their appearance.

Whatever the influences affecting the Phrygian illuminees, we find Paul declaring in a most energetic manner the superiority of Christ over any imaginable category of angel:

> Yes, in him all created things took their being, heavenly and earthly, visible and invisible: what are thrones and dominions, what are princedoms and powers? They were all created through him and in him; he takes precedence of all, and in him all subsist. He too is that head whose body is the Church (Col. 1:16–18).

> (God) raised Christ from the dead, and bade him sit on his right hand above the heavens, high above all princedoms and powers and virtues and dominations, and every name that is known, not in this world only, but in the world to come. He has put everything under his dominion, and made him the head to which the whole Church is joined, so that the Church is his body, the completion of him who everywhere and in all things is complete (Eph. 1:21–23).[8]

[7] See p. 80 above, n. 1; see also Cerfaux, *Gnose préchrétienne et biblique,* SDB, 690, 700; Benoit, RB, 1937, 342-61, 506, 525.

[8] St. Paul here shows the influence of Jewish doctrines concerning the angels, but does not add to them any new elements. The nature of the Powers which are less than Christ is not clearly specified. They were not, it seems, fundamentally evil, but had in some way gone astray, having abused their authority over the world in the administration of the Mosaic law. Christ nailed the law to the cross and stripped these Powers of their influence (Col. 2 : 14-15; Eph. 1 : 21-22).

The idea of the head is brought in here in relation to heavenly powers. Christ is their head, exercising over them an irresistible authority (Col. 2 : 10, 18-19; Eph. 1 : 20-22). This is, furthermore, the normal use of the metaphor of the head in Semitic terminology. But Christ is head not only of the angels, but also of the Church (Eph. 1 : 22-23; Col. 1 : 18) and the idea of authority is in the latter case supplemented by that of vital principle. We must unite ourselves to "that head of ours, on whom all the body depends, supplied and unified by joint and ligament, and so growing up with a growth which is divine" (Col. 2 : 19). We must grow in the Head which is Christ: "On him all the body depends; it is organized and unified by each contact with the source which supplies it; and thus, each limb receiving the active power it needs, it achieves its natural growth, building itself up through charity" (Eph. 4 : 16). This idea of the head as a vital principle that also nourishes does not come from the bible but from Platonism and stoicism and St. Luke, the beloved physician and companion of St. Paul, must have found it a particularly attractive notion (Col. 4 : 14). The conception of a vital principle —which does not, of course, exclude the idea of authority— undoubtedly comes as an enrichment to St. Paul's thought. It emphasizes well the distinction between the members and the Head. The latter is in heaven where the members are destined to join him. They are not with him in a relationship identifying themselves absolutely with him, but in a union the great intimacy of which depends upon infusion of the vital principle that is communicated to them.[9] The apostle's teaching on the

---

[9] Christians thus live at one and the same time in the old world and in the eschatological world. They are dead in Christ but are destined to die once more (Rom. 6 : 3-13; Col. 2 : 20; 3 : 5). Their resurrection is already realized through their union with the risen Christ (Col. 2 : 12; 3 : 1; Eph. 2 : 5-6), but it is nevertheless still in the future (Rom.

gift of the Holy Spirit and the contact with Christ's body in the sacraments shows that this is indeed his thought on the matter. The comparison with marriage in Eph. 5 : 22–32 has the same significance and is no less realistic in its approach.

Christ is thus both the chief and the head of his Mystical Body. This does not apply to the Powers which are nowhere described as his body and in connection with which we have merely to retain the idea of supremacy and authority. Only men are united by the sacraments to the dead and risen body of Christ. The Powers are influenced only indirectly by the redemption. They are reconciled with God (Col. 1 : 20) solely in the very general sense of the restoration of all things to a right order. They are henceforth subordinated to Christ just as, in a sense, the material universe itself is incorporated into the new order, into the new creation resulting from the redemption. Christ is all in all (Col. 3 : 11). "Everything must be summed up in Christ as in one unique chief (Eph. 1 : 10), a chief who is recognized and is even a head providing nourishment for some, but imposed by force on others."[10]

It seems, then, that the action of Christ the Redeemer touches the whole of creation. St. Paul indicates this when he declares that it pleased God that the whole pleroma, the whole completeness, should dwell in Christ (Col. 1 : 19). The term "pleroma" is borrowed from stoicism but is purified from any pantheism and the Old Testament had already used it, adapted to monotheism (Ecclus. 16 : 29; 43 : 27; Wisdom 1 : 7; 7 : 24; 8 : 1). In these passages, the pleroma is not equivalent to the Godhead because Jesus does not become divine. He is divine by nature as Son of God. The pleroma seems

6 : 5, 8), and remains the object of hope (Rom. 8 : 23-25; Phil. 3 : 11). In our conclusion, we shall have occasion to return to this paradox of the Christian message, so clearly brought out by St. Paul, this fundamental unity and continuity between the life of the Christian and the glorified life, hereafter. [10] RB, 1956, 31.

to be the universe, the framework in which redeemed humanity moves, and Christ the Redeemer assumes responsibility for it at the same time as he assumes responsibility for redeemed humanity. Scripture, in fact, often represents the Cosmos as being filled with divine presence and divine action (Isa. 6 : 3; Ps. 23 : 1). "Having by his incarnation summed up in himself the whole universe, divine, human, and even cosmic, divided as it was by sin, Christ was able, by his expiatory death and resurrection, to reconcile all things and to restore peace.... It was by reconciling and pacifying all the divided parts of this Universe through the death of Christ that God made it 'dwell' in Christ as in a new Being, the New Creature, where All, God and the World, find themselves restored to order."[11] By bringing the Powers under his authority, he becomes head of the whole universe. "There thus dwells in him all 'Completeness' – the 'Completeness' of God which he is by nature, and of the World which he has finally brought back into a state of obedience."[12] We can understand in the same sense what St. Paul says a little further on: "In Christ the whole plenitude of Deity is embodied, and dwells in him, and it is in him that you find your completion; he is the fountain head from which all dominion and power proceed" (Col. 2 : 9-10). The plenitude of Being, of God and of the world, dwells in Christ in a corporal mode: first, certainly, through the individual body he assumed at the incarnation, but also in his uniting himself in the redemption and the resurrection with the regenerated humanity that his glorified body fills with the Spirit and also by his uniting to himself indirectly the whole universe, which is the framework of the new humanity. Christians benefit in a privileged way from the life of Christ united with the pleroma, which he communicates to them in baptism (Col. 2. 10-12).

[11] Ibid. 38.   [12] Ibid. 38.

In the epistle to the Ephesians, St. Paul, leaving out of account the errors of the Colossians, deals particularly with the question of the Church as the body of Christ. This builds itself up little by little on earth and thus completes the Plenitude of Christ (Eph. 1 : 22-23; 2 : 20-22; 4 : 12-13, 15-16). The supreme fulfilment of the redemptive work of Christ is "all the completion God has to give" (3 : 19), to which he will join the members of the Church. This doctrine is perfectly consistent, in spite of the varied elements of diverse origins that St. Paul incorporates in it: "Sacramental union of the body of Christians to the risen body of Christ; the constitution through this of a Body of Christ, which is the Church and which is increasingly building itself up; the government and vivification of this Body by Christ considered as its Head, first in the sense of a chief who gives the orders, but also as a nourishing principle; the extension of this influence of Christ to the whole universe, which he carries in himself with the divinity, in a pleroma where all things are reconciled in unity; finally the Completeness of God himself who, through Christ, is at the beginning and end of this work of re-creation."[13]

[13] RB, 1956, 43-4. The teaching we have just outlined does not take its origin from the gnostic myth of the *Urmensch*. This idea appears only in texts later than St. Paul and, far from it being true to say that his own thought derives from it, the gnostic doctrine itself may have been influenced by St. Paul. We must look for the sources of the Pauline doctrine in the Old Testament where Adam represents the whole of humanity, inspiring by way of contrast the theme of the New Adam, and we also look to a Semitic realism which cannot conceive of a man without his body. But this is a long way from the myth of the anthropos-saviour. The primordial Being, according to this theory, had to descend from heaven to deliver souls, gather them together and take them to heaven. This is a purely cosmic conception of the redemption and we can see at a glance how far it is from Christian redemption. See RB, 1956, 17-8. Goossens, *L'Église corps du Christ d'après s. Paul*, Gabalda, 1949, 90-8. The doctrine of the body of Christ offers a close analogy with the gospel allegory of the vine and the branches (John 15 : 1-8). See Kittel κεφαλή, III, 678-82 (Schlier).

13

UNION WITH THE BODY OF CHRIST THROUGH THE EUCHARIST

*"Is not the bread we break a partici-
pation in Christ's body?" (1 Cor. 10:16).*

WRITING to the Corinthians in 55 or 56 A.D., St. Paul was
led to remind them of the doctrine of the Eucharist in order
to put an end to the disorders that had grown up in the
conduct of the religious meetings (1 Cor. 11 : 1-22). The
dress of the womenfolk was not all it should be. They had
taken to praying with their heads uncovered, as though they
wanted to emancipate themselves from dependence on their
husbands. The apostle invited them to observe greater modesty,
using arguments of unequal value, some of which were not
free from a teasing irony, and finally based himself on
the custom of the churches. But, what was more serious,
the meal preceding the Eucharistic celebration was too often
conducted in a selfish and individualistic way, incompatible
with the spirit of charity demanded by common participation
in the Body of the Lord. The faithful gathered together in little
groups, taking their meal without bothering about each other,
in such a way that some did not have enough while others
became fuddled. Paul condemned these abuses vigorously,
recalling in doing so the institution of the Eucharist. His
account is of the greatest importance because it is earlier than
that of the gospels, except perhaps the Aramaic version of St.
Matthew's gospel.

The tradition which I received from the Lord, and handed on to you, is that the Lord Jesus, on the night when he was betrayed, took bread, and gave thanks, and broke it, and said, *Take, eat; this is my body (given up) for you. Do this for a commemoration of me.* And so with the cup, when supper was ended, *This cup,* he said, *is the new testament, in my blood. Do this, whenever you drink it, for a commemoration of me.* So it is the Lord's death that you are heralding, whenever you eat this bread and drink this cup, until he comes; and therefore, if anyone eats this bread or drinks this cup of the Lord unworthily, he will be held to account for the Lord's body and blood (1 Cor. 11:23–27).

Was St. Paul referring here to a direct revelation from Christ? The words in the Greek do not necessarily require this interpretation. They can be understood as referring to an indirect transmission, but going back, in fact, to our Lord. Father Allo paraphrases the passage in this way: "I have received through a tradition that comes from the Lord, what I have also passed on to you (that is to say I have passed it on in the way it was transmitted to me). It is that the Lord Jesus..."[1] It would not seem that a direct revelation was needed. It is inconceivable that immediately after his conversion Paul should have failed to receive instructions from Ananias or from others in the essential elements of the faith he was to preach and, when he was writing, the Eucharist had already been celebrated for a long time in all the churches (Acts 20 : 7). Those who regard this passage as affirming an immediate revelation are forced to admit either that it represented for St. Paul the simple confirmation of what he already knew, or else that it related only to the dispositions necessary for a

---

[1] See Allo, *Première aux Corinthiens,* 309-16. The shortness of the account leads us to think that it repeats a liturgical formula or is at least inspired by one. If that is so, we are provided with the thought of the early communities as well as that of the apostle.

worthy participation in the Eucharist. None of these hypotheses is definitely established.[2]

The formula for the consecration of the bread is in itself quite clear: "This is my body for you." St. Luke provides the verb that St. Paul left to be understood and which completes the sense: "This is my body, given for you" (Luke 22 : 19). The general context makes it certain that the allusion is to the Passion. St. Matthew (26 : 26) and St. Mark (14 : 22) say simply: "This is my body." For the wine, St. Paul uses a double metonymy: "This cup is the new testament, in my blood."[3] He takes the cup for its contents, the blood of Christ, and the testament for the blood in which it is sealed. The mention of testament in the blood presumes the blood to be really present in the cup, all the more so since the allusion is to the old covenant concluded in the blood of victims, through Moses (Exod. 29 : 3-8, quoted in Hebrews 9 : 18-22). In each case, there is a covenant linked with the sacrifice of a victim. This context makes it impossible to interpret the words of the Saviour metaphorically, and chapter 6 of St. John, together with the constant tradition of the Church, should remove any hesitation on the point. The following verses, moreover, strongly support the realistic interpretation: to communicate unworthily is to make oneself guilty of the body and

[2] Huby, 262; Cerfaux, *The Church in the Theology of Saint Paul,* 262.

[3] In John 6 the word "flesh" is used in the place of "body". In the Greek, the word for body, σῶμα, is preferred, even though it may be a less literal translation of the Aramaic word employed by our Lord, because it has no pejorative implications. "The body lives through the blood which is its vital principle; the two together signify the whole man. In the context of the Passion, it is a question of the body which is to be put to death and of the blood which is to be shed" (Dupont, *Ceci est mon corps,* NRT, 1958, 1030). We are dealing here with a symbolic rite in so far as it relates to the Passion, but a rite that is efficacious, containing the reality it signifies (ibid. 1034-40).

blood of Christ (verse 27). Failure to make a distinction between the sacred body and profane food is to eat and drink damnation to oneself (verse 29). The mysterious rite of the Eucharist is thus a true sacrifice, intimately linked to the Passion with which it effects the new covenant that was announced by the prophet Jeremias (31 : 31-34), and that was destined to bring about the forgiveness of sins and a deeper union with God.

St. Luke's description (22 : 19-20) closely resembles that of St. Paul, as we should expect from one of the apostle's own disciples. The parallel is striking, particularly in the part relating to the chalice and in the order in which the words of the Eucharistic celebration are repeated, in memory of the Saviour. St. Matthew and St. Mark do not allude to this order and, in the case of the chalice, say simply, "This is my blood". It is perhaps merely a matter of preserving simplicity and literary balance in the words used. The words adopted by St. Paul and St. Luke seem to us more archaic and are probably the original ones.[4] But Matthew and Mark add that the blood is the blood of the testament shed for many (Mark 14 : 24) and Matthew also says that it is shed unto the remission of sin (Matt. 26 : 28). It will be seen that the four texts all agree in affirming the sacrificial character of the rite instituted by the Saviour, "the night that he was betrayed".

Another passage in the epistle (10 : 14-22), gives testimony in the same sense. It deals with the use of the idolothyta or meats offered to the idols. Paul considers that it is licit to eat of them when one is invited to a pagan's house. The origin of the food gives no ground for scruple since the idols count for nothing. But there would be reason to abstain in order to

---

[4] Some commentators nevertheless believe that the tradition followed by St. Mark is the older one.

avoid giving scandal to Christians not well instructed in the matter (8 : 7-13; 10 : 28). On the other hand, there must be no participation in meals within the precincts of the temples. Sitting down at the table of demons makes it impossible to sit down afterwards at the Lord's table. Whoever associates himself with a sacrifice also associates himself, at least morally, with the divinity to whom the sacrifice is offered. The pagans entered into communion with the demons to whom the cult of idols was in reality directed. The Jew who eats the victims unites himself to God, symbolized by the altar. The Christian unites himself closely with Christ: "We have a cup that we bless; is not this cup we bless a participation in Christ's blood? Is not the bread we break a participation in Christ's body?" (10 : 16). In every case, there is a victim sacrificed and the eating of that victim. In the case of the Eucharistic feast, participation in the body and blood of Christ is as real as was the eating of the idolothyta and of the victims offered in the Jewish temple. The eucharistic feast has an additional sacrificial character because the victim is presented in an immolated form, shown by the separate mention of the body and the blood. The doctrine is the same as that given in the account of the Last Supper, which ends, moreover, with a declaration that in eating the bread and drinking the Eucharistic cup, we are "heralding the Lord's death". We recall and proclaim the Lord's death as though it were happening at this very moment.

There is thus the real presence of Christ and a sacrifice actually taking place and not merely symbolic. At the last supper, Christ offered by anticipation his own immolation in a bloody manner. He accepted it in advance with all the dispositions of obedience to the Father and of redeeming love for men which were to be his on the cross. Since his glorification, he continues to offer this same sacrifice through the

Church and in the same dispositions. This is assuredly a mystery, both in relation to the real presence and in relation to the sacrificial offering, but it is one proclaimed by the apostle from the beginning, to which we must submit in a spirit of faith. The role of theology would subsequently be to examine all its aspects and strive to clarify its nature, but the essential was already clearly taught by St. Paul.[5]

The use of the world communion (κοινωνία) in the body and blood of the Lord emphasizes the affirmation of the real presence and of the intimate union resulting from it. We are faced not only with the union of each individual with Christ but with a union of the faithful among themselves, in such a way that the Eucharist strengthens the unity of the Church and completes the effect of baptism: "The one bread makes us one body, though we are many in number; the same bread is shared by all" (10 : 17. Compare Gal. 3 : 26-28; 1 Cor. 10 : 1-4; 12 : 13). There is but one bread, which is strictly the sole of its kind (τοῦ ἑνὸς ἄρτου). The sacramental species, being plural, cannot be understood in this way, but only the indivisible body of Christ.[6] We become united among ourselves in the highest degree because we are identified collectively and individually with the unique body of the risen Christ. We are identified with the substantial and individual Christ who gives us life. There is thus a mystical identification of the Church with the body of the risen Christ, arising from the communication of the same life. But it is an imperfect identity because the two parts of it remain distinct. That is

[5] Uniting us, as it does, with the sacrificed and glorified Christ, the Eucharist has a paschal character. The allusion in 1 Cor. 5 : 7-8, taken in conjunction with other texts, gives sufficient indication of this.

[6] St. Paul might equally well have taken the chalice as the basis of his argument, but "the solid conveys better the idea of a concentrating force, uniting the faithful in a compact body" (Allo, 240).

what we mean when we use, for want of a better term, the expression "mystical identity".[7] We may even ask ourselves whether it is not the Eucharistic communion that did most to reveal to St. Paul the identification of the Church with the glorified body of the Lord.[8] However it may be on this point, the doctrine of unity through the Eucharist manifestly has a spiritual richness, all the more profound in that it cannot be other than a unity in charity and the Holy Spirit. We find both individual and collective fruit at the same time. Contemporary pastoral theology rightly stresses the second aspect without overlooking the first.

From each follow certain obligations to which the apostle does not refer explicitly, but which can easily be deduced from the warnings he adds to his reminder of the Eucharistic institution. Each person should examine his own conscience before approaching the Lord's table. To receive the Eucharist without discerning the sacredness of the body of the Lord is to eat and drink one's own damnation, to make oneself guilty towards the body and blood of the Lord (1 Cor. 11 : 28 and 27). God would be justified in holding those responsible to account for this sacrilege as he held Cain to account for the blood of Abel. The unworthy communicant makes himself in a sense the accomplice in murder. He fails to recognize the significance of the body of Christ, the efficacy of his

[7] See also DT, *Messe*, 830-1; Cerfaux, *The Church in the Theology of St. Paul*, 246-7, 268, 277-8, Bonsirven, *Théologie du Nouveau Testament*, 357-8; *Évangile de Paul*, 272-3. Compare St. John Chrysostom, in 1 Cor. hom. XXIX, PG LXI, 200. The order of repetition in the Eucharistic formula having been communicated only to the apostles, it is legitimately concluded that the celebration throughout the centuries is reserved to their successors in the priesthood.

[8] See Benoit in RB, 1956, 14, n. 1. The fact that the two aspects, Eucharistic and mystical, are envisaged in the first epistle to the Corinthians (10 : 17; 12 in its entirety) is doubtless not merely an accident.

death, the love that inspired his sacrifice, and the union which should exist between those who partake of the one bread. The sacred gifts[9] should not be received except with a strong faith, a pure conscience and a burning resolve to observe fraternal charity, — what Guardini calls the "feeling for the Mystical Body" — a profound sense of the Church as Christ's body. Paul attributes to disrespectful or sacrilegious communions the fact that an unusual number of the faithful in Corinth had been struck by illness or death. Each member of the faithful should therefore strive to avoid meriting similar punishment through imperfect dispositions and to avoid the final sentence of damnation, falling upon the world in enmity with God (11 : 28-32). They were, moreover, enjoined to wait for each other at the celebration of the Eucharist, satisfying their appetites beforehand in their own homes (11 : 33-34). Paul gives permission before the Eucharistic celebration for no more than a moderate meal, later to be known by the well chosen name of *agape*. Some commentators consider, indeed, that the apostle prohibited as an abuse any kind of preliminary meal. Clear evidence of the *agape* does not appear until the beginning of the second century and the practice quickly disappeared.[10]

The Eucharist is a source of unity, not only in space, if we may put the matter thus, but also in time: "So it is the Lord's death that you are heralding, whenever you eat this bread and drink this cup, until he comes" (1 Cor. 11 : 26). The Eucharist is the link between the past appearance of our Lord and his glorious return at the end of time. It perpetuates his sacrifice and his presence between these two comings.[11] It is a

---

[9] At the present time in Athens the Corpus Christi procession is referred to as the procession of the "Holy Gifts".

[10] See SDB, *Agape*. [11] See de Montcheuil, *Signification eschatologique du repas eucharistique*, RSR, 1946, 10-43; Durrwell, 374-80.

reminder and reiteration of the Last Supper and is at the same
time the joyous anticipation of the eternal Messianic repast
in the kingdom of the Father: "And I tell you this, I shall
not drink of this fruit of the vine again, until I drink it with
you, new wine, in the kingdom of my Father" (Matt. 26 : 29).
The Eucharist thus brings about the marvellous presence of the
glorified Lord (1 Cor. 2 : 8) in the efficacious representation
and continuation of his sacrifice, and it appears as the privileged means of applying to us the fruits of that sacrifice through
the imparting of the body and blood of him who died on the
cross. St. Paul is careful to remind us implicitly of the fact
that there is no participation in Christ's glory without participation in his cross. It is only by proclaiming Christ's death
that we prepare ourselves for his glorious coming, but the
proclamation of his death leads henceforward to his mysterious
and hidden coming, in the expectation of his solemn coming
on the last day. This makes the Eucharist both a possession
and a waiting. As St. Thomas says, "The whole mystery of
our salvation is summed up in it".

We may ask ourselves if the union with the body of Christ in
the Eucharist is any different from the incorporation inaugurated by faith and realized in baptism, of which St. Paul speaks
a little further on (1 Cor. 12 : 12-13). Incorporation in
Christ through baptism unites to the body of Christ by secur-
ing entry into the Church (Eph. 5 : 26-30) which is his
body and his completion (Eph. 1 : 23), and is entirely in-
fused with his life. The glorified body of Christ is given in
the Eucharist and, if we may express it in this way, it becomes
present, as it were, in a given place. The Eucharistic presence
thus brings about a more intimate union. Through their reception of "the one bread", the Lord more than ever transforms
Christians into himself, both individually and collectively

201

(1 Cor. 10 : 17). The effect of baptism, which already united to his death and resurrection (Rom. 6 : 1-11), is prolonged and intensified. The sacramental presence of Christ is, as we know, only temporary, but its effect remains as an imparting of his life and this is the object of his presence. The body of Christ, "life-giving spirit", impregnates us once more with the Holy Spirit whom it possesses in all fullness and by the Spirit we become more perfectly identified with Christ's glorified humanity and with his life. His sacred humanity becomes the means whereby we are assimilated more completely to Christ in and through his Spirit. We find in the Eucharist, as in the whole life of grace in general, the common action of Christ and of the Spirit, the aim of which is to unite the faithful to Christ by making them members of his body, so that henceforth they are one with him (Gal. 3 : 26-28).[12]

St. Paul spoke of the Eucharist only in connection with abuses that he had to repress. It was in this context that he came to refer to the real presence and the sacrificial character of the sacrament. But he does not develop this doctrine, assuming it to be well known, nor does he attempt to prove it. He simply recalls the institution of the Eucharist in order to show the dispositions needed for the Lord's supper. Even so, he manages to say all that is essential. His statement of the link between the two comings of the Saviour constituted by the Eucharist fully justifies the exceptional importance accorded to the Eucharist by the Church. The Church lives through Christ's sacrifice, which is made present within the Church in its final glorious form but exteriorized in the sacramental rite; and this hidden coming of Christ is a preparation for his final spectacular coming.[13]

[12] See chapter 10, p. 164 and Durrwell, 212,257.
[13] See Durrwell, 374-80.

The "breaking of bread" was practised from the very beginning (Acts 2 : 42) and Paul is careful to repeat this characteristic expression (Acts 20 : 7; 1 Cor. 10 : 16; 11 : 24). He is not, therefore, pretending to be an innovator. Had he done so, neither the other apostles nor the early Christian community would have tolerated it. He himself denies attempting to build on any other foundation than that of Christ, of whose mysteries he is merely the dispenser (1 Cor. 3 : 11; 4 : 2). He is even careful to show the Eucharist prefigured in the manna and in the water, gushing miraculously from the rock in the desert (1 Cor. 10 : 3-4). This rock was Christ, already mysteriously present and active. The true nourishment and the true spiritual drink, the body and blood of Christ, are now given to God's new people who are marching towards the true Promised Land.[14]

[14] There is nothing whatever to suggest that St. Paul has borrowed anything, even unconsciously, from the pagan mysteries. See Allo, 298-300; SDB, *Eucharistie,* 1164-7; 1196-1209 (Coppens).

14

THE CHURCH AS THE BODY OF CHRIST

> *"He has put everything under his domination, and made him the head to which the whole Church is joined, so that the Church is his body"*   *(Eph. 1:22-23).*

THE term Church, ἐκκλησία, is used in the Greek bible of the Seventy to designate the whole of the Jewish people gathered together in prayer. St. Paul uses it to refer only to Christians, first those in the community in Jerusalem and afterwards those in the local churches. Finally, in the epistles written during his captivity, he extends it to all Christians of the universal Church.[1]

To the extent that it applies to the whole body of Christians, St. Paul treats the Church as synonymous with the body of Christ. Christ is "that head whose body is the Church" (Col. 1 : 18). God made Christ "the head to which the whole Church is joined, so that the Church is his body, the completion of him who everywhere and in all things is complete" (Eph. 1 : 22-23). Speaking in the same sense, the apostle declares that he completes in his own flesh what is lacking in the afflictions of Christ, for the sake of his body, the Church (Col. 1 : 24).

This last text probably refers to the sufferings endured

---

[1] See Cerfaux, *The Church in the Theology of St. Paul.*

by Christ during his mortal life. God requires the efforts and sufferings of the apostolic labourers in order to apply the merits of these sufferings of Christ. Communion in suffering obtains from God communication of Christ's merits, in a beautiful realization of what the apostle's creed and theologians unite in calling the *communion of saints* – the mutual edification (in the Latin sense of the word) of the members of the Mystical Body. This communion is realized in a variety of ways, not only through suffering but also through prayer and almsgiving. The fact is shown in many passages in the epistles (Eph. 1 : 16-17; 6 : 18-19; Col. 4 : 3; Rom. 15 : 30; 2 Cor. 8 : 13-15; etc.). A constant interdependence in good works is thus established between the different members of the Church, contributing to the growth of the whole body and providing for its *edification* in charity (Eph. 4 : 16). The interdependence unfortunately also relates to evil works. The unhealthy members cause suffering to the rest (1 Cor. 12 : 26) and the acts of disrespect committed towards the Eucharist unleashed in Corinth illnesses that were sometimes fatal.

All that is postulated about the Mystical Body can thus be said equally about the Church, as long as we make the necessary distinctions.

We can describe the Church as the completion of Christ (Eph. 1 : 23), for if Christ fills redeemed humanity with his life, he is, in a way, filled out and completed by the growth of the Church,[2] which, as we have seen above, can be said to

---

[2] This form of words must be properly understood. The Church does not complete Christ in an active sense. It receives everything from him and participates in his completeness (Col. 2 : 10). The body thus does not complete the head in the strict sense of the word. It is simply the recipient of the life with which the glorified body of Christ is filled, in such a way that Christ is, in reality, the whole body as well as the head. See Durrwell, 254-5.

draw the world after Christ. "Christ showed love to the world and gave himself up for it in order to sanctify it... . He would summon into his own presence the Church in all its beauty, without stain or wrinkle or disfigurement; but holy and immaculate" (Eph. 5 : 25-27).[3] Besides being the bride of Christ, the Church is also a spiritual building whose corner-stone is Christ and whose foundations are the apostles and the prophets. In Christ, "all the building, being framed together, groweth up into a holy temple in the Lord" (Douai). All the faithful enter into the construction of this building and become the dwelling place of God in the presence of the Spirit (Eph. 2 : 20-22). The Holy Spirit is the soul of the Church, as he is of the Mystical Body. He reveals the reality and universal extension of the Church (Eph. 3 : 5) and he gives life to all its members by making the inward man grow in them (Eph. 3 : 16), by setting his seal on them (Eph. 1 : 13), by giving them access to the Father (Eph. 2 : 17), by incorporating them in the body of Christ, of whose unity, both interior and exterior, he is the foundation (1 Cor. 12 : 12), by his profound action (Eph. 4 : 4), and by the charismata (1 Cor. 12 : 7-11).

From a more direct point of view, the Church is the visible society of the faithful in its exterior unity and provided with a hierarchical organization. The expression "Mystical Body", on the other hand, lays stress on the life common to the head and members, on the common life between members, and on the inner unity. But the aspect represented by the Church and that represented by the Mystical Body are not mutually exclusive. So much is this so that the apostle goes

[3] Translator's own rendering. The union of Christ and the Church is, of course, a more perfect one than that of a husband and wife and the Church did not exist before Christ as the woman does before a marriage. See Durrwell, 201, 210-11.

constantly from one to the other. The visible Church has for its aim the sanctification and salvation of the members composing it, the growth within them of the inner man, their rooting in charity, and the indwelling of Christ in their hearts (Eph. 3 : 16-17). These are equally the characteristics of the Mystical Body, and the Church, far from absorbing the individual, opens men to the action of Christ and of the Spirit[4] in order to lead all, individually and severally, to the state of perfection appropriate for those who make up the body of Christ (Eph. 4 : 13).

It is, nevertheless, through the medium of the visible Church that the Powers receive the revelation of the universality of the redemptive plan (Eph. 3 : 10-11) and we are not normally incorporated in the Mystical Body except through the Church. If Christ is the head of all those who are justified, it nevertheless seems that those who, though in good faith, are not members of the visible Church are his members only potentially. They have only an implicit wish to become effective members of Christ through baptism and membership of the Church; and they are deprived of numerous graces that the Church alone can dispense.[5]

The Church is born of the redeeming blood and resurrection of Christ (Rom. 4 : 24). Its existence was fully manifested at Pentecost in the abundant outpouring of the Spirit. From that time forth, the new people has come into being, God's true Israel (Gal. 6 : 16), and the blessings accorded to Abraham are extended to all nations (Gal. 3 : 9, 14). For, if the

---

[4] See Cerfaux, *The Church in the Theology of St. Paul*, 320-33.

[5] This seems to be the teaching contained in the encyclical *Mystici Corporis* of Pius XII. There is now a tendency to refrain from using the expression "soul of the Church" in referring to those who do not belong to the visible Church.

infant Church was at first made up of Jews, it was not long before it was joined, and in much greater numbers, by pagans of all kinds. By his sacrifice, Christ had broken down the wall of hate forming a barrier between Jew and Gentile, so that all thenceforth constituted a single new man and a single people (Eph. 2 : 13-18). Those Jews who became Christians abandoned any claim to special racial privileges and special customs. They passed from the order of the flesh to that of the spirit, dying and rising in Christ, not merely as individuals, but as a people.[6] St. Paul repeats in a number of different ways the truth that God is the God of all (Rom. 3 : 29), that he wishes to save all men (1 Tim. 2 : 4), that all distinctions between Jews and Gentiles are abolished (Gal. 3 : 26-28; Rom. 10 : 11; Col. 3 : 11). The great mystery he is privileged to announce is precisely the call to the Gentile peoples to embrace the faith. They are admitted to the same inheritance and are made beneficiaries of the same promises as Israel (Eph. 3 : 6-9), and they too possess Christ, their hope of glory (Col. 1 : 27). If, up to the time of which St. Paul speaks, Israel shows itself a rebel against the gospel, that unhappy attitude will endure only for a time. A day will come when the chosen people, recovering from their hardness of heart, will give themselves to Christ (Rom. 11).[7]

The universal character of the call to salvation implies also the universality of the Church, or in other words, its *catholicity*. All preachers of the gospel and all Christians should work to give effect to this catholicity, which is still only imperfectly realized. They should do so in order that, throughout the world, the third human race, which is vivified by the redeeming blood and constitutes the new creature, shall substitute

---

6 See Durrwell, 235-7.
7 See chapter 4 above.

itself for the first two races, that of the pagans in the flesh, and that of the circumcised in the flesh (Eph. 2 : 11). Catholic spirit and missionary spirit are equivalent terms and a fruitful anxiety will continue to operate in the hearts of true Christians as long as the gospel has not been preached to the whole human kind.

The universality of the Church requires its *unity*. There is but one Christ and one body of Christ, just as there is only one gospel of Christ. What we have said earlier about the Mystical Body and about its members shows how deep this unity is. It is the exterior unity of the one Lord Jesus, of the common faith in Jesus and of the one baptism, uniting us to him in the confession of that faith. It is also the interior unity of the unique Spirit which animates and sustains the Church by the unique hope of eternal blessings of which the Spirit's presence constitutes the first realization. It is also the transcendental unity of the one God and Father who is in all and acts in all and is the foundation both of the exterior and of the interior unity (Eph. 4:2-6). The unity of the Church is thus linked with the unity of God himself, of whom the faithful constitute the one family (Eph. 2 : 19-22).[8] It reaches perfection in the common participation in the one body of Christ in the Eucharist (1 Cor. 10 : 17) and must be continually strengthened by the practice of unremitting charity (Eph. 4 : 1-3; 5 : 2). It will, moreover, be safeguarded by holding fast to the deposit of the faith received from the apostles, in submission to the hierarchy established by them.

The exterior unity of the Church is clearly intended to preserve the interior unity composed of unity in holiness, in participation in the Spirit and in the very life of Christ. When Paul calls the faithful "saints", he is not simply using the

[8] Compare John 17 : 20-26.

word in the etymological sense of those who are separated from pagans, but is also referring to a positive holiness, consisting of conformity with Christ, the need for which he ceaselessly reaffirms. Eminently holy in its Chief, the Church must also be holy in its members, to whom it offers the most efficacious means of salvation, through the incessant action of the Spirit and through its sacraments.

The Church's apostolic character is too clear for there to be any need to insist upon it. With Christ, the apostles are its indispensable foundation (Eph. 2 : 20). The gospel is announced by them and by their disciples and it is by them that the Church is governed and that its members are guided towards their eternal destiny.

Strictly speaking, the apostles are the Twelve whom Christ chose, and who were the companions of his earthly life and witnesses of his resurrection (see Acts 1 : 15-25 dealing with Matthias, elected to replace Judas). By a special exception, Paul is himself also an apostle. He saw the risen Saviour (1 Cor. 9 : 1; 15 : 8) at the time of the marvellous vision which was responsible for his conversion. He thus received his apostolic mission from Christ and from God the Father (Gal. 1 : 1; Rom. 1 : 5). The fact that he later wanted to explain his "gospel" to those who had been apostles before him, lest he should be found to have run for nothing (Gal. 1 : 18, et seq.), does not imply the least doubt about the authenticity of his vocation or of his teaching (Gal. 1 : 8-9). It was, rather, because the exercise of his ministry made it necessary for his agreement with the authorities in Jerusalem to be attested. He declares himself the least of the apostles, unworthy to bear the name because he had been a persecutor, but he nevertheless claims an authority equal to theirs, proudly adding that he had worked harder than all the rest, not indeed he but the grace of God with him (1 Cor. 15 : 9-10). Later, at Antioch, St. Paul did not shrink from withstanding St. Peter to his face (Gal. 2 : 11, et seq.), when he felt it his duty to oppose the head of the apostles whose attitude was threatening to divide the Christian community[9] and to lead people to suppose that he still considered the Mosaic law binding. The strong and varied opposition he was destined to meet, particularly in Corinth, induced St. Paul to defend his rights as an apostle with unequalled vigour and eloquence (2 Cor. 10-12), uniting a moving humility with a merited sternness towards those whom he ironically refers to as "the great apostles" (2 Cor. 11 : 5 [Douai]) and towards those mediocre Christians whose conduct was a scandal (1 Cor. 5 : 1-5; 6 : 1-11). He acted with equal authority when he gave orders concerning the conduct of the meetings of the faithful, whether it was a question of the apparel of the women, or respect due to the Eucharist, or of the use to be made of charismata (1 Cor. 11 : 12, 14).[10] When, in the pastoral epistles, he put the government of the churches on a hierarchical basis, he again exercised his authority. In proclaiming himself the apostle of Christ at the beginning of each of his epistles, he is not using a vain formula.

Alongside the Twelve, St. Paul recognizes the existence of apostles in a wider sense and he places this category at the head of two lists of charismata (1 Cor. 12 : 28; Eph. 4 : 11). He uses the term to describe chosen disciples, such as

[9] The dispute did not concern doctrine. Peter's excessive condescension towards the Judaizing Christians was liable to give a false impression of his real thought on the matter. It is a mistake to regard this episode as constituting an objection to the primacy of Peter whose authority was, on the contrary, so great that Barnabas, Paul's companion in the evangelization of the heathen, felt obliged to follow his example. See Roiron, RSR, 1913, 507-18. [10] See chapter 11 above.

Titus and Timothy, who were entrusted with the task of organizing the churches. He expects from everyone what he was himself the first to provide — absolute sincerity, true humility, unalloyed with timidity, complete unselfishness, a generosity in the service of the faithful that shrinks at no sacrifice, overflowing charity, and paternal tenderness towards the faithful. We could find passages to illustrate this in all the epistles.[11] The apostles are as the light and incense of Christ (2 Cor. 2 : 15). They are intimately united with the Saviour and their tribulations are at the same time part of the tribulations of Christ, which would remain incomplete if the passion of his members were not joined to the Passion of the head: "I am glad of my sufferings on your behalf, as, in this mortal frame of mine, I help to pay off the debt which the afflictions of Christ still leave to be paid for the sake of his body, the Church" (Col. 1 : 24). The apostles carry in their own bodies the sufferings of Christ's death. They are ready to shed their blood in order that the converts shall give themselves to God as a sacrifice and offering worthy of acceptance (Phil. 2 : 17; Rom. 15 : 16). But their sufferings increase the life of Jesus in them and procure the pouring out of his life on those to whom they preach the gospel (2 Cor. 4 : 10-12). To these unforgettable expressions of apostolic devotion and of the doctrine of the communion of saints, Paul joins the statement that Christ's sufferings in him multiplied his consolations (2 Cor. 1 : 5). Joy, which is the flower of a generous sacrifice, comes as a crown, to reward his labours even at this stage. There is a superabundance of joy in the midst of his tribulations (2 Cor. 7 : 14), and he calls upon the faithful to show themselves ever joyful and to live in thanks-

---

[11] In the light of this, it is worth while re-reading 1 Thess. 1-3; 2 Cor. 1-4; and 11-12. Compare Gal. 4 : 12-20; 1 Cor. 4 : 4-17.

giving and peace (Phil. 4 : 4-7; etc.). He wants the whole of Christian behaviour to bear the mark of an optimism founded on a deep faith, on unshakeable confidence in the promises of divine help, and on the conviction that nothing can deprive us of the love that Christ bears us (Rom. 8 : 35-38).[12]

Apostolic authority had necessarily to take a *hierarchical* form as the local churches grew and multiplied.

From the beginning, we find the apostles, with Peter in the front rank, governing the Church in Jerusalem. They soon appointed deacons to help them in the material administration (Acts 6 : 1-4), as well as to preach (Acts 7-8; 8 : 5) and to baptize (Acts 8 : 12-13, 36-39). St. Paul appointed "elders" in the communities of Asia Minor and conferred their powers upon them by the rite of the laying on of hands (Acts 14 : 23; 20 : 7), following the example of the apostles in the case of the deacons (Acts 6 : 6). The Thessalonians were called upon to obey those "who have charge of you in the Lord and give you directions" (1 Thess. 5 : 12-13) and St. Paul's orders to the Corinthians clearly suggest the existence of men in authority, to see that they were complied with. In the opening words of the epistle to the Philippians, the apostle greets the bishops and the deacons and this is the first explicit mention of a hierarchy composed of two orders. The pastoral epistles show that he instituted such a hierarchy everywhere.

The presbyter-bishops — the two terms are equivalent (Acts 20 : 17, 28; Titus 1 : 5, 7) — and the deacons are all consecrated by the ancient rite of the laying on of hands, accompanied by prayers (1 Tim. 4 : 14; 2 Tim. 1 : 6-7; Acts 6 : 6). In these rather fleeting references, we can fairly readily

---

[12] For a further treatment of the Pauline conception of the apostolate, see *Enseignement de saint Paul,* II, 146-8; 229-38. Referring to the spirit of sacrifice necessary, Durrwell speaks of the Church's character as a victim (p. 276).

discern the essentials of the sacrament of Orders, consisting as it does of the laying on of hands and a form of words, determining the significance of the act accomplished. The college of priests imposed hands at the same time as the apostle, but it seems that this was merely a concomitant rite which could be dispensed with (1 Tim. 4 : 14; 2 Tim. 1 : 6). The apostle gives a fairly long list of the qualities to be sought in these presbyter-bishops and deacons (1 Tim. 3 : 2-7; Titus 1 : 6-9; 1 Tim. 3 : 8-13). His requirements may not seem to us particularly stringent. He required only what was reasonably possible in the recently established communities. Those responsible were enjoined not to grant ordination too hastily and the presbyters were not to be neophytes. St. Paul also required that they should have married no more than once, should enjoy a good reputation with all men, even the pagans, should conduct their own homes well and be of a completely upright life. His requirements for deacons are similar. In particular, they must be free from all the vices to which their tasks in temporal administration might constitute a temptation. St. Paul's immediate representatives, Titus and Timothy, were given more detailed instructions, consonant with their greater authority. These related not only to their personal conduct, but also to the vigilance necessary in combating errors. The errors themselves are not very clearly defined, but they threatened the purity of the faith by their advocacy of magic practices and of a dubious asceticism, going so far as to condemn marriage, and they included allegorical interpretations of the scriptures, giving rise to fancies and endless disputes (2 Tim. 2 : 15, 22-25; 5 : 5; Titus 1 : 10-16; 3 : 9-11; 1 Tim. 4 : 1-8; 2 Tim. 3 : 1-5, 9; 4 : 1-4).

What exactly were the functions of the different ranks of the hierarchy? The apostle was the only bishop in the full sense of the word, enjoying complete authority over the churches he founded. Titus and Timothy are delegate-bishops, depending on the apostle and entrusted with the government in his name of certain communities and with the appointment there of presbyters (1 Tim. 5 : 22; Titus 1 : 5). We have next to ask ourselves whether the latter are priests or bishops in the modern acceptance of the words. That is to say, had they the power to ordain other priests? The answer is not very apparent and all sorts of plausible theories have been advanced. It is not certain, moreover, that the organization of the local churches was everywhere exactly the same. But at least some of these dignitaries must have had the power to appoint successors, otherwise the hierarchy would have disappeared after apostolic times. We cannot be sure, either, whether, in St. Paul's time, the government of each of the churches was by an individual chief or by a college. The fact that in the pastoral epistles reference to the bishop is exclusively in the singular (1 Tim. 3 : 2; Titus 1 : 7), which seems to mark him out from the priests (1 Tim. 5 : 17; Titus 1 : 5), would incline us to think that one of the priests was made responsible for governing the church, but we must not build too much on these details. The singular noun used for bishop may merely denote the category. Whatever the truth about the early organization, it marked the beginning of an evolution that would naturally end, after the death of the apostles, in the establishment in all the churches of a monarchical episcopate. The letters of St. Ignatius of Antioch leave no doubt about the position at the end of the first century. From this time onwards, a threefold hierarchy of bishops, priests and deacons is definitely to be seen in office, the bishop alone possessing jurisdiction and the fullness of the priesthood.[13]

[13] See in the encyclopedia, *Catholicisme*, IV, 781-3, the author's article on bishops, followed by a bibliography. In apostolic times, there

The powers of the apostles and of those who helped them, directly or indirectly, did not constitute an end in themselves. Everything was ordered towards the sanctification and salvation of the faithful and, at all its various levels, the hierarchy was at the service of the faithful (2 Cor. 4 : 5). Far from acting as a barrier between Christ and the faithful, the members of the hierarchy were entrusted with the task of announcing Christ's gospel to them in all its purity and of transmitting his life to them. The purpose of their authority, which was exercised in a paternal and no wise despotic fashion, was to form Christ in them (Gal. 4 : 19) and to allow the Holy Spirit to act in their hearts. From this point on, as Father de Grandmaison puts it, the hierarchy's authority leaves "the creature with the Creator", without any indiscreet interference in the privacy of men's souls. This was the harmonious union of a religion of authority and a religion of the spirit. Even so, the religion of the spirit must be preserved from error and illusion and to ensure this is the function of the Church's *magisterium*. The *infallibility* of the Church is, in fact, a necessary guarantee for the faithful who commit their entire lives and eternal future to their trust in the Church's teaching.

St. Paul offered this assurance in the highest degree to the infant Christian community. He did so in the first instance by basing his teaching on the authority of the scripture. Towards the end of his life, he wrote to Timothy: "Everything in the scripture has been divinely inspired, and has its uses; to instruct us, to expose our errors, to correct our faults, to

---

may also have been a kind of charismatic priesthood, receiving its powers directly from the Holy Spirit (1 Cor. 12 : 4-11 and 28-29). This priesthood would have been subordinate to the apostles in the exercise of its functions (1 Cor. 14 : 26-40) and would soon have been incorporated in the ordinary hierarchy, established by them. (See the same article, 782).

educate us in holy living; so God's servant will become a master of his craft, and each noble task that comes will find him ready for it" (2 Tim. 3 : 16).[14] Thus, the scripture has God for its first author because it is inspired, literally breathed, by him. That is why St. Paul relates his teaching so repeatedly to the Old Testament, in order to establish it or confirm it. We find this in almost every page of his epistles, where he is either borrowing definite arguments from the sacred texts or translating his own statements into scriptural language.[15] Following our Lord's example, he recognizes in the inspired Word the heralding, either literal or through types, of the Messiah and of the realities of the New Testament.[16] Christ is the end of the law (Rom. 10 : 4), the limit towards which it led and before which it must efface itself. The Jews, who in their reading of scripture misunderstood this essential truth, had a veil over their eyes and hearts and could not appreciate its true sense. On conversion to Christ, the veil fell (2 Cor. 3 : 14-16) and the truth of the scripture appeared in all its splendour.[17] But it follows from the superiority of the new covenant that scripture is not restricted to the Old Testament. The writings of the New Testament were soon accorded an equal authority and the second epistle of St. Peter, admitting,

[14] About the same time, or a little later, a similar doctrine, echoing the constant thought of our Saviour, was taught in the second epistle of St. Peter (1 : 20-21). (See, for example, Matt. 21 : 42; 22 : 29, 43; 26 : 54; Luke 4 : 24; John 5 : 39; 10 : 35). Among the four evangelists, this doctrine is set out with particular clearness in the gospels of St. Matthew and St. John.

[15] See chapter 2 above.

[16] An example of the literal announcement of the Messiah is to be found in 1 Cor. 15 : 3-4. Through types, that is, prophetically and figuratively: Gal. 4 : 21-31; 1 Cor. 10 : 1-6, 11.

[17] This doctrine is magnificently illustrated by the Strasbourg statues which represent the Synagogue blindfolded and the Church with eyes uncovered.

no doubt for our encouragement, that St. Paul's letters were difficult to understand, complains about those who twist them "into a wrong sense... to their own undoing", as they do "with the rest of scripture" (3 : 16). Later, the Church will be found unhesitatingly placing the writings of apostolic origin[18] on the same plane as the books of the Old Testament. Both "can instruct thee to salvation, by the faith which is in Christ Jesus" (2 Tim. 3 : 15 [Douai]) and make the men of God able to accomplish perfectly their task.

In both will be found the patience and consolation characteristic of the scriptures and the strength they impart to our hope (Rom. 15 : 4).

But the epistles were only a tiny part of St. Paul's teachings. The apostle claims for his oral preaching the same infallible authority that the Church attributes to his writings. The apostles were prophets and their words were inspired by God like the words of the prophets of old. Paul was vividly aware of this. His gospel, he affirms, owed nothing to human inspiration. He had received it by a revelation from Christ (Gal. 1 : 11-12). If an angel from heaven, or the apostle himself were to announce a different gospel, both would merit an anathema (Gal. 1 : 8-9). He praised the Thessalonians for having received the word he announced to them not as a human word, but for what it was in truth, the Word of God, showing forth his power (1 Thess. 2 : 13). He made known to the Corinthians the redemptive plan which was the true wisdom revealed by the Spirit of God and the very thought of Christ (1 Cor. 1 : 6-16). He presented himself to them as Christ's ambassador. It was as though God exhorted through him. Christ spoke in him (2 Cor. 5 : 20; 13 : 3). He was the

[18] Whether this origin was directly apostolic or only indirectly so as in the case of the epistle to the Hebrews and probably in that of 2 Peter.

privileged prophet of the great Mystery of the universal call to salvation (Col. 1 : 26-27; Eph. 3 : 1-12). We could give many more examples.[19]

But Paul's gospel is not a personal teaching. It is the gospel of Christ, common to Paul and the other apostles (Gal. 2 : 2, 9; 1 Cor. 15 : 10-11). Later, enlarging his outlook, he asserts to Timothy that the Church of the living God is "the pillar and foundation upon which the truth rests" (1 Tim. 3 : 15) and in face of threatening errors, he enjoins his disciple to keep intact the deposit of the faith. "Keep the good thing committed to thy trust by the Holy Ghost who dwelleth in us" (1 Tim. 6 : 20; 2 Tim. 1 : 14 [Douai]). An explicit statement of the meaning of these words, taken in conjunction with the implications of the attitude of the apostles, would enable us to conclude that both they and the Church as a whole could not err in the transmission of the traditional deposit, the revelation brought by Christ and completed by the Holy Spirit, the precious and immutable παράδοσις.[20] The gospel preached by the apostles assures salvation on condition that it is kept free from all deterioration (1 Cor. 15 : 1-2; 1 Tim. 4 : 16), that they hold firm in the faith (1 Cor. 16 : 13; Col. 2 : 7), rejecting all errors of purely human origin (Col. 2 : 4, 8, 18; 1 Tim. 6 : 20-21, etc.). He requires an indefectible faithfulness (2 Tim. 3 : 14). Shipwreck in the faith would be the worst of misfortunes (1 Tim. 1 : 19; 4 : 1). Each must nourish himself unceasingly through the apostolic teaching (1 Tim. 4 : 6), the sound principles of our Lord Jesus Christ (1 Tim. 6 : 3) and the

[19] In his teaching, Paul distinguishes carefully between Christ's own revelation and precepts (1 Thess. 4 : 15; 1 Cor. 7 : 10), the official interpretation of these (1 Cor. 7 : 12), and what is simply counsel (1 Cor. 7 : 6, 25).

[20] Immutable in its essence but subject to more precise definition and to development. St. Paul himself furnishes the proof of this.

teaching which God our Saviour has revealed (Titus 2 : 10). That is why apostasy is regarded as an almost irreparable catastrophe (Heb. 6 : 4-6; 10 : 26-31) and Paul adjures Timothy to announce the true doctrine in season and out of season, to entrust the teaching of it only to men he can trust and to condemn error tirelessly (2 Tim. 4 : 1-5; 2 : 2). He himself did not hesitate to excommunicate and "make over to Satan" those responsible for heresy, whom he described severely as blasphemers (1 Tim. 1 : 20).[21]

The repeated affirmations of St. Paul and the other apostles are proved by the miracles that set the seal on their teaching. Paul performed a large number of cures (Acts 19 : 11-12) and, at Troas, even raised a dead person to life (Acts 20 : 9-12). He often recalls in the epistles the miracles of all kinds that accompanied the preaching, and discreetly underlines their probative character (Gal. 3 : 5). They were the distinctive signs of his mission (2 Cor. 12 : 12) and gave him full assurance to preach the gospel (1 Thess. 1 : 5). They are the work of the Holy Spirit and the undoubted sign of his intervention (1 Cor. 12 : 10; Rom. 15 : 19). The efficacious presence of the Spirit appears finally in the transformation of souls. Formerly prey to the vices of paganism, the faithful have been justified, purified and sanctified (1 Cor. 6 : 11). They are henceforth the hope of the apostle, his joy, and his crown of glory (1 Thess. 2 : 19; Phil. 4 : 1).[22]

For those who study the early days of the Church without prejudice, the intervention of the Spirit must be manifest. If confirmation of the divine origin of the apostolic teaching

[21] Médebielle in SDB, *Dépôt de la foi* and Kittel εὐαγγέλιον, II, 726-33 (Friedrich) are worth consulting on this point.

[22] Compare Heb. 2 : 4. Additional reading: SDB, *Apostolat* (Médebielle), *Église* (Médebielle); 388-91; 654-60; *Évêques* (Marchal); Kittel, ἐκκλησία III, 507-16 (Schmidt).

were needed, it would be provided by its nobility and grandeur, by its consistency, richness and depth, and by the light cast upon each other by the various dogmas it proclaims. Those converted by the apostles had good reason for seeing in the Church, the holy and well-loved bride of Christ (Eph. 5 : 22-32), the depository of "the great mystery we worship". "Revelation made in human nature, justification won in the realm of the Spirit; a vision seen by angels, a mystery preached to the Gentiles... accepted by faith... taken up into glory" (1 Tim. 3 : 16).

15

A COMPLEMENTARY ASPECT OF THE DOCTRINE
OF THE BODY OF CHRIST

> *"One mediator between God and men,*
> *Jesus Christ, who is a man like them"*
> *(1 Tim. 2:5).*

THE doctrine of the redemptive incarnation is central to the teaching of St. Paul concerning salvation.

Christ is everything for St. Paul. The apostle understood right from his conversion that he who had risen was the Saviour of the World. He is the second head of the human race, the "second first man". Adam precipitated the whole human kind into sin and death. The new Adam repairs the ravages caused by the fall and brings life to those who believe in him. All die in Adam, but all will find life in Christ. By one man death came into the world and by another came the resurrection of the dead (1 Cor. 15 : 21-22). The action of the second Adam is incomparably more powerful and efficacious than that of the first because he is God's own Son (Rom. 8 : 32). "As our fault was amplified, grace has been more amply bestowed than ever; that so, where guilt held its reign of death, justifying grace should reign instead, to bring us eternal life through Jesus Christ our Lord" (Rom. 5 : 20-21). God wished, then, to bring about the salvation of the human race through a man who was possessed of a real body, capable of feeling, and who was mortal, so made "in the fashion of our guilty nature" (Rom. 8 : 3) that outwardly he seemed no more than a man (Phil. 2 : 7) and most of the witnesses of his earthly life failed to recognize in him the Son of God.

The religious institutions existing before his coming were only a shadow. "The reality is Christ's body" (Col. 2 : 17).[1] By this, St. Paul means his human nature, the instrument of the redemption, for the body is here taken as the equivalent of the whole man.[2] It was his body, his human nature, that made it possible for the Son of God to be a high priest, feeling for us and showing mercy (Heb. 2 : 17; 5 : 2) and that enabled him to offer himself as a sacrifice and to reconcile us with the Father. At the resurrection, his humanity was glorified and penetrated by the life of the Spirit in order to transmit it to men. His body was thenceforth a spiritual body (1 Cor. 15 : 44-45). Everything in him that was mortal and that bore resemblance to our guilty nature was finally consumed: "The death he died was a death once for all to sin" (Rom. 6 : 10). What was destroyed did not represent a deprivation, being only weakness and the limitations of the mortal body. The destruction of the body of sin (Rom. 6 : 6 [Douai]) is merely the reverse aspect of the magnificent exaltation in glory, the immortality, the superabundance of imperishable life and the fullness of the Spirit. "Christ, now he has risen from the dead, cannot die any more.... The life he now lives is a life that looks towards God" (Rom. 6 : 9-10). His glorification is as much for us as for himself. His risen body, his glorified humanity, becomes the source of spi-

---

[1] Translator's own rendering.

[2] To belong to the body is to belong to Christ (1 Cor. 12 : 13) and put on Christ (Gal. 3 : 27). There is a similar thought in the prologue to St. John's gospel: "The Word was made flesh", that is to say made man (1 : 14).

223

ritual resurrection and a guarantee of bodily resurrection for all who are redeemed.

This is a constant factor. The sanctified humanity of Christ, which is the means of redemption, is also the means of transmitting the fruit of the redemption to men. It is by being incorporated in the risen body of Christ, by becoming members of this body, that we attain salvation. We have, we believe, shown sufficiently clearly that the Mystical Body of Christ is not simply a social unit but is, in fact, his body, concretely and individually. Our redemption takes place through the union with the body of Christ, inaugurated through faith and realized through baptism which is an introduction into the Church, and it is brought to perfection by the reception of the Eucharist, while waiting to be completed by the resurrection on the last day.[3] In the light of this, Christ's body can be seen to be the permanent source of sanctification and the vital centre of the Church. Its role is soteriological in the act of the redemptive sacrifice, ecclesiological in the uniting with the Church, Eucharistic in the sacramental giving, and eschatological in that it places a seed in us and brings us a guarantee of resurrection. There is an admirable rehabilitation of the body, of the matter associated with the work of salvation, and this rehabilitation extends to glorification, because the "spiritual" body, penetrated though it is by the Spirit, remains a real body. Certain important consequences follow from this for our bodies themselves and for the whole of the material world.

Greatly saddened by a scandal which dishonoured the community in Corinth, St. Paul, showing his usual vision, reminded his readers of the reasons for Christian chastity (1 Cor. 6 : 12-20). A member of the faithful is not the master of

---

[3] See chapter 14. SDB, *Médiation*, 1037-83 (Spicq).

his own body. His body belongs to the Lord, who destines it for eventual resurrection. He is a member of Christ, and it is a sacrilege to make a member of Christ the member of a harlot, in a shameful union with which the apostle eloquently contrasts the union between Christ and one who, respecting his own body, forms a single spirit with Christ. In conclusion, the apostle points out that fornication profanes the body in the highest degree in the sources of the transmission of life. The body of a Christian is the temple of the Holy Ghost, sanctified by grace and worthy of all respect, and the gift of the Spirit has been bought by the blood of Jesus Christ. The Christian should, therefore, consider himself as "officiating in the temple of his body".[4] We cannot fail to admire such an exalted outlook and no one can be unaware of the enormous influence Christian chastity exercises in the conversion of the world.

Clearly, the relationship between husband and wife should be marked by a delicate purity (1 Cor. 7 : 1-16). Everyone is not required to adopt the virgin state and it is better to marry than to burn with desire while living a celibate life. The fulfilment of conjugal duties is obligatory for husbands and wives and, if they want to abstain, they can do so only by mutual agreement, for a limited time and in order to give themselves to prayer. The conjugal union is indissoluble. Separation does not confer freedom to contract a new marriage. To this the apostle promulgates only a single exception. If one of the marriage partners becomes a Christian and the pagan, refusing to live peacefully, wishes to separate, the ending of the marriage is permissible and often preferable to life together, accepted in the uncertain hope of converting the partner remaining pagan.

[4] Cf. Cerfaux, *The Church in the Theology of St. Paul,* 148.

In St. Paul's view, besides Christ's own positive precept (Matt. 19 : 3-12; Mark 10 : 2-12), the indissolubility of marriage follows from the exalted significance of the conjugal union as an image of the perfect union between Christ and the Church: "Husbands show love to your wives, as Christ showed love to the Church and gave himself up for it so as to hallow it.... That is how husbands must love their wives, as if they were their own bodies. In loving his wife, a man is but loving himself."[5] The husband should surround his wife with signs of affection as Christ does the Church. "That is why a man will leave his father and mother and will cling to his wife, and the two will become one flesh. Yes, those words are a high mystery, and I am applying them here to Christ and his Church. Meanwhile, each of you is to love his wife as he would love himself, and the wife is to pay reverence to her husband" (Eph. 5 : 23-33). Marriage, then, is eminently holy and we can readily understand that the ending of a marriage is not to be contemplated. Can any Christian husbands and wives fail to be exalted on reading this passage in St. Paul?

But virginity is a higher state and one that the apostle wishes to see adopted more frequently (1 Cor. 7 : 7, 35), while recognizing that it implies a special gift from God. The underlying reason for preserving virginity is that this makes it possible to belong more perfectly to God: "He who is unmarried is concerned with God's claim, asking how he is to please God; whereas the married man is concerned with the world's claim, asking how he is to please his wife; and thus he is at issue with himself" (1 Cor. 7 : 32-34). The ideal proposed to generous souls is that of being undivided and of belonging only to the Lord. The shortness of life, looked

---

[5] Translator's own rendering.

at in relation to eternity, with, in the background, the possible imminence of the Parousia should bring us to realize that the fashion of this world passes and that we must use the world as though we were not using it. That is what virginity helps to accomplish in a complete holiness of body and mind. Paul is nevertheless careful to avoid providing pitfalls. He is content to recommend the complete gift of oneself to the Lord (1 Cor. 7 : 35). A father who gives his daughter in marriage commits no sin;[6] but he would do better if he refrained from doing so (1 Cor. 7 : 36-38).

For similar reasons, widows would be better advised to remain in a widowhood respected by men and blessed by God. They could, nevertheless, remarry, provided it was to a Christian (1 Cor. 7 : 39-40). Later, St. Paul altered the emphasis of his advice. To young widows unmindful of their determination to devote themselves to God, he recommended remarriage in preference to life as unemployed and indiscreet gossips and he ordered Timothy to put on the list of widows helped by the Church only women of at least sixty who had been married but once, and were to be recommended for their good works (1 Tim. 5 : 9-16).

St. Paul's dominant thought is, then, always to ensure that the faithful shall belong as perfectly as possible to God and to the body of Christ. They should live holy lives in the different states to which they are called (1 Cor. 7 : 5) because they are members of Christ (1 Cor. 6 : 15; Eph. 6 : 30).

The action of the sanctified body should certainly not be regarded as confined to the present life. Christ's resurrection is the guarantee of our own, of which it gives us the certainty

---

[6] Some writers believe that St. Paul had in mind a kind of unconsummated marriage of a Christian who decided to allow his wife to remain a virgin, giving to her virginity a safeguard that was clearly not without its danger.

(1 Cor. 6 : 14; 15 : 20; et seq., etc.).[7] Going much further, we can say that the doctrine according to which Christ is all in all (Col. 3 : 11), head of the angelic Powers (Col. 1 : 16, 20; 3 : 15), and in whom dwells all Completeness (Col. 1 : 19; 2 : 10) implies that Christ's action extends to material creation which is introduced by the redemption into the new order inaugurated by the sacrifice of Calvary. It even seems that, at the time of the resurrection of the body, the material world will reach a better state. "The whole of nature, as we know, groans in a common travail all the while" (Rom. 8 : 22). The universe, linking itself with man, is, as it were, awaiting impatiently the glorification of the children of God, who has associated it with man's destiny and, following the first sin, has imposed upon it a curse (Gen. 3 : 17-18). It is "subject to vanity" [Douai]. Man's sin has turned it away from its goal and it would like to be freed from this "tyranny of corruption", to participate in "the glorious freedom of God's sons" — that is, to be no longer used and dominated by man except for the glorification of the Creator (Rom. 8 : 20-21). The redemption will thus have a certain repercussion on the material world.

We should note, finally, that redemption relates also to the just who died before the coming of Christ. St. Peter speaks of the descent of Christ's sacred soul into hell between the Passion and the resurrection, doubtless in order to apply the merits of his sacrifice to them (1 Peter 3 : 19-20 — the text is hard to interpret).[8] St. Paul seems to be referring to the same thing when he says that before he ascended into heaven, Christ had already descended into the lower regions

[7] These various questions will be referred to again at the end of chapter 19. Cf. Viard, *Expectatio creaturae*, RB, 1952, 337-54.

[8] See Selwyn, *The first Epistle of St. Peter*, London, Macmillan, 1947, 313-62.

of the earth (Eph. 4 : 9), and when he asserts that thenceforth every knee will bend before the name of Jesus in heaven, and on earth and under the earth (Phil. 2 : 10).[9]

Christ becomes Lord of the whole universe in a new way. All completeness dwells in him and, "in the blood of his cross", God has reconciled to himself all things on earth and in heaven, re-establishing the order upset by sin (Col. 1 : 19-20). It remains to make this renovation effective in each and every one of us and to sum up everything in Christ ($\dot{a}vaxεφαλαιώσασθαι$), the centre, vital link, and principle of universal unity (Eph. 1 : 10). By creation, he has brought all things into being (Col. 1 : 16-17). By the redemption, he unites all creatures separated from God by sin, and reconciles them with him. Redeemed man, for whom Christ is not only chief and lord but also the head of the Mystical Body of the Church (Col. 1 : 18), must act as a true member of the body of his Saviour by persevering efforts from which the whole body will gain. Through charity, we must grow in every way in him who is the head, the Christ, working thus to build up fully the frame of his body (Eph. 4 : 12). The growth of the Church will be due to the unceasing striving of each Christian, so that, in the unity of the faith and in full knowledge of the Son of God, we shall reach full manhood, proportioned to the completed growth of Christ (Eph. 4 : 13). To the extent that each one of us grows spiritually, Christ's body will be completed and the redemptive incarnation will bring forth its fruits in the world.

In the light of this, we can appreciate that the action of Christ's body is universal, but the aspect differs widely according to whether we contemplate Christ's relations with

---

[9] Bonsirven, *Théologie du Nouveau Testament,* 410 is worth consulting on this point.

the angelic Powers, with the material world, or with redeemed man. The Church shows its admirable understanding of the central character and efficacy of the redemptive incarnation by placing at the heart of its worship the Eucharist, in which the sacrifice of the cross is continued and which, through the presence of the glorified Christ, already unites the present world and the future world (1 Cor. 11 : 26). This understanding is also illustrated by the fact that the Church regards the Eucharist as the most perfect means of strengthening the unity of the Mystical Body. Above all else, it is in the body and blood of Christ that the divine life grows among the faithful, that the Holy Spirit spreads forth the abundance of his gifts and that already all things are renewed. Communion in the body and blood of Christ, the forming of one body by the sharing in the one bread (1 Cor. 10 : 16-17), the heralding of the glorious return of the Lord: these things surely constitute, albeit imperfectly, "God all in all" (1 Cor. 15 : 28).[10] Truly, as our Saviour indicated in mysterious words which were not understood by the apostles until after the resurrection,[11] his body is in the highest degree the Temple of the new law, the spiritual axis of the redeemed world.

[10] See above, chapter 13, 199-204.
[11] John 2 : 19-22.

PART FOUR

THE ATTAINMENT OF SALVATION

16

CHRISTIAN HOPE

"Nor does this hope delude us" (Rom. 5:5).

THE Pauline conception of salvation is of impressive breadth. It extends from the eternal plans enshrined in God's foreknowledge to the gift of glorious immortality and to the resurrection of the body at the second coming of Christ. The divine plan of the redemption, formerly mysterious and hidden and now revealed to the apostles, and particularly to Paul (1 Cor. 2 : 7; Rom. 16 : 25-26; Col. 1 : 26-27; Eph. 3 : 3-6), had been prepared and willed from all eternity. Contemplating it, the apostle cannot restrain his admiration and gratitude: "Blessed be that God, that Father of our Lord Jesus Christ, who has blessed us, in Christ, with every spiritual blessing, higher than heaven itself. He has chosen us out, in Christ, before the foundation of the world, to be saints, to be blameless in his sight, for love of him; marking us out beforehand (so his will decreed) to be his adopted children through Jesus Christ" (Eph. 1 : 3-5). This is "the hidden purpose of his will. It was his loving design, centred in Christ, to give history its fulfilment by resuming everything in him, all that is in heaven, all that is on earth summed up in him. In him it was our lot to be called, singled out beforehand to suit his purpose, (for it is he who is at work everywhere, carrying out the designs of his will); we were to manifest his glory" (Eph. 1 : 9-12). And again: "All those who from the first were known to him, he has destined from the first to be moulded into the image of his Son, who is thus to become the eldest-born among many brethren. So predestined, he called them; so called, he justified them; so justified, he glorified them" (Rom. 8 : 29-30).

It is by anticipation that Paul mentions the final stage of salvation. We are not yet glorified in an ultimate and immutable manner, though we are gradually transformed into the image of our Lord's glory, which will be reflected in our faces as in a mirror (2 Cor. 3 : 18). We are, as yet, saved only in hope, awaiting patiently the glorification of our bodies, which is the final phase of salvation (Rom. 8 : 23-25). In this world, we have only the earnest of the Spirit, waiting for total redemption and entry into the heavenly inheritance (Eph. 1 : 14; 2 Cor. 1 : 22; 5 : 5). We journey by faith and not with clear vision (1 Cor. 13 : 12; 2 Cor. 5 : 7). We bear the seal of the Spirit with a view to the day of redemption (Eph. 4 : 30), and this gift of the Spirit places in our hearts a hope which cannot delude us and which is not in any way weakened but is, rather, strengthened by tribulations endured for the sake of the gospel (Rom. 5 : 3-5). We rightly take pride "in the hope of attaining glory as the sons of God" (Rom. 5 : 2). But hope, after all, is not possession (Rom. 8 : 24), in spite of the fundamental identity between the earnest and the full gift of the Spirit and the continuity of justification and glory. The apostle constantly speaks of hope and wishes his readers a firm and joyous hope. "May God, the author of our hope, fill you with all joy and peace in your believing; so that you may have hope in abundance, through the power of the Holy Spirit" (Rom. 15 : 13). The faithful must not be saddened by the thought of their death as are the pagans who are without hope (1 Thess. 4 : 13), strangers to the divine promises and without God in the world (Eph. 2 : 12). They must remain firm in the hope brought by the gospel (Col. 1 : 23), founded on the love that God and Christ show for us (2 Thess. 2 : 16) and the indefeasable character of their promises (Heb. 10 : 23). All must fix their hopes on eternal life, "promised to us long ages since by the God who cannot fail us" (Titus 1 : 2), eternal life guaranteed by the justification mercifully granted to us (Titus 3 : 7), exalted by the expectation of "a new dawn of glory, the glory of the great God, the glory of our Saviour Jesus Christ" (Titus 2 : 13). Hope keeps us in a state of fruitful tension, one in which a deep desire for eternal life, detaching us from perishable goods, prepares us to receive imperishable blessings, the weight of everlasting glory that will recompense passing effort (2 Cor. 4 : 17). The epistles are full of this thought, which never fails to console and strengthen the Christian on his way to salvation. In the letter to the Hebrews, it is given particularly striking expression. The redemptive designs have been the object of a divine promise confirmed by oath, so that their immutable character cannot be denied. God wished thus to give us "the strongest comfort, we who have fled for refuge to hold fast the hope set before us, which we have as an anchor of the soul, sure and firm, and which entereth in even within the veil: where the forerunner Jesus is entered for us, made a high priest for ever" (Heb. 6 : 18-20 [Douai]). The glorification and heavenly intercession of Christ (Rom. 8 : 34; Heb. 7 : 25), together with divine fidelity, make the hope of our own glorification unshakeable.

These beautiful texts convey a complex notion whose principal aspects may be summed up as follows. Hope is essentially linked with the Christian "vocation" (Eph. 4 : 1), founded on the eternal election of the faithful, their call to the faith and to eternal life. It implies the impatient waiting for future blessings and confidence that they will be obtained. These "blessings that still lie in the future" (Heb. 9 : 11) and which constitute the object of hope consist of salvation and eternal life, the entry into the inheritance and the heavenly kingdom, the vision of God face to face (1 Cor. 13 : 12), the glorious return of Christ and, above all, God's glory towards which everything is ordered. This last point brings out the fact that Christian hope is not a selfish and calculating one, solely concerned with the eternal reward. It is inspired by unselfish love, though it is certainly part of the pattern that good works are rewarded and sins punished. Paul insists on this point several times. "A man will reap what he sows" (Gal. 6 : 7-9; Col. 3 : 25). At the judgement seat of Christ, he will be dealt with as he merits, according to whether he has done good or evil (2 Cor. 5 : 10). Hope of reward and fear of damnation are often evoked in order to exhort and sustain the faithful (1 Thess. 4 : 6; 2 Thess. 1 : 5–10; 1 Cor. 3 : 17; 6 : 9-10; etc.). But this consideration never excludes others and the apostle's basic thought is on an entirely different plane. With him, it is a question of being with the Lord for ever, avoiding rejection far from his face (1 Thess. 4 : 17; 2 Thess. 1 : 9; cf. 2 Cor. 5 : 6, 8), and sharing his risen life – a sharing which, as we have seen in studying baptism and grace, is already fundamentally realized.[1] And more particularly, the union by virtue of which Christ lives in us implies our own total submission, imitating the redemptive love even to the extent of the supreme sacrifice (Eph. 5 : 1-2). It also implies conformity with his feelings and, as it were, continuation of his Passion through the sufferings entailed by apostolic labours (Phil. 2 : 5; Col. 1 : 24; 2 Cor. 5 : 14). St. Paul's claim to credit is in having freely announced the gospel (1 Cor. 9 : 14) and the great unselfishness which the love of Christ arouses in him makes him prefer to help the faith-

[1] Chapters 8-10.

ful by carrying on with his apostolate rather than meeting death at an earlier date, which would be to his gain. "I long to have done with it, and be with Christ, a better thing, much more than a better thing; and yet, for your sakes, that I should wait in the body is more urgent still" (Phil. 1 : 23-24). "Starting with the wish to merit a happy eternity, man enters into an intimate relationship with Christ, into a sharing of Christ's life. This brings about a change of direction. The orientation of man's activity becomes different. It is no longer the attraction of an exterior reward that counts. The activity becomes obedience to an interior prompting which pushes him forward. The Christian is no longer seeking his own interests. In him Christ, who has not sought his own delectation, hastens to serve men for the glory of the Father".[2] Man cannot and must not abandon the search for his own salvation, but he will make it the more certain, the more completely he lives and acts out of love for the Saviour. All the aspirations and strivings of the faithful should have as their purpose the glorification of the name of Christ and the glorification of the faithful themselves in Christ (2 Thess. 1 : 11-12), the two things being inseparably linked.[3]

From this, we can understand how it is that St. Paul considers the motives for Christian hope so solid. They are the divine promises, the death and glorification of Christ, the gift of the Spirit, who himself intercedes sovereignly for us "with groans beyond all utterance, demanding our glorification better

[2] Didier, *Désintéressement du chrétien. La rétribution dans la morale de s. Paul*, Aubier, 1955, 228. The whole conclusion is worth reading. The author rightly shows that a similar chain of reasoning emerges from the gospel.

[3] Hope is thus seen to be closely linked with charity. It is not less closely linked with faith "which gives substance to our hopes" (Heb. 11 : 1).

than we are able to do so ourselves" (Rom. 8 : 26-27). Hope should thus fill the Christian with confidence (2 Cor. 3 : 12) and be for him a helmet to protect him (1 Thess. 5 : 8) against temptations and all obstacles to his salvation. Paul's own hope never failed and he was able to write to Timothy, when awaiting martyrdom: "As for me, my blood already flows in sacrifice; the time has nearly come when I can go free. I have fought the good fight; I have finished the race; I have redeemed my pledge; I look forward to the prize that is waiting for me, the prize I have earned. The Lord, the judge whose award never goes amiss, will grant it to me when that day comes; to me, yes, and all those who have learned to welcome his appearing" (2 Tim. 4 : 6-8).[4] But how shall we receive this crown of justice? How are we to envisage the accomplishment of salvation in relation to death, to the resurrection, and to the return of Christ? The Christian is a man who waits. How is he to wait?

---

[4] Spicq, *La révélation de l'espérance dans le Nouveau Testament*, Avignon, Aubanel, 1931, 1-59. Grossouw, *L'espérance dans le Nouveau Testament*, RB, 1954, 508-32. Hope will continue in eternity as an attitude of filial confidence, being no longer a waiting for promised blessings. Faith will continue also "as the reception of God's gift, an attitude of being ready ... for his Son who animates us with his Spirit and transmits to us his charity". But faith will clearly no longer take the form of imperfect knowledge enfolded in an enigma. This seems to be the meaning of 1 Cor. 13 : 13. See D. Laucan, *Les trois qui demeurent*, RSR, 1958, particularly 340-2.

17

DEATH AND JUDGEMENT

"Death is swallowed up in victory"
(Isa. 25:8; quoted in Cor. 15:54).

IN a penetrating passage in which he describes the meaning
and end of Christian life, St. Paul writes to the Romans: "Now
that you are free from the claims of sin, and have become God's
slaves instead, you have a harvest in your sanctification, and
your reward is eternal life. Sin offers death, for wages; God
offers us eternal life as a free gift, through Christ Jesus our
Lord" (Rom. 6 : 22-23). By his sin, the first man unleashed
in the world the baneful empire of death (Rom. 5 : 12-14).
Sin is death's sting (1 Cor. 15 : 56).[1] The passage deals with
bodily death and with spiritual death, both direct consequences
of sin and having eternal death as their final end, if the sinner
is not converted. The person who is justified remains subject
to bodily death because of his link with the first man (Rom.
8 : 10) and death remains the supreme enemy, the last obstacle to Christ's rule, which Christ will conquer and abolish
on raising the dead to life when he comes again in glory
(1 Cor. 15 : 26).

Death's defeat does not take place only on the last day.
Accomplished in principle by the triumphant death and the
resurrection of the Saviour, the way is prepared for it in every

---

[1] See chapter 5, section 1.

Christian by death to sin and, paradoxically, it becomes effective at the moment of bodily death, while waiting to be completely fulfilled in the resurrection.

At baptism, the old man is crucified in union with the redeeming death of Christ, in order that the body enslaved to sin shall be destroyed (Rom. 6 : 6). All Christian asceticism is aimed at this mystical death which renders escape possible from the slavery of sin and forms an introduction to the new life in union with the risen Saviour (Rom. 6 : 4-5). It is the flesh with its passions and concupiscences that has to be crucified (Gal. 5 : 24) in order to permit life according to the Spirit (Rom. 8 : 13). We strip off the old man only to put on the new (Col. 3 : 9-10), and — as we cannot repeat too often — there is no really true and fruitful asceticism outside union with the crucified and glorified Christ[2] (Rom. 8 : 17; 2 Cor. 4 : 10). Asceticism prolongs the Passion of Christ in his members, not only for their own sanctification, but also for the benefit of the whole Church (Col. 1 : 24),[3] in order that the elect may have their part in salvation and eternal life (2 Tim. 2 : 10). It is a sacrifice inspired by love (Rom. 12 : 1). It has a social as much as an individual aspect and like the whole of the Christian life is inseparable from the communion of saints. The persevering effort of the ascetic to reduce his body to slavery is not an inhuman mutilation but a liberation designed to gain for him the imperishable crown (1 Cor. 9 : 25-27). Mystical death opens the way to life (Rom. 8 : 12-13) in such a way that weakness becomes strength. "Weakness brought him to the cross, but the power of God brought him life; and though it is in our weakness

---

[2] St. Paul condemns a false and superficial asceticism advocating practices inspired by Judaism and the pagan philosophers and not arising from union with Christ (Col. 2 : 16-23).

[3] See chapter 9 above.

that we are united to him, you will find us too, as he is, alive with God's power" (2 Cor. 13 : 4; compare 12 : 9-10).[4]

By an astonishing paradox, bodily death is itself an opening to life and fear of death ceases to hold the world in thrall (Heb. 2 : 15). "Guilt makes no more claim on a man who is dead" (Rom. 6 : 7). When he died on account of our sins, Christ entered into glory and his life became from that time forth a life for God (Rom. 6 : 10). There was no longer anything in him resembling our guilty nature (Rom. 8 : 3). In his risen humanity, he possessed the completeness of life in order to communicate it to regenerated humanity, unhindered by any limitation of time and space. In the same way, in dying, the Christian escapes from the domination of sin. He consummates in physical death, accepted as a supreme purification, the sacramental death of baptism. He is freed from our guilty nature. If indeed he is dead in Christ he will from that time onwards live and reign with him: "We are to share his life, because we have shared his death.... We shall reign with him" (2 Tim. 2 : 11-12). Death destroys itself, at is were, by enabling those whom it touches to escape from sin and damnation.[5] But we have now to ask ourselves how far the Christian who has returned to Christ lives with him before his glorious return and the resurrection.

Some of the more recent texts of the Old Testament had shown considerable progress in the revelation concerning retribution accorded in the after-life. The psalms (16: 81--; 49 : 16; 73 : 23-26) express desire for eternal life with God. The Book of Wisdom (3 : 1 et seq.), marking the happy influence of Platonic philosophy, showed, in contrast with the opinion of the foolish, the souls of the just in God's hand, living in peace and in his love, apart from any question of resur-

---

[4] See Durrwell, 390-6.   [5] See Durrwell, 298-9.

rection and this implied firm belief in the survival and immortality of the soul.[6] The witness of the Jewish tradition was similar, placing the just, as it did, in Abraham's bosom after their death, and separating them for ever from the sinners who were delivered over to the flames.[7] St. Paul in turn affirms that the reward is given to the just after death, without awaiting resurrection.

Describing Christ's glorious second coming to the Thessalonians, he declares — at least according to a possible interpretation — that the Saviour "will take with him those who are dead" (1 Thess. 4 : 14) and from the fact, moreover, that he describes them as being dead in Christ, (4 : 16) it is to be inferred that they were already with him. A little later, the apostle makes his thought clearer in writing to the Christians of Corinth: Our physical and mortal body is only a temporary habitation, a tent to be raised to go to another camping ground and one that is condemned to destruction, but "God, we are sure, has a solid building waiting for us, a dwelling not made with hands, that will last eternally in heaven" (2 Cor. 5 : 1). That is to say the glorified body of Christ who, by uniting us with himself in baptism, places in our body the seed of resurrection or, according to other interpretations, our glorified body, prepared in advance in heaven, indestructible and possessed already in hope.[8] Like all men, however, St. Paul was apprehensive of death and would like to escape from it and put on his immortal body without having to strip off the corruptible body: "Yes, if we tent-dwellers here go

[6] See Lagrange, *Le Judaïsme avant Jésus-Christ*, Gabalda, 1931, 343-51. Bonsirven, *Le Judaïsme palestinien*, Beauchesne, 1934, 322-40, 538-41. SDB, *Judaïsme*, 1228-30.

[7] See Allo, *IIᵉ Épître aux Corinthiens*, 157, n. 1. See also 1 Thess. 3 : 13 and Col. 3 : 4.

[8] But this interpretation seems to be contradicted by Col. 3 : 1-4 and Phil. 3 : 20-21.

sighing and heavy-hearted, it is not because we would be stripped of something; rather, we would clothe ourselves afresh; our mortal nature must be swallowed up in life. For this, nothing else, God was preparing us, when he gave us the foretaste of his Spirit" (2 Cor. 5 : 4-5). It is certain that in the long run we shall not find ourselves naked: the separation of soul and body will be only passing. The presence of the Spirit gives us the certain assurance of this. Death is therefore not to be feared. To fear it would be to show a weak faith. Death should on the contrary be desired, because "we recognize that our spirits are exiled from the Lord's presence so long as they are at home in the body.... We take heart, I say, and have a mind rather to be exiled from the body, and at home with the Lord" (2 Cor. 5 : 7-8).[9] Death thus takes on the character of a deliverance which makes it something to be looked forward to, even while it does not eliminate the tragic aspect due to its character as a final accounting.

During his first imprisonment, when he was facing possible martyrdom, the apostle returned to the same teaching: "For me, life means Christ; death is a prize to be won. But what if living on in this mortal body is the only way to harvest what I have sown? Thus I cannot tell what to choose; I am hemmed in on both sides. I long to have done with it, and be with Christ, a better thing, much more than a better thing; and yet, for your sakes, that I should wait in the body is more urgent still" (Phil. 1 : 21-24). These moving confidences all strike the same note. There can be no doubt that in St. Paul's view leaving this world by death meant going to Christ, passing from the rule of faith to that of clear vision (2 Cor. 5 : 7; compare 1 Cor. 13 : 12). With complete unselfishness, he was willing

---

[9] See Feuillet, *La demeure céleste et la destinée des chrétiens* (2 Cor. 5 : 1-10), RSR, 1956, 161-92. 360-402.

to live in exile from the Lord in order to continue a fruitful apostolic ministry. But he had in his heart a great desire to live with Christ. In the uncertainty of the future, there is but one preoccupation: to strive to please the Lord during the present life in order to be united with him in the future one: "At home or in exile, our ambition is to win his favour" (2 Cor. 5 : 9). In this way would we realize the fine ideal of loyalty and Christian serenity expressed in the epistle to the Romans: "None of us lives as his own master, and none of us dies as his own master. While we live, we live as the Lord's servants, when we die, we die as the Lord's servants; in life and in death, we belong to the Lord. That was why Christ died and lived again; he would be Lord both of the dead and of the living" (Rom. 14 : 7-9).

A dominion so authentic that each one is judged by our Lord at the moment of death. "All of us have a scrutiny to undergo before Christ's judgement seat, for each to reap what his mortal life has earned, good or ill, according to his deeds" (2 Cor. 5 : 10). St. Paul is not referring here to the Parousia but to the situation of each person at the moment he leaves his body. He thus asserts, at least implicitly, the fact of a *particular judgement* following death. This judgement will introduce us into the company of Christ in a manner proportionate to the merits we have acquired or it will, on the contrary, exclude us.[10] If one is not prepared to admit that the passage amounts to an explicit affirmation, it must at least be conceded that a judgement is implied by the happy or unhappy outcome of the appearance before Christ.[11]

It may be objected that it is normally to the general judgement that Paul is referring when he speaks of the Parousia.

---

[10] See Allo, *11e Épitre aux Corinthiens,* 133-59; Cerfaux, *Le Christ,* 46; SDB, *Jugement* (Mollat), 1374; Dupont, *L'Union avec le Christ,* de Brouwer, 1952, 157. [11] Thus Prat, II, 43-7. The interpreta-

We shall return to this point in dealing with the time of the Parousia and we shall then show that the apostle did not assert its imminence. There is no contradiction in his thought on this subject. It is inconceivable that, after having regarded the return of Christ as near at hand, he should have changed his mind on such an important point without warning his readers, and that when he came to write his second epistle to the Corinthians, he should suddenly have adopted the view that the Parousia was not at hand and thus be led to speak of

tion of Heb. 9 : 27, is also disputed. Was St. Paul thinking of Christians appearing before Christ with faults too small to entail damnation, but requiring the temporal purification to which theologians give the name purgatory? This idea was, it seems, not unknown at the Machabean period. On the morrow of a battle, Judas had an expiatory sacrifice offered in Jerusalem in order that the dead might be loosed from their sins (2 Mach., 12-46). At the time of Christ, Judaism admitted the name purgatory. This idea was, it seems, not unknown at the Machabean existence for certain types of sinners of a temporary Gehenna. See SDB, *Judaïsme*, 1270. In 1 Cor. 3 : 10-15, the apostle pictures the preachers of the gospel building on the only foundation on which anybody can lay – Christ – with precious materials such as gold, silver, and stones of great price, or with base materials, such as wood, hay and straw. The fire of judgement will reveal the quality of their work. He whose building stands up will be rewarded, whereas he whose building is burnt will receive no reward but will himself be saved "only as men are saved by passing through fire". The judgement symbolized by the fire is described in very general terms and the punishment of the mediocre workers for the gospel can be related equally well to the future life and to the present. This text can therefore be used to support the doctrine of temporary punishment for venial faults that do not merit damnation. See Prat, I 112-3; Huby, *Ie aux Corinthiens* (Verbum salutis), 112; Allo, *Ie aux Corinthiens*, 62-3; 66-7. If *baptism for the dead*, mentioned in 1 Cor. 15 : 29, was a rite intended to benefit their souls, this text would provide a further argument. But we can do no more than speculate on the meaning. See Allo, op. cit., 412-4.

We cannot agree with Cullmann, who looks upon the state of the Christian after death as a kind of sleep in the expectation of bodily resurrection, a sleep in which possession of the Holy Spirit brings him, nevertheless, closer to Christ (*Immortalité de l'âme ou résurrection des morts?*, Delachaux, 1956, particularly 74-8).

what would happen to the faithful immediately after death. It has been argued that the persecutions he had suffered (2 Cor. 1 : 8-9) led Paul to abandon hope of being present for the triumphant return of Christ and that this brought a sudden and complete change in his teaching. In fact, however, Paul was, like all of us, ignorant of when the Parousia will take place. He looked upon it as being at hand or delayed, each theory having arguments to support it, and his mind passed constantly between the two.[12] Events led him to dwell on the delay in his second epistle to the Corinthians and in the epistle to the Philippians, but in this he was not proposing any new doctrine. The teaching is perhaps implicit in the first epistle to the Thessalonians (4 : 14, 16; compare 5 : 10),[13] which St. Paul in fact wrote during his first stay in Corinth. Apart from this, his use of the words "we are sure" to introduce his first outline of individual eschatology (2 Cor. 5 : 1), indicates a doctrine already known, at least in an elementary form. This provides a valuable addition to the collective eschatology, which remained present in the apostle's mind, after as well as before he came to write his second epistle to the Corinthians. In his second epistle to Timothy, realizing that death was near, the end of the fight, the finish of the race, he nevertheless links to it the crown of justice, expected at Christ's final coming: "I look forward to the prize that is waiting for me, the prize I have earned. The Lord, the judge whose award never goes amiss, will grant it to me when that day comes; to me, yes, and all those who have learned to welcome his appearing" (2 Tim. 4 : 8; compare 1 : 6, 7). He takes in at a single glance both his particular judgement and the general judgement, but he does not confuse them, for the first is the prelude to the second.

[12] See chapter 19. [13] See p. 243 above, and Allo, *IIe Épitre aux Corinthiens*, 158; Bonsirven, *Évangile de Paul*, 310-5 and 343.

From the beginning, the *general judgement* formed one of the essential points in the apostolic teaching. Before baptizing Cornelius and his family, Peter declared: "And he gave us a commission to preach to the people, and to bear witness that he, and none other, has been chosen by God to judge the living and the dead" (Acts 10 : 42). In his speech to the Gentiles in Athens, Paul uses similar language: "God ... has fixed a day when he will pronounce just judgement on the whole world. And the man whom he has appointed for that end he has accredited to all of us, by raising him up from the dead" (Acts 17 : 31). He is constantly preoccupied with the need to proclaim the judgement, the different aspects of which are numerous. In the second epistle to the Thessalonians, we find a particularly thought-provoking text, full of reminders of the Old Testament:

> Our own boasting, as we visit the churches of God, is of your perseverance and your faith amidst all the persecutions and trials which you have to endure. It will be a proof of the just award God makes, when he finds you worthy of a place in his kingdom for which you are prepared to suffer. Or do you doubt that there is justice with God, to repay with affliction those who afflict you, and you, the afflicted, with that rest which will be ours too? But that is for the day when the Lord Jesus appears from heaven, with angels to proclaim his power; with fire flaming about him; as he pours out vengeance on those who do not acknowledge God, on those who refuse obedience to the gospel of our Lord Jesus Christ. They will be condemned to eternal punishment, far from the presence of the Lord, and the majesty of his power, when he comes to show how glorious he is in his saints, how marvellously he has dealt with all the faithful (2 Thess. 1:5–10).

The judgement, comfort that it is for persecuted Christians, will be applied with strict justice. It will be the work of God accomplished by Christ, descending in glory from heaven. Men will be judged according to their attitude towards

God and their obedience to the gospel of Christ. The punishment of sinners will be eternal, consisting in separation from God, far from his presence and the majesty of his power. The faithful, on the other hand, will be admitted to the heavenly kingdom and will enjoy repose in return for the afflictions they have endured. The first letter to the Thessalonians had laid it down that they would be "with the Lord for ever" — a capital feature of the eternal reward. Paul insists too on the universality of the judgement. All will appear before the judgement seat of God (Rom. 14 : 10). Sentence will be passed on men's most hidden actions (Rom. 2 : 16; 1 Cor. 4 : 5) and its irrevocability will be dramatic (Heb. 6 : 2; compare 10 : 26-31 which refers to the terrible punishment of apostates).

The strict equity of the divine judgement means that men will be judged according to the light they have received, rudimentary in the case of the pagans and fuller in that of the Jews (Rom. 2 : 12). Each man will reap what he has sown, a perishable harvest if nature is his seed ground, eternal life if his seed ground is the spirit (Gal. 6 : 7-8; Col. 3 : 25; Eph. 6 : 8). The imperishable crown of faithful Christians will be a crown of justice (1 Cor. 9 : 25; 2 Tim. 4 : 8). Their intimate union with Christ (1 Cor. 1 : 9) will fill them with a joy beyond anything that the heart of man can conceive (1 Cor. 2 : 9). Faith will have given place to seeing face to face (1 Cor. 13 : 12). They will share in the victory of God and of Christ (1 Cor. 15 : 24-28) and with Christ will judge not only the world but also the angels (1 Cor. 6 : 2-3). But beforehand, they will have had a share in the glorious resurrection of the Saviour and seen their miserable bodies transformed into glorified bodies.[14]

---

[14] For the Jewish conception of the judgement and reward, see Bonsirven, *Le Judaïsme*, I, 486-538; for the similarity betw. St. Paul's teaching and that of the gospels, SDB, *Jugement*, 1344-59, 1379, 1385.

18

THE RESURRECTION

*"And first of all the dead will rise up,
those who died in Christ" (1 Thess. 4:16).*

THE resurrection of the dead, which comes as an addition to
and completion of salvation, is closely connected with Christ's
own resurrection and constitutes, as it were, the first phase
of his glorious return.

The doctrine of the resurrection was accepted with difficulty in the Hellenic world. To the extent that the teachings of
Socrates and Plato led to an increasing belief in the immortality of the soul, repugnance to the idea of resurrection grew.
Death was regarded as a liberation, an entry into a more perfect life. The body became regarded as the soul's tomb or
prison and it was not thought in the least desirable to return
to it from beyond the grave. All kinds of objections were
raised to the idea of resurrection, or to the way in which it
was to be achieved. The Athenians shrugged their shoulders
and ceased to listen to Paul as soon as he mentioned it (Acts
17 : 32).[1] Among the Jews, the Pharisees believed in the
resurrection, while the Sadducees rejected it and considered they
had made a valid objection when they produced for our
Lord the fable of the woman who had seven husbands (Matt.
22 : 23-32 and parallel passages). Finally, the false doctors

---

[1] See Cerfaux, *Christ*, 77, n. 9; Festugière, *L'idéal religieux des
Grecs et l'Évangile*, Gabalda 1932, 143-69.

opposed by St. Paul in his pastoral epistles alleged that the resurrection had already taken place, understanding it in a purely spiritual sense (2 Tim. 2 : 18).

The apostle's thought concerning the resurrection remains constant. After his arrest, he proclaimed the hope of it before the Sanhedrin, thus cleverly setting the Pharisees and the Sadducees against each other (Acts 23 : 6-8). A little later, at Cesarea, he told the governor, Felix, that there would be a resurrection of the dead "both just and unjust" (Acts 24 : 15).[2] The letter to the Hebrews (6 : 2) presents the resurrection as one of the articles in the elementary baptismal catechism. The epistles frequently speak of it (1 Cor. 6 : 14; 2 Cor. 4 : 14; Rom. 8 : 11; etc.). The two most important texts are to be found in the first epistle to the Thessalonians (4 : 13-17) and in 1 Cor. 15.

St. Paul speaks of the dead as "those who sleep". We need not take our analysis of the expression too far since it was current both in classical antiquity and in the Old Testament and Judaism. It seems, however, to have been used intentionally in the context in which we find it. The resurrection of the faithful is there asserted on the strength of their interdependence in Christ and the presence in them of the Holy Spirit.

The Thessalonians needed to be strengthened in their faith in the resurrection and were asking themselves what would be the lot of their dead when Christ returned. Paul reassures them in a few words: "We believe, after all, that Jesus underwent death and rose again; just so, when Jesus comes back, God will bring back those who have found rest through him" (4 : 14). And at the Parousia, "the Lord himself will come

[2] The epistles generally speak only of the resurrection of the just, which is the only normal end for the Christian. But that of sinners is implicitly affirmed in the announcement of their eternal punishment (2 Thess. 1 : 9-10; Rom. 2 : 5-6).

down from heaven... and first of all the dead will rise up, those who died in Christ" (4 : 16). The lot of the dead will be similar to that of those who survive. All will join in the cortege of the triumphant Saviour and will henceforth be always with him.

The doubts of the Corinthians concerning the resurrection were much stronger and St. Paul sets out to provide them with a formal demonstration. After recalling briefly[3] Christ's apparitions to the apostles and to himself (1 Cor. 15 : 3-8), he stresses the irreparable damage that would be caused to the faith by any rejection of the doctrine of the resurrection. "How is it that some of you say the dead do not rise again? If the dead do not rise, then Christ has not risen either; and if Christ has not risen, then our preaching is groundless, and your faith, too, is groundless" (12-14). If resurrection is an impossibility, it is one for everybody, not excepting Christ. In that case, the preaching of the apostles and the Christian faith are empty and without object since Christ's resurrection is an essential article of both. The apostles themselves become false witnesses and impostors because, if the resurrection of the dead is denied, their testimony that God raised Christ to life must be regarded as disproved. The whole work of redemption then collapses. "And if Christ has not risen, all your faith is a delusion, you are back in your sins. It follows, too, that those who have gone to their rest in Christ have been lost" (17-18). If Christ is not risen as he foretold, giving the resurrection as the chief sign of his divine mission, then he is only a false prophet. He is neither Son of God nor Saviour. Faith and baptism are without efficacy. The believers are back in their sins, for if Christ has been defeated by death, which is the punishment for sin, sin retains its sovereignty and

---

[3] See chapter 6 at the beginning of section III.

pardon for it has not been obtained. The faithful are the most unfortunate of men, for they have no purification from sins here below and no hope of future life. What would immortality amount to if it excluded resurrection? It would be an immortality without glory or joy. The most apparent punishment of sin would remain, and sin with it. It would, in fact, be final death, with salvation rendered impossible. It would be as well to banish all anxiety about the future life and make the most of the present one.

The apostle dwells on this terrible prospect only to dismiss it immediately. "But no, Christ has risen from the dead, the first-fruits of all those who have fallen asleep" (15 : 20) and "this was the first birth out of death" (Col. 1 : 18). There cannot be first-fruits without a harvest. God willed that death should come through a man and that life should also come through a man. "Just as all have died with Adam, so with Christ all will be brought to life" (1 Cor. 15 : 22). The solidarity for life in Christ repairs the evil effects of the solidarity for death in Adam. This constitutes a brief reminder of the parallel between Adam and Christ that St. Paul must have taught to the Corinthians and that he repeats in the letter to the Romans (5 : 12-21). On the day of Christ's return, then, his resurrection will entail our own. It is the model and guarantee of it. Again, the catechumens who had themselves baptized on account of the dead — in a rite the nature of which we do not know and on whose value St. Paul does not pronounce — can be regarded as bearing witness to their faith in the resurrection as Judas Machabeus had done when he had an expiatory sacrifice offered for the dead (2 Mach. 12 : 44). And finally, what good were the works and sufferings of the apostles, who risked their lives every day, if the dead do not rise? Of what good, especially, were the struggles of St. Paul at Ephesus, which he compares with a fight against the beasts?

Would it not be better to live like the Epicureans waiting for death in which, in practice, all things ended, if one could envisage only a pseudo-immortality, uncrowned by resurrection (29-32)? In a word, was it to be suggested that Christian hope rested on a man swallowed up by death and as powerless to preserve others as he was to save himself? It was to this that one would be reduced by denying the resurrection of the dead.

Besides this, Paul takes a delight in linking Christ's resurrection and our own with the power manifested by the Father in an admirable way when he made his Son sit at his right hand in heaven (Eph. 1 : 20). "And God, just as he has raised our Lord from the dead, by his great power will raise us up too" (1 Cor. 6 : 14). "He who raised Jesus from the dead will raise us too, and summon us, like you, before him" (2 Cor. 4 : 14). God will give life to the bodies of the faithful through the action of the Holy Spirit whose gifts they constantly experience (Gal. 3 : 5; 1 Thess. 5 : 19-20). "And if the Spirit of him who raised up Jesus from the dead dwells in you, he who raised up Jesus Christ from the dead will give life to your perishable bodies too, for the sake of his Spirit who dwells in you" (Rom. 8 : 11). And the Holy Spirit will not indefinitely permit the corruption of the bodies which he has made his temple. The "first-fruits of the Spirit", which are a partial gift, are in fact given with a view to the resurrection (2 Cor. 5 : 5) which will complete the work of redemption in us (Eph. 1 : 15). The apostle shows with great eloquence that the completion of the redemption by the glorification of the body is looked forward to by inanimate creation, which would like to be part of a better world, entirely subject to God (Rom. 8 : 19-22). We, too, possessing the first-fruits of the Spirit and under his influence, groan in expectation of the redemption of our bodies. The strength of our desires is so much in conformity with divine plans that the Spirit himself intercedes for us with "groans beyond all utterance" helping us to formulate the prayer that we do not know how to express (Rom. 8 : 23-26). Finally, God, who makes himself ready to grant "the Spirit's intent" and to grant us the complete glorification of which justification has placed in us the seed, is all the more inclined to hear our prayer in that Christ the Redeemer intercedes for us (Rom. 8 : 27-33).[4] This co-ordinated and universal effort to ensure the glorification of the believer should place an indefeasible hope in his heart.

It would seem that the Corinthians did not repudiate this hope entirely, but they failed to overcome the difficulties arising in their minds from speculation on the nature of the risen body. What kind of body would the dead wear (15 : 35)? Would it be in skeleton form, or corrupt? How was this disturbing mystery to be solved?

Showing what he derives from Jewish tradition,[5] Paul turns very appropriately to the comparison of the sowing. The grain thrown into the earth must die in order to live again.[6] It gives birth to a plant which, though very different, retains a certain identity with it. The wonderful variety of the vegetable kingdom, repeated in the animal kingdom and found to an even greater extent among the stars, referred to as heavenly bodies, should help us to understand that God can create spiritual bodies that are more perfect than corruptible bodies (15 : 36-41). That is what will happen at the resurrection of the dead. "What is sown corruptible, rises incorruptible; what is sown unhonoured, rises in glory; what is sown in weakness,

---

[4] Thus, in the resurrection of the body as in the sanctification of souls, there is a common action of Christ and the Spirit.

[5] Bonsirven, *Judaïsme palestinien*. I, 483-6.

[6] Compare John 12 : 24.

is raised in power; what is sown a natural body, rises a spiritual body" (15 : 43-44).

The body will rise again, transformed but fundamentally the same, like the plant issuing from the sowing. It will no longer be subject to corruption, will shine in glory, full of agility and strength. In a word, it will be a spiritual body like to the body of the risen Christ. After solidarity in Adam, solidarity in Christ is pressed to its logical conclusion: "Mankind begins with Adam who became, as Scripture tells us, a living soul; it is fulfilled in the Adam who has become a life-giving spirit" (15 : 45). In union with Adam, the body is moved by a soul which is the principle of life according to the flesh, in a natural and sentient form; in union with Christ, having become a life-giving spirit, it participates in the qualities of his glorified body (compare Phil. 3 : 20-21). The risen Christ has the fullness of the divine status which he gave up at the moment of the incarnation (Phil. 2 : 6-7). He is henceforth completely spirit, entirely penetrated by the Spirit in his humanity, in order to transmit the Spirit to men. His body is a spiritual body, delivered from all the weaknesses and limitations of our guilty nature and overflowing with the Spirit. Christ is henceforth the divine Spirit (2 Cor. 3 : 17) — without being in any way confused, as we have seen above, with the Holy Spirit.[7] He exercises the fullness of divine power. He is in very truth the heavenly man who has come after the earthly man. "And it remains for us, who once bore the stamp of earth, to bear the stamp of heaven" (1 Cor. 15 : 49). Adam was able to transmit to his posterity only an earthly and mortal life Christ has given us a spiritual life, one which is in a certain manner heavenly and will have as its final effect the resurrection of our bodies. It will be the same for all the

---

[7] See chapter 10, pp. 162-66.

faithful, living and dead, for flesh and blood, the corruptible and mortal body can have no part in the kingdom of God (15 : 50, 53). But when the body has taken on incorruption and immortality, death will be swallowed up in Christ's victory (15 : 54) and the salvation of believers will be fully accomplished by a complete share in his victory.

The nature of the risen bodies remains a mystery but what the epistles say about Christ's glorified body gives us some idea. A spiritual body does not mean an immaterial one. Matter will be penetrated by the spirit and by divine power. It will escape from wasting and corruption without ceasing to be material. Paul can talk without contradiction about spiritual body because, for him, spirit is force, light and divine holiness rather than immateriality strictly speaking. It is the supernatural aspect that predominates in his thought.[8] Not separating body from soul but considering man in the unity of his person, he can refer to the person as carnal or spiritual according to whether he considers it as animated or not by the Spirit of Christ. Sin reduces human nature, body and soul, to the carnal state. Through the action of the Spirit, the body itself becomes spiritual on the day of the resurrection. It has been shrewdly pointed out[9] that what makes the body dangerous is that it is not sufficiently united to the soul and partially escapes from it. At the resurrection, the glorified soul will penetrate the body with such force that it will turn it away from the carnal and corruptible state and make it a perfectly adjusted instrument which will no longer resist the soul in any way. The supernatural transformation of man will strengthen the unity of the composite human being in a harmony that nothing will in future upset (compare Matt. 22 : 30 and parallel texts).

[8] See Cerfaux, *Christ*, 77.   [9] Mouroux in RSR, 1943, 168-9.

The two main texts we have quoted concerning the resurrection teach in addition that the last generation of humans living at the time of the Parousia will be transformed without dying:

> This we can tell you as a message from the Lord himself; those of us who are still left alive to greet the Lord's coming will not reach the goal before those who have gone to their rest. No, the Lord himself will come down from heaven to summon us, with an archangel crying aloud and the trumpet of God sounding; and first of all the dead will rise up, those who died in Christ. Only after that shall we, who are still left alive, be taken up into the clouds, be swept away to meet Christ in the air, and they will bear us company. And so we shall be with the Lord for ever (1 Thess. 4:15–17).
>
> Here is a mystery I will make known to you; we shall not all die but we shall all be transformed in a moment, in the twinkling of an eye, when the last trumpet sounds. For the trumpet will sound, and the dead will rise again, free from corruption, and we shall be transformed (1 Cor. 15:51–52).[10]

It is surprising that there should be any hesitation about the meaning of declarations as clear as these. Paul says elsewhere that Christ "is to be the judge of living and dead" (2 Tim. 4 : 1) and this form of words, repeated in early creeds, implied an exception to the general rule of death, all the more so since the apostle expressed elsewhere his desire to put on the second garment over the other, that is to say to enter into possession of his glorified body without having to strip off the mortal body (2 Cor. 5 : 3-4). What scripture – and Paul himself (1 Cor. 15 : 22; Rom. 5 : 12; 6 : 23; Heb. 9 : 27) – have to say about the universality of death and the punishment of all sin has been strictly interpreted. But though undeniable taking humanity as a whole, it does

---

[10] Translator's own rendering.

not apply to the witnesses of the Parousia. Some commentators have thought that the last human beings would die while they were being taken through the air to meet Christ and would arise from the dead immediately afterwards... . This was an error for which the Latin Fathers and theologians can be excused for, in the Vulgate, they had like ourselves an inaccurate translation of 1 Cor. 15:51.[11] But the sense of the authentic text is not in doubt. "We shall not all die but we shall all be transformed", we shall all be transformed that is, in the same way as those who are risen, for corruption can have no share in incorruption. Those whom Christ will find living when he returns in glory will put on "in the twinkling of an eye", without preliminary death, the spiritual and immortal body that the dead will assume at the end of their waiting in the grave.

[11] The Vulgate reads: *omnes quidem moriemur, sed non omnes immutabimur;* in the context, this means we shall all die but shall not all undergo change, in the sense of the glorious transformation. The assertion is true but it is not in conformity with the thought St. Paul is here expressing.

19

THE PAROUSIA

"The Lord himself will come down from heaven" (I Thess. 4:16).

WITH the resurrection which will accompany it, the glorious return of Christ, or Parousia, is an additional stage in redemption and the completion of salvation. This explains its extreme importance in the apostle's thought.

He uses a number of terms to express this impressive reality. That of Parousia, or presence, παρουσία, was employed in the Hellenic world to designate the state entry of a sovereign, or the special manifestation of gods. The New Testament sometimes uses it in a secular sense but also in the technical sense of the coming of Christ in glory which will represent his presence in the highest degree (1 Thess. 2 : 19; 3 : 13; 4 : 15; 2 Thess. 2 : 1). The context makes it clear which is intended. We also find the word epiphany (ἐπιφάνεια) used in the epistles with the same meaning to describe the first (2 Tim. 1 : 10) and above all the second coming of Christ (2 Thess. 2 : 8; 1 Tim. 6 : 14; 2 Tim. 4 : 1, 8; Titus 2 : 13) and we find revelation, ἀποκάλυψις, in various senses, but also with that of the final coming of Christ (2 Thess. 1 : 7; 1 Cor. 1 : 7).[1] Finally, corresponding with the Day of Jahveh mentioned by the prophets (for example

[1] See B. Rigaux, *Épîtres aux Thessaloniciens* (Études Bibliques), Gabalda 1956, 196-206.

Amos 5 : 18), the glorious coming of Christ is represented as the Day *par excellence* (2 Tim. 1 : 12, 18; 4 : 8), the decisive and last intervention, the day of the Lord Jesus Christ (1 Thess. 5 : 2; 2 Thess. 1 : 10; 2 : 2; 1 Cor. 1 : 8; 3 : 13; 5 : 5; 2 Cor. 1 : 14; etc.). We know the strength of the desire among Jews for the Day of Jahveh, for the coming of the Messiah which would, it was thought, be a signal for the end of the world.[2]

The two passages we have already studied in the first epistle to the Thessalonians and in the first to the Corinthians contain a brief description of the resurrection and of the Parousia. To these must be added the well known but obscure second chapter in the second epistle to the Thessalonians. St. Paul there borrows more or less word for word from the Old Testament: Psalms 16 and 72; the second part of Isaias; Daniel 7 : 13-14; 12 : 1-4; and from other prophetic passages concerning the judgement and the end of time; 2 Mach. 12 : 43-46. There are also passages reminiscent of the Jewish apocryphas and the Qumrân texts.[3] But it is with the eschatological passages of the New Testament that the resemblances are greatest and in particular with the words of our Saviour about the ruin of Jerusalem and the end of the world, particularly in the version given by St. Matthew.[4]

[2] Jewish eschatology is somewhat incoherent in this respect. It was not clear whether there would be an earthly reign of the Messiah, if so whether it would take place between two judgements and two resurrections, what would be its nature, and what would be its duration etc. See *Enseignement de saint Paul*, II, 181-3.

[3] For example, the 4th Book of Esdras, 8 : 1; the Apocalypse of Baruch 18 : 50, etc. See Lagrange, *Judaïsme* 343-53; Bonsirven, *Judaïsme palestinien*, I, 310-19. For Qumrân, see above, chapter 2, p. 42.

[4] See the comparison of texts and discussion in Rigaux, *Épître aux Thessaloniciens*, 94-105. He does not believe that St. Paul was influenced by the earlier writings but that the apostle and the synop-

The first epistle to the Thessalonians is dominated by the prospect of the second coming. St. Paul invites his readers to await the appearance from the heavens of the risen Christ who will deliver us from the anger to come (1 : 10). He consequently exhorts them to lead a life worthy of God and asks the Lord to make them irreproachable in holiness against his coming (2 : 12; 3 : 13) so that their whole being, spirit, soul and body,[5] will be found without stain when Christ comes (5 : 23). They will then be St. Paul's delight and his title to glory (2 : 19). These brief indications provide a framework to the text in which the apostle strives to calm the apprehensions of the Thessalonians. He first of all reminds them that Christ's resurrection is the guarantee of our own, then shows that at the time of the Parousia the dead and the living will receive the same glorious reward of life with Christ.

> This we can tell you as a message from the Lord himself; those of us who are still left alive to greet the Lord's coming will not reach the goal before those who have gone to their rest. No, the Lord himself will come down from heaven to summon us, with an archangel crying aloud and the trumpet of God sounding; and first of all the dead will rise up, those who died in Christ. Only after that shall we, who are still left alive, be taken up into the clouds, be swept away to meet Christ in the air, and they will bear us company. And so we shall be with the Lord for ever (4:15–17).

The message of the Lord to which the apostle solemnly refers could be Christ's revelation about the end of time,

---

tics all referred to the same words of our Lord. 1 Thess. 4 : 15 seems to hint at this.

[5] On the trichotomy which seems implied in 5 : 23, see Festugière, *Idéal religieux des Grecs*, 196-220. Rigaux in I rejects the idea that St. Paul was indicating a trichotomy. He considers that the word "spirit" refers to the higher powers of the soul and "psyche" to the lower.

incompletely reported in the synoptics or, less probably, a particular revelation (compare 1 Cor. 15 : 51). Its precise purpose is to show that those who are living at the time of the Parousia will have no advantage over the dead. The latter will rise first, then the living will be taken with them in the clouds to meet Christ and to remain for ever with him. The arrival of Christ is described in language showing the influence of the theophany of Sinaï (Exodus 19 : 10-18), of the prophets and of the Jewish apocalyptic writings.[6] The second epistle (1 : 7-8) adds that the Lord will be accompanied by angels to proclaim his power, with fire flaming about him. The signal, the voice of the archangel and the divine trumpet are a triple expression of the divine command. The Lord will then descend from heaven and, even before he arrives on earth, the dead who will have risen and the living who will have been transformed will be taken into the clouds to meet him. The details of this description, which is, indeed, expressed with restraint, are evidently not to be interpreted literally. They are of a kind habitually found in the apocalypses and are inspired by a rudimentary cosmology, the only one the apostle could have known. The essential points are the link between Christ's resurrection and our own and the identical nature of the fate of the dead and the living. The dead will even have the advantage because they will be raised first. The fears of the Thessalonians are thus unfounded and Paul adds that it matters little whether we are dead or alive when the Lord comes because all will be preserved from anger and will have a share in the salvation that his death has merited for them, will be with him always and will live with him (5 : 9-10). They will be for ever with him, living through God in him (Rom. 6 : 8-11). The prospect of judgement is

---

[6] References in Rigaux, *Épître aux Thessaloniciens*, 230.

merely implicit in this passage, but is clearly shown in 2 Thess.
1 : 8-10. The passage does not deal either with what happens
to the dead before the Parousia. Paul explains this later in his
second letter to Corinth (2 Cor. 5 : 1-10).[7]

In his first epistle, he was brought to speak again of the
Parousia. After insisting that the resurrection of Christ is the
essential basis of Christian faith, he declares that Christ is
risen, "the first-fruits of all those who have fallen asleep".
Those who belong to him will rise again in the same way
when he comes (15 : 20, 23). The end will then follow. It
will come as an immediate consequence without any interval.
The context gives no indication of a lapse of time[8] which is,
moreover, excluded by the way the ideas are linked together.
The last enemy, death, will have been defeated. All hostile
powers will have been annihilated. Christ will have subjected every creature to himself and, one by one, God will have
placed all his enemies under his feet, in conformity with the
psalms, (9 : 5-7 and 109 : 1). "Then the Son himself will
become subject to the power which made all things his sub-
jects" and will place "his kingship in the hands of God, his
Father" (15 : 24-28) in a magnificent gesture. Thus God
will be all in all. All beings will be absolutely and completely
subject to his power. But it is only as Messiah and
Mediator, wresting men from the power of sin and death,

[7] See chapter 17.

[8] Verses 24-28 do not indicate that Christ's struggles to overcome
his last remaining adversaries are to be placed between the resurrection
of the just and that of the damned. It is before the Parousia that Christ
is to annihilate his enemies (compare Eph. 1 : 22). There is no trace
here of "millenarism" or of the idea of a double resurrection (the
same applies to the Apocalypse 20 : 1-10, correctly interpreted). It
would be hard to understand why a second resurrection, that of the
damned, should be followed by a chant of victory (54-58). See Allo,
Ière Épître aux Corinthiens, 441-7; Kittel, βασιλεία, I, 581-92
(Schmidt).

that Christ will cease to rule. His domination, up to then militant, will become exclusively triumphant and will no longer be distinct from the universal domination of God with whom he will reign indivisibly. Paul speaks elsewhere of "the kingdom of Christ and of God" (Eph. 5 : 5),[9] from which sinners will be excluded. Christ will be more than ever Lord and life-giving spirit (15 : 45) — his sacrifice will have brought forth all its fruits. The Church will have attained its fullness and the members of the Mystical Body will have reached "perfect manhood, that maturity which is proportioned to the completed growth of Christ" (Eph. 4 : 13). The destruction of death will coincide with the placing of the Kingdom in the hands of the Father and the establishment of the eternal order. This prospect leads Paul to give a fresh description of the Parousia:

> Here is a mystery I will make known to you: we shall not all die but we shall all be transformed. It will happen in a moment, in the twinkling of an eye, when the last trumpet sounds. For the trumpet will sound, and the dead will rise again, free from corruption, and we shall be transformed. This corruptible nature of ours must be clothed with incorruptible life, this mortal nature with immortality. Then, when this corruptible nature wears its incorruptible garment, this mortal nature its immortality, the saying of scripture will come true: Death is swallowed up in victory. Where then, death, is thy victory; where, death, is thy sting? It is sin that gives death its sting, just as it is the law that gives sin its power; but thanks be to God, then, who gives us victory through our Lord Jesus Christ (1 Cor. 15:51–57).[10]

The apostle here sets out more clearly the sudden transformation of the living which will take place at the same time as the resurrection of the dead and is necessary for partici-

[9] Translator's own rendering.
[10] Ibid.

pation in the Kingdom of God (50). Both will henceforth be incorruptible and immortal. Death will have been finally conquered and with it sin, which was its sting and without which it would never have fallen upon men (Rom. 5 : 12). Paul is able to give voice to a hymn of triumph and to give thanks to God who gives us victory through Christ. The faithful will then enter into the Kingdom of God of which, up to that time, they will have had only an imperfect possession (Col. 1 : 13) thus fully putting into effect the divine plan calling them to this possession (1 Thess. 2 : 12; 2 Tim. 4 : 18). This will represent for them the full divine adoption of sons in the glorification of their bodies (Rom. 8 : 23). Their life, hitherto hidden in God with Christ, will appear in glory at the coming of the Lord, himself sovereignly glorious and living (Col. 3 : 4).

Anxious that their dead should have a share in the solemn return of Christ, the Thessalonians reckoned on remaining alive until the last great accounting. Some of them thought it was at hand and, that being the case, considered themselves free to live idle lives. Jewish theories, according to which the coming of the Messiah would be a signal for the end of the world, may have influenced them. St. Paul reminded them of the obligation to work (4 : 11-12). But, in his description of the Parousia, he seemed to number himself among those who would survive and would be witnesses of it and he says twice: "Those of us who are still left alive to greet the Lord's coming" (4 : 15, 17). Did the apostle share the unfounded belief of his readers? We know how thoroughly the question has been discussed and, even today, it is still the subject of vigorous controversy. Catholic exegesis seems, however, able to provide a reasonable and objective solution.

The Saviour, questioned by the apostles concerning the

time of his return, refused to reply to them, declaring, paradoxically, that it was unknown to him (Mark 13 : 32 and parallel passages). At the time of the ascension, he again refused to answer the question (Acts 1 : 6-8). It would be very strange if St. Paul should fail to take account of Christ's attitude and, in fact, he does not. He was as ignorant as the rest of us of the date of the glorious coming. The texts in which he makes known his views sometimes look on the Parousia as at hand and sometimes as far off and this is an understandable attitude on the part of one who, being in ignorance, thought that each hypothesis had something to be said for it.

In the first epistle to the Thessalonians, after placing himself among the possible survivors, he immediately adds an exhortation to vigilance.

> You are keeping it clearly in mind, without being told, that the day of the Lord will come like a thief in the night. It is just when men are saying, all quiet, all safe, that doom will fall upon them suddenly, like the pangs that come to a woman in travail, and there will be no escape from it. God has not destined us for vengeance; he means us to win salvation through our Lord Jesus Christ, who has died for our sakes, that we, waking or sleeping, may find life with him (1 Thess. 5:2–3; 9–10).

The comparison with the thief is plainly a reminder of the gospel (Matt. 24 : 43-44; Luke 12 : 39-40) and rests on the uncertainty of the last day. Whether we are found dead or alive, one thing matters — to achieve the salvation which the death of Christ has merited for us and live together with him. The apostle does not know when Christ will return and it is reasonable to suppose that in placing himself among the living, he was merely expressing a hope and desire and did not know whether it would be fulfilled. Witnessing death strike round him at Corinth where he then was and at

266

Thessalonika (1 Thess. 4 : 13-15; 1 Cor. 11 : 30), could he think that all his readers would escape? Some months later, when he was faced with the growing anxiety of the Thessalonians, he had to remind them that the Parousia would be preceded by an apostasy and by the revelation and the coming of the man of sin, which, to say the least, considerably enlarged the perspective (2 Thess. 2 : 1-12).[11] In all the epistles in which St. Paul speaks of the Parousia, we shall find the same juxta-position of various impressions, combining to show the same ignorance regarding the date.

In the first epistle to the Corinthians (15 : 51-52), Paul declares: "We shall not all die but we shall all be transform-ed".[12] A few pages earlier, he had said: "And God, just as he has raised our Lord from the dead, by his great power, will raise us up too" (6 : 14).[13] The use of the first person to cover the two eventualities is significant. In the second epistle (5 : 1-10), the apostle is even more explicit when, after having revealed his own hope of escaping death and putting on the second garment over the first, he turns to an individual eschatology, which he places beside the collective eschatology, and says that it would be better for him to leave the body in order to go and dwell immediately with the Lord. The same preoccupations, shot through with uncertainty, occupied his mind during his first captivity, as he shows in the epistle to the Philippians. He is, so to speak, caught between two con-tradictory desires: to go in order to be with Christ and to live on in the body to continue his apostolate (1 : 23-24). Such vagueness in his expressions of hope would not make sense if the apostle thought the Parousia was at hand. Clearly, he did not know when it was to take place. Nevertheless, it is per-

[11] This text will be studied later.
[12] Translator's own rendering.
[13] Compare 2 Cor. 4 : 14.

manently on the horizon of his thought as the final completion of salvation, for which the preliminary phases are merely
a preparation and a journeying. A little further on, he writes:
"...whereas we find our true home in heaven. It is to heaven
that we look expectantly for the coming of our Lord Jesus
Christ to save us; he will form this humbled body of ours
anew, moulding it into the image of his glorified body, so
effective is his power to make all things obey him" (Phil.
3 : 20-21). But he cannot be saying whether this will be
a transformation excluding death because he speaks also of his
"hope of achieving resurrection from the dead" (3 : 11). Thus,
when, in the same epistle, he asserts that "the Lord is near"
(4 : 5), we have to ask ourselves whether he is not thinking
of the active presence of Christ and of the advent of death as
much as of the Parousia or whether, according to the common
practice of prophetic language, he is not moving from one
period to another without worrying about the time scale.

The same applies to the pastoral epistles, written at the
end of the apostle's career. The coming of Christ may take
place during the lifetime of Timothy, but its date remains a
divine secret. Paul invites his disciple to fulfil faithfully the
directions he gives him, "until the day when our Lord Jesus
Christ appears. God will reveal him in due time, the blessed
God who alone enjoys dominion; he is King of kings, and
Lord of lords" (1 Tim. 6 : 14-15). Just before his martyrdom,
knowing that the time of his departure was near, he looked
forward to the reward of his faithfulness, which he would
receive from the just judge – salvation in the heavenly kingdom, on the supreme day, as though personal reward were
postponed until the final settlement (2 Tim. 4 : 7, 8, 18).
But the second epistle to the Corinthians (5 : 10) shows us
that this was not what he thought.[14] He never loses from sight,

14 See chapter 17.

268

however, the supreme Event, towards which all things are ordered. He adjures Timothy to fulfil his ministry "in the name of his coming and of his kingdom" (2 Tim. 4 : 1) and he asks that Christians striving after holiness should be looking forward "in our hope, to the day when there will be a new dawn of glory, the glory of the great God, the glory of our Saviour Jesus Christ" (Titus 2 : 13).

Other aspects of St. Paul's thought provide evidence of a similarly complex outlook. The apostle places the preaching of the gospel to the Gentiles and the conversion of at least a part of Israel before the Parousia (Rom. 9-11) and he announces that the Parousia will also be preceded by a crisis — the apostasy and the appearance of Antichrist. This thing could hardly take place in a short period of time (2 Thess. 2 : 1-12). Even if he thought that the evangelization of the Roman Empire would be fairly rapidly accomplished (Rom. 10 : 14-18), he could hardly expect that developments of such importance would take place in the restricted compass of one generation. Moreover, his frequent allusions to the glorious coming do not prevent him from organizing the churches, from laying the foundations of a new society, preaching submission to the established authorities (Rom. 13 : 1-7), laying down the rights and duties of married couples (Eph. 5 : 21-33), of children and of slaves (Eph. 6 : 1-9; Col. 3 : 18 to 4 : 1), calling upon Christians to live an upright and industrious life (1 Thess. 4 : 11-12; 2 Thess. 3 : 6-12) and describing the divine plan for universal salvation (Eph. 2 : 11 to 3 : 13; Col. 1 : 26-27). But these sweeping, though necessarily distant perspectives do not prevent Paul from presenting the last days, *the day,* the final tribulations, and the disappearance of the world as having already started (1 Cor. 7 : 29; 10 : 11; Rom. 13 : 12; Phil. 4 : 5; 2 Tim. 3 : 1-5; Heb. 1 : 2; 4 : 7; 9 : 26). In fact, these expressions refer to

269

the whole of Messianic times, from the incarnation until the end of the world, and not simply to the final event which is the Parousia. We are in the last age in which history finds its fulfilment (Gal. 4 : 4; Eph. 1 : 10), in the final period of redemption and salvation, but these modes of presentation do not give us any means of determining whether it will be long or short.

The same uncertainty, producing the same vagueness and the same literary processes, is to be found in the other eschatological passages of the New Testament. St. Peter says in his first epistle that "the end of all things is close at hand" (4 : 7). But he explains in his second that "with the Lord a day counts as a thousand years, and a thousand years count as a day" (3 : 8). They must not be surprised that the Parousia should be delayed, for Christ would come like a thief. In the Apocalypse, St. John seems to regard the period of the Church's struggles as destined to be long, symbolized by the figure of a thousand years (20 : 1-10), but he ends his book with an apparent announcement of the approaching return of the Lord: "Indeed I am coming soon. Be it so, then; come, Lord Jesus" (22 : 20). The analogy with what we have read in St. Paul is striking and is to be explained by the same ignorance concerning the last day. The actual presence of Christ, so keenly felt by the apostles, is a hidden and mysterious Parousia which heralds and prepares the glorious and shining coming.[15] We are concerned with a single reality which approaches its apogee, but as no one can say when it will arrive there, the eyes of the inspired writers are sometimes directed towards the dawn and sometimes towards the full day of which this dawn gives promise and for which it arouses a desire (Rom. 13 : 12), the dawn and the day being, as it were, fused in a single perspective.

[15] See Durrwell, 328-9.

270

How can we sum up these over-long reflections? There can, it seems, be no doubt that St. Paul very much wanted to be alive at the time of Christ's return and that the strength of his desire sometimes made him look forward to a rapid sequence of events, which did not, in fact, take place. In the ignorance in which he was, and in which we remain, a case could be made both for the imminence of the Parousia and for its indefinite delay. St. Paul favoured the first hypothesis. Experience of the incomplete evangelization of the world after twenty centuries inclines us to the second, but in each case, it is a question of theories and possibilities. As long as there is no intellectual judgement and no claim to be enunciating an assured doctrine, there can be no accusation of error. "For Paul, salvation itself in the new religion and perseverance until death are intimately linked with the final accounting. The question of the time lying between was God's secret. Want, hope, desire, wish, regard as possible – yes. But to believe the Parousia already present, to leave the established order, to cease working, as though the date were known and ecclesiastical and civil organization useless, all that would be a mistake and it is one that Paul does not make."[16] Nor do we make it when we consider it probable that it will be many centuries before Christ comes, always provided that we affirm nothing. There is thus nothing here to call into question the inerrancy of scripture and we can only subscribe to the decree of the Pontifical Biblical Commission made on 18th June, 1915, according to which Paul has said nothing that is not perfectly consistent with ignorance of the time of the Parousia – an ignorance proclaimed by Christ and common to all men. How, moreover, would the Church have

---

[16] Rigaux, *Épître aux Thessaloniciens*, 227. See also our own commentary, 262-72, and, in a rather different vein, Bonsirven, *Évangile de Paul*, 338-43.

managed to overcome the set-back that would have been occasioned by the delay in the second coming had Paul formally proclaimed its imminence?

This misunderstanding was threatening to become a serious matter among the Thessalonians when Paul sent them his second epistle, a few months after the first. Some turbulent members of the faithful were upsetting the community by asserting that the day of the Lord was already imminent. They were basing their contention on alleged revelations of the Holy Spirit and the apostle was afraid lest they should also base themselves on a misunderstanding of his own words or on a letter falsely attributed to him (2 : 1-2). They refused to work, living in idleness and as a burden on their brethren. Paul reproved them with merited severity. He invoked the example of his own labours and declared roundly that anyone not willing to work should not eat either (3 : 6-15). While recalling these agitated souls to a more sensible attitude, he took the opportunity of correcting their erroneous interpretation of his previous epistle and completed the doctrine contained in his oral preaching.

> Do not let anyone find the means of leading you astray. The apostasy must come first; the champion of wickedness must appear first, destined to inherit perdition. This is the rebel who is to lift up his head above every divine name, above all that men hold in reverence, till at last he enthrones himself in God's temple, and proclaims himself as God. Do not you remember my telling you of this, before I left your company? At present there is a power (you know what I mean) which holds him in check, so that he may not show himself before the time appointed to him; meanwhile, the conspiracy of revolt is already at work; only, he who checks it now will be able to check it, until he is removed from the enemy's path. Then it is that the rebel will show himself; and the Lord Jesus will destroy him with the breath of his mouth, overwhelming him with the brightness of

his presence. He will come, when he comes, with all Satan's influence to aid him; there will be no lack of power, of counterfeit signs and wonders; and his wickedness will deceive the souls that are doomed, to punish them for refusing that fellowship in the truth which would have saved them. That is why God is letting loose among them a deceiving influence, so that they give credit to falsehood; he will single out for judgement all those who refused to the thuth, credence and took their pleasure in wrongdoing (2:3–12).

St. Paul declares in the first place that, before the Parousia, there will be an apostasy, as there had no doubt been at the time of the persecution of Antiochus Epiphanus. This theme occurred frequently in the apocryphal texts and is to be met again in the Qumrân documents. No details are given but a serious and somewhat general crisis was obviously in question. Apostasy clearly presupposes previous conversion and this opens a wide field. The apostle will be found once more announcing this daunting defection in his pastoral epistles (1 Tim. 4 : 1-3; 2 Tim. 3 : 1-9; 4 : 3; et seq.). There are also allusions to it in the gospels (Matt. 24 : 11-12; 23-24; Luke 18 : 8).

Before the Parousia, moreover, there will appear the champion of wickedness, the heir of perdition, the great adversary, who will pit himself alone against God. He is described in terms similar to those used by the prophets (Ezech. 28 : 2; Dan. 11 : 36-38). The idea that he will enthrone himself in the Temple is not to be interpreted literally. St. Paul intends simply to indicate that he will try to substitute himself for the true God and have himself worshipped. We may wonder whether the reference is to a person or to a group that is personified. Father Rigaux insists that it must be to an individual person.[17] It is permissible to disagree. In the eschato-

[17] *Antéchrist*, Gabalda, 1932, 250-90; *Épître aux Thessaloniciens*, 259-73.

logical passages our Saviour foretells a series of false Christs and
false prophets (Matt. 24 : 11, 12, 24). St. John's epistles also
speak of several antichrists (1 John 2 : 18-22; 2 John 7), and
the general view is that the two beasts of the Apocalypse
(13 : 17, 18) symbolize all the persecutors and false prophets.
Finally, provided the "mystery of iniquity", which is already at work, has to be equated with the rebel, the collective
character of the impious one will be found sufficiently indicated in Paul's writings. On any interpretation, and whoever
the protagonists may be, an enormous struggle is in question
with no doubt fluctuating fortunes and the Church will be
engaged in it until the coming of the Saviour.

The parousia of the impious one is delayed by a mysterious obstacle referred to in turn by the neuter word κατέχον
and by the masculine κατέχων, which rather clearly suggests
a group. We are left to guess at the nature of this manifestation. Paul gave a partial explanation in Thessalonika, but does
not repeat what he then said. He has been taken to be referring
to St. Michael, Satan's great adversary (Apoc. 12 : 7-9), to
the charismata of the early Church, to the Roman Empire, to
Christian civilization, which grew out of it, etc. Abandoning
hope of a better explanation, Father Rigaux asks himself whether the apostle was not simply referring to an obstacle the
nature of which he himself did not know.[18] In an article which
attracted some attention, Father Buzy[19] suggested that the obstacle was composed of all the preachers of the gospel. St.
Matthew's gospel (24 : 14) seems to give some support to
this interpretation: "This gospel of the kingdom must first
be preached all over the world, so that all nations may hear
the truth; only after that will the end come." In more specific terms, the Apocalypse (11 : 1-12) cites two witnesses,

[18] *Épître aux Thessaloniciens*, 277-8.
[91] *L'adversaire et l'obstacle*, RSR, 1934, 402-31.

likened by their demeanour to Moses and Elias, whose miracles preserve them from their enemies and prevent the Beast from appearing. But *when their testimony is completed,* the Beast will vanquish them and kill them. His victory, however, will be short, for God will raise them again afterwards. These two witnesses, it is suggested, are the preachers of the gospel, in the first place, St. Paul himself, and the apostles, who resist the mystery of iniquity by their action and constitute the obstacle delaying the appearance of the impious one. This is a comforting outlook for all those who work for the Kingdom of God. Even so, when the struggle reaches its paroxysm, they will be reduced to impotence and will disappear. The obstacle will be set aside. This final point remains irremediably obscure and the mystery will be ultimately solved only by the fulfilment of the prophecy. However that may be, and in spite of the deceitful prodigies that accompany them, the activities of Satan and his minions will lead astray only those from whose hearts love of the truth is lacking and who will consequently be abandoned by God to their guilty deviation. But the Parousia of the Antichrist will be no more than an apparent triumph without any future to it. The glorious coming of the Lord Jesus will destroy the impious one. Jesus will destroy him with the breath of his mouth, that is to say, in a moment and with the greatest ease (compare Isa. 11 : 4). The pessimism apparently contained in the prediction of terrible struggles thus gives way to final optimism. Christ's victory is assured.[20]

A little reflection will show us that the uncertainty of the date of the Parousia was and remains extremely beneficial because it sustains vigilance, encourages apostolic labours and

[20] See Amiot, *Épitre aux Thessaloniciens,* 272-81.

excites in those who are spiritually inclined a keen desire for Christ's final triumph and for the supreme glory of the Father. Ignorance of the day of the anticipated Parousia constituted for each one of us by death is no less salutary. In both cases, the believer is preserved in a noble state of tension and eager hope. No doubt, there had at various times been bouts of emotional instability, brought about by impatience and worked upon by persecutions and calamities.[21] St. Paul knew how to re-establish order as the Church has known how to do so after him. The desire for "the second coming of the Word", as Father de Condren has said, should be close to the heart of every Christian who sincerely wishes for the completion of the redemption and the fullness of God's reign.

Finally, we may ask ourselves whether the glorious coming of the Saviour and the resurrection of the dead will change the present state of inanimate matter. St. Paul makes a brief reference to the question in Rom. 8 : 19-22, a passage we have already considered.[22] Creation impatiently awaits the showing forth of the children of God. It would like to be free from the slavery of corruption and to share in the glorious liberty of the children of God. It groans in the travail of childbirth. Is the apostle looking forward to the physical transformation of the material world? Some passages in Isaias (65 : 17; 66 : 22) foretell a new heaven and a new earth. A number of Jewish aprocrypha seem to suggest a renewal of the world. St. Matthew (19 : 28), St. Peter (2 Pet. 3 : 13) and the Apocalypse (21 : 1-5) all provide echoes of the passages in

[21] During Paul's lifetime there appear to have been serious troubles only at Thessalonika. There is no evidence of anything similar in the towns in which he stayed for the longest periods, such as Corinth and Ephesus.
[22] Chapter 18.

276

Isaias. It is difficult to say whether these are merely literary devices, associating the material world with the divine intervention, or whether they constitute the formal prediction of a new world. St. Paul asserts elsewhere (Col. 1 : 15-20; Eph. 1 : 10) that the redemption has an effect on the whole universe, Christ's humanity having no doubt the same relationship with the lower creatures that unites them with the rest of humanity. Are we to believe, in these circumstances, that our risen bodies will not have an appropriate material setting? Will God destroy inanimate creation and are we to form an exclusively spiritual conception of the future life? These are all questions to which it is difficult to reply. The balance and harmony of the world will be restored, but we cannot say that this means transformation of material creation, which may not have been intrinsically modified by the fall. The apostle's thought is predominantly religious. He asserts the moral link between nature and man's destiny without teaching us anything in the realm of science. Perhaps it is wise to stop here without claiming to exclude whatever divine goodness may bring about in the material world itself when sin will have been annihilated and with it "the tyranny of corruption"[23] (Rom. 8 : 21; compare Acts 3 : 21).

[23] See Lagrange's commentaries Gabalda, 1961 and Huby Beauchesne, 1957 on the epistle to the Romans. See also Viard, *Expectatio creaturae*, RB, 1952, 337-54; Dubarle, *Le gémissement des créatures et l'ordre divin du Cosmos*, RSPT, 1954, 445-65; Boismard, *Prologue de saint Jean*, Cerf, 1953, 141-2.

There is a good summary of St. Paul's eschatological doctrine in Allo, *Vivre et penser*, RB, 1940, 169-85, and in *IIe aux Corinthiens*, 155-60.

20

THE PRESENT AGE AND THE FUTURE ERA

"So justified, he glorified them"
(Rom. 8:30).

THE death and resurrection of Christ are the most important events in history. While the Greek conception of time was cyclic, with an unending series of fresh beginnings like the perpetual return of the seasons, Jews and Christians joined in looking upon time as linear, though their outlooks were not entirely similar. For Judaism, the central point in time still lies ahead. It is the moment of the future coming of the Messiah, who will inaugurate the new world. The Christian places the central point in the past. The decisive moment arrived when Christ appeared on earth and it divides the history of humanity into two parts. History will go on until the Parousia, at the threshold of a glorious eternity. But this eternity begins to be realized in the world in which we are living since, for the believer, redemption is the beginning of salvation through an initial participation in eternal blessings. There is an interpenetration between the present era and the future, a continuity between the earthly life of the justified Christian and eternal life.[1] It will be useful, taking an overall view, to give further consideration to this unity of the life

[1] See Cullmann, *Christ et le temps,* Delachaux, 1947. St. Paul often uses expressions denoting time such as day, hour, moment, time, age and so on. For him the present age is both historic time and the evil

278

of grace and life after glorification, to the unity between the initial realities of salvation and the completion of salvation which so often underlies what St. Paul says, or is affirmed by him.

God sent his Son when the fullness of time was come (Gal. 4 : 4), after a long time devoted to the preparation of humanity and particularly to that of the Jewish people. With Christ's death and resurrection, the redemption is in principle complete. It remains for man, so disposed by grace, to participate in it by giving himself completely to the Saviour through faith and through a life lived in conformity with the gospel. There is no salvation except in the Name of Jesus (Acts 4 : 12), preached everywhere by the apostles. The time of pardon and the day of salvation have begun (2 Cor. 6 : 2). By listening to the "message of salvation" everyone may enter the road leading to it (Acts 13 : 26; 16 : 17). We are coming to the fulfilment of history (1 Cor. 10 : 11). We are entering the world's final era, which will receive its crown at the glorious coming of Christ on the great Day, the true day of Jahveh, announced by the prophets. Their message, however, is now given more precisely and in greater detail. It is in the person of his Son that Jahveh will come. He will come on behalf of the new Israel, the Israel of those who believe in Christ, which enfolds all nations.

world in which we live, marked by sin (Gal. 1 : 4; Rom. 12 : 13; 1 Cor. 1 : 20; 2 : 6, 8; 3 : 18; 2 Cor. 4 : 4; 1 Tim. 6 : 17; 2 Tim. 4 : 10). He only rarely refers to future ages (Eph. 1 : 21; Heb. 6 : 5), but the idea denoted by the term is frequently met with. The future age is the era that will follow the Parousia, an eternity freed from sin which will see the blossoming forth of the fruits of the redemption and God's reign. But the future age overlaps the present since the decisive battle is already won through the redeeming death of Christ, although hostilities still continue. We come across the same expressions in the synoptic gospels: Matt. 12 : 32; Luke 16 : 8; 18 : 30; 20 : 34; etc. See Kittel I, article dealing with the word αἰών (Sasse).

The glorified Christ will continue to act unceasingly in history until his final intervention to raise those who sleep, judge the living and the dead and place the kingdom in the hands of his Father. We are saved henceforth by the merits of his blood, but our entry into the era of salvation brings about only a partial share in the divine blessings which go to make up salvation. Faith constitutes the foundation of our hope (Heb. 11 : 1) and of what will be given us in eternity. We are saved, but only in hope as, for the time, we possess only the first-fruits and an earnest of the Spirit (Rom. 8 : 22-24), and the Spirit has marked us with a seal which we shall bear against the day of final redemption (Eph. 4 : 30). We await the appearance in the heavens of the Lord who will make our miserable bodies like his own glorified body (Phil. 3 : 20-21). In the present life, the hope of salvation is like a helmet which, together with faith and charity, protects us against the attacks of sin (1 Thess. 5 : 8).

God does not destine us to wrath but to the possession of salvation (1 Thess. 5 : 9). It was with a view to this that he elected us in Christ from before the creation of the world, predestining us to become his adopted children in Christ (Eph. 1 : 4-5). But the road to salvation is completed by stages. These are the call to faith, progress in faith, life with Christ after death, resurrection and glorification. They are the various phases of a single reality whereby, right from the beginning, the Christian is introduced into the future world even while he remains in the present world, and the inspired authors sometimes take in these various phases at a single glance.[2] St. Paul is also not afraid to regard the Christian's glorification as in a sense already achieved here below, not only through a prophetic anticipation, but because the life

[2] See Durrwell, 309-12.

280

of grace is the seed and the guarantee of life in glory. It differs from it in degree but not in nature. "All those who from the first were known to him, he has destined from the first to be moulded into the image of his Son, who is thus to become the eldest-born among many brethren. So predestined, he called them; so called, he justified them; so justified, he glorified them" (Rom. 8 : 29-30). And again: "How rich God is in his mercy, with what an excess of love he loved us! Our sins had made dead men of us, and he, in giving life to Christ, gave life to us too; it is his grace that has saved you; raised us up too, enthroned us too above the heavens, in Christ Jesus. He would have all future ages see, in that clemency which he showed in Christ Jesus, the surpassing richness of his grace" (Eph. 2 : 4-7). The glorification of the Head is bound to bring about that of the members, already achieved in principle through his redemptive death.

The idea of a preliminary share in salvation, a kind of adumbration of salvation, is to be found in all the great Pauline passages dealing with Christian life, passages which are closely related to each other.

Divine justice transmitted through Christ's merits (2 Cor. 5 : 21), the fruits of which fill souls (Phil. 1 : 11), is responsible for a share in the very life of Christ (Gal. 2 : 20; Rom. 5 : 18) and leads to eternal life (Rom. 6 : 22-23) under the new dispensation of grace (Rom. 5 : 20-21; 6 : 14). The Christian lives for God with the risen Christ and in him (Rom. 6 : 10-11). Justice and holiness (1 Cor. 1 : 30; Eph. 4 : 24) open the way to a favourable judgement on those who remain faithful (2 Thess. 1 : 5; Rom. 8 : 33-34). Justice means a share in the Holy Spirit, in the first-fruits of the Spirit while awaiting the complete gift (Eph. 1 : 13-14) and while awaiting the resurrection which will be his work

(Rom. 8 : 11). The Spirit who is Christ's Spirit makes the one in whom he dwells like Christ and makes him an adopted child and heir of the Father (Gal. 4 : 6-7). The right to an inheritance will produce its effect at the end of a life united to Christ's Passion, which is the condition of the union with his glorification (Rom. 8 : 17; Eph. 1 : 14; 5 : 5; Col. 3 : 24; Heb. 9 : 15). All these supernatural blessings constitute a spiritual share in the risen life of the Saviour (Rom. 6 : 4, 8, 11) and bodily resurrection will be the crown of this participation (1 Cor. 15 : 20-22). Redemption thus takes its effect from now onwards (1 Cor. 1 : 30; Col. 1 : 14; Eph. 1 : 7). But it is incomplete because its fruits can be lost through sin and it has still to be completed by the resurrection, "the ransoming of our bodies" (Rom. 8 : 23; Eph. 1 : 14; 4 : 30). We are transferred to the kingdom of his beloved Son (Col. 1 : 13); we will enter it fully and finally after a life that is holy and free from sin (Gal. 5 : 21; 1 Cor. 6 : 9; Eph. 5 : 5). We shall enter it when, having reached heaven, we share in Christ's reign (1 Thess. 2 : 12; 1 Cor. 15 : 24; 2 Tim. 4 : 1, 18). Then God's glory, the reflection of which was already on us and which transformed us little by little into the image of the Lord (Rom. 3 : 23; 2 Cor. 3 : 18; 4 : 6), will penetrate our entire being (Rom. 5 : 2; 8 : 18; 1 Cor. 15 : 43; 2 Cor. 4 : 17; Eph. 1 : 18; Col. 1 : 27; 1 Thess. 1 : 12; 2 Thess. 2 : 14). We shall be with Christ for ever and shall live with him (1 Thess. 4 : 17; 5 : 10). This will bring the complete revealing and showing forth of the Lord (2 Thess. 1 : 7; 1 Cor. 1 : 7). On the supreme day, he will appear in glory and will join to himself all the members of his Mystical Body (Col. 3 : 3-4).

The Christian who, from this life onwards, benefits from the eternal blessings should live blessed in his hope to the day when there will be a new dawn of glory, the glory of the great God, our Saviour Jesus Christ (Titus 2 : 13). This will be the crowning piece of divine bounty. The Christian is a member of the heavenly Jerusalem (Gal. 4 : 26), finding his true home in heaven (Phil. 3 : 20). He is already in heaven in the person of Christ with whom he is intimately linked. He must look forward with all his soul to the glorious ending which will make this union indissoluble, the ending to which God has predestined him (Rom. 8 : 29-30) and which his own infidelity can alone prevent him from achieving. He belongs to the future age at the same time as he belongs to the present. The Church is his guide in his journey towards eternity and the Eucharist, strengthening his union with Christ and his brethren (1 Cor. 10 : 17), helps him to be always ready for the coming of the Lord (1 Cor. 11 : 26, 32) by giving him for his nourishment Christ's body, present in the continuation of his sacrifice, and in the eternal glory of his resurrection.[3]

Christ's disciple should, therefore, use this world as if he used it not (1 Cor. 7 : 31). He should work for the fulfilment of his salvation in careful and generous vigilance (1 Thess. 5 : 4-11). He should bear without surprise and with courageous patience the inevitable persecutions and tribulations which will make him an imitator of Christ and of the apostle (1 Thess. 1 : 6; 2 : 14; 2 Thess. 1 : 4; et seq.; 2 Cor. 11 : 21-38; etc.). He should not allow himself to be worried by the baneful activities of the mystery of iniquity and the works of Satan (2 Thess. 2 : 7-12). These are merely rearguard actions. Christ has won the victory and he will make those who follow him conquerors with him (Rom. 8 : 37).

That is why, in spite of the hardness of the struggles that oblige him to work for his salvation in fear and trembling

[3] See Durrwell, 374-80.

(Phil. 2 : 12), the believer is able to live in joy and peace.
"I cannot contain myself for happiness, in the midst of all
these trials of mine" (2 Cor. 7 : 4). "Joy be with you
always.... Joy to you in the Lord at all times; once again I
wish you joy.... So may the peace of God, which surpasseth
all our thinking, watch over your hearts and minds in Christ
Jesus" (1 Thess. 5 : 16; Phil. 4 : 4-7). God's kingdom is
"justice and peace and joy in the Holy Spirit" (Rom. 14 : 17
[Douai]). "May God, the author of our hope, fill you with
all joy and peace in your believing... through the power of
the Holy Spirit" (Rom. 15 : 13). This joyful hymn fills the
epistles and breaks forth in thanksgiving for divine blessings:
"So that grace made manifold in many lives may increase
the sum of gratitude which is offered for God's glory" (2 Cor.
4 : 15; compare Phil. 4 : 6; 1 Tim. 2 : 1; 4 : 3-4). "Blessed
be that God, that Father of our Lord Jesus Christ, who has
blessed us, in Christ, with every spiritual blessing" (Eph.
1 : 3). Paul is carried away with enthusiasm at the thought
of the rewards of the future age, the eternal weight of glory,
bearing no relation to the trials of a moment (2 Cor. 4 : 17),
and which will be beyond anything that the human heart
could conceive (1 Cor. 2 : 9). The hope of the Christian
cannot fail:

> Who can be our adversary, if God is on our side? He did not
> even spare his own Son, but gave him up for us all; and must
> not that gift be accompanied by the gift of all else? Who will
> come forward to accuse God's elect, when God acquits us? Who
> will pass sentence against us, when Jesus Christ, who died, nay,
> has risen again, and sits at the right hand of God, is pleading
> for us? Who will separate us from the love of Christ? Will
> affliction, or distress, or persecution, or hunger, or nakedness, or
> peril, or the sword...? Of this I am fully persuaded; neither
> death nor life, no angels or principalities or powers, neither what
> is present nor what is to come, no force whatever, neither the

height above us nor the depth beneath us, nor any other created thing, will be able to separate us from the love of God, which comes to us in Christ Jesus our Lord (Rom. 8:31–39).

The love of God is not external to us. It is spread forth in our hearts by the gift of the Holy Spirit (Rom. 5 : 5). Through the Spirit, we live in the future age, in the era of salvation, for salvation is death to sin through Christ and in Christ. It is life in Christ. It is union with Christ. Salvation will reach its completion when the union with Christ becomes unbreakable and when the risen body will be glorified together with the soul. But it has started now and goes towards its final stage: "You have undergone death, and your life is hidden away now with Christ in God. Christ is your life, and when he is made manifest, you too will be made manifest in glory with him" (Col. 3 : 3-4). One who has given himself to Christ and is sustained by grace can hardly fail to press on with all his strength towards that which lies ahead in order to gain "the prize, God's heavenly summons in Christ Jesus" (Phil. 3 : 14). We are not left in darkness for our journey towards the light. Already the light illuminates our hearts (2 Cor. 4 : 6). The night is far on its course and the Day draws near (Rom. 13 : 12).

21

TO THE GLORY OF GOD THE FATHER

> *"Filled with the fruit of justice, through
> Jesus Christ, unto the glory and praise of
> God"*   *(Phil. 1:11 {Douai}).*

OUR study has shown us the completely objective and deeply religious character of St. Paul's thought.

For him, the facts concerning our Lord are the necessary foundation of any valid witness. There is first of all the reality of the incarnation. Christ was born of a woman under the rule of the law (Gal. 4 : 4). He took the nature of a slave and was fashioned in the likeness of man (Phil. 2 : 7). He took on the fashion of our guilty nature (Rom. 8 : 3), was subject to suffering and death and descended, in respect of his human birth, from the line of David (Rom. 1 : 3). Next to be considered is the reality of the redemptive sacrifice. The apostle speaks of it constantly and in so vivid a way that the image of Christ crucified was, as it were, set before the eyes of his hearers (Gal. 3 : 1). Jesus bore witness to his great claim when he stood before Pontius Pilate (1 Tim. 6 : 13), confessing that he was the King-Messiah and freely accepting death for the salvation of men, in an act of sovereign obedience which has repaired the ravages of the disobedience of Adam[1] (Rom. 5 : 19). Finally, there is the reality of the

---

[1] See chapter 6, section II.

glorification. Christ was laid in the tomb and raised on the third day, in accordance with the scriptures. He appeared to the apostles and to Paul himself, who is in consequence qualified to bear witness to the resurrection (1 Cor. 15 : 3, 8; 9 : 1). The glorified Saviour has entered the heavenly sanctuary (Heb. 9 : 12, 24), where he sits on the right hand of God and intercedes for us (Rom. 8 : 34; Heb. 1 : 2; 7 : 24; etc.). All creatures must confess that the Lord is equal to Jahveh[2] (Phil. 2 : 11). Witness has been born to all these facts at the appointed time (1 Tim. 2 : 6) and we have not forgotten with what assurance St. Paul reminded the Corinthians of the appearances of Christ, declaring that if he were not truly risen the apostles would be false witnesses and impostors (1 Cor. 15 : 3-8, 15). He was later to say with the same certainty in his speech to Agrippa: "The King knows about all this well enough.... . None of this, I am sure, is news to him; it was not in some secret corner that all this happened" (Acts 26 : 26). Paul declared that this dead man called Jesus was alive (Acts 25 : 19) and he was able to challenge his questioners to prove him a liar.

Thus, God intervened in history and sent his own Son as sole mediator between himself and men in order that all might be saved (1 Tim. 2 : 4-5), by associating them with the death and the life of him who has risen. The divine intervention is a work of immense love and a love that is in no way merited (Eph. 2 : 4-9). But in the glorification of Christ and in the salvation of men, this intervention has and could only have as its ultimate purpose God's glory.

St. Paul says this in a number of different ways. He continually points out God's ineffable transcendence and the gratuitousness of all his gifts. It is out of pure goodness that he

[2] See chapter 6, section III.

made his Son an expiatory victim (Rom. 3 : 24), not only for Israel, once the object of his gifts and of his attentions, but for all peoples, whom nothing would henceforth separate from the chosen people, so that they would all be but one new creature in the blood of Christ (Eph. 2 : 13-18). What is true of nations is equally so of individuals. The essential personal initiative of faith is impossible without grace. It consists of the conscious and intended giving which tears us from ourselves to submit us to God, but which none the less remains a free gift, emanating from God (Eph. 2 : 7-9; Rom. 11 : 6). Its merciful character should fill us with gratitude (Titus 2 : 4-7). Thus man has no ground for self-glorification, as though salvation were his own work. No creature can boast in the presence of God (1 Cor. 1 : 29; Rom. 3 : 27-28). It is legitimate to glorify oneself only in the Lord and in his blessings (1 Cor. 1 : 31; 2 Cor. 10 : 17). Taken as a whole, Israel failed to understand this truth and spent itself in a vain search for justification, claiming to rely on observance of the law and not on faith (Rom. 9 : 30-32). The drama of the Jewish people, obstinate in their faithlessness, which so tortured St. Paul that he would have been ready to be anathema for the sake of his kinsmen by race (Rom. 9 : 1-3), is a drama of pride, a tragic misunderstanding of the free nature of divine blessings. In his struggle against temptations (1 Cor. 10 : 13) and in every effort towards his own sanctification (2 Cor. 3 : 5, etc.), the Christian, sustained as he is by the presence and action of the Holy Spirit (1 Cor. 12 : 3, 11; Rom. 8 : 5-8, 14; etc.), is also accompanied by this merciful and free generosity. "He who has inspired this generosity in you will bring it to perfection, ready for the day when Jesus Christ comes" (Phil. 1 : 6).

Paul himself is the first to give an example of this necessary humility and works only for Christ's glory. He is able to bear witness that he has worked more than the other apostles, but adds immediately afterwards: "Or rather, it was not I, but the grace of God working with me" (1 Cor. 15 : 10). And he readily boasts of his own weaknesses in order that Christ's power should dwell in him (2 Cor. 12 : 9) and his own labours should be more clearly recognized as the effects of Christ's strength. He lives in the intense conviction that he can do nothing without grace and that he owes everything to Christ who loved him and who delivered himself up for him and lives in him even more than he, Paul, lives in himself (Gal. 2 : 20). Whether he lives or dies, he has the single desire; that this body of his shall do Christ honour through the spiritual growth of the faithful for which it will be the instrument (Phil. 1 : 20, 25). He will always rejoice to see Christ proclaimed, even if some preachers are inspired by rivalry and jealousy towards Paul himself (Phil. 1 : 17-18). The whole of the Church's mission is designed to proclaim the glory of the name of the Lord Jesus and the glory in him of the faithful, through the effects of the grace that comes from God and from Christ (2 Thess. 1 : 11-12).

Christ himself seeks above all things the glory of his Father in the redemptive work, in his life, in his death, in his triumph. If every tongue must proclaim that he is the Lord equal to Jahveh, it is doubtless because this title in his as Son of God and Redeemer. It is thus ultimately the sovereign glorification of God the Father (Phil. 2 : 11), author of Christ's resurrection in his ineffable splendour and power (Rom. 6 : 4; Eph. 1 : 20). When Christ will have finally destroyed every principality and every dominion and will have overcome death, the last enemy, when God will thus have put everything under his feet, he will hand over his kingdom to the Father, so that God shall be all in all, reigning perfectly over all (1 Cor. 15 : 24-28). This royal gift will be the supreme glorification of the Father – and of the Son, reigning indivisibly with him – in the completed redemption, the salvation of men crowned by the resurrection of the body, the final submission to its Creator of the world, which the sin of man will no longer turn away from the aim it is meant to achieve (Rom. 8 : 19-22). "Everything is for you", says the apostle in another passage, "whether it be Paul, or Apollo, or Cephas, or the world, or life, or death, or the present, or the future; it is all for you, and you for Christ, and Christ for God" (1 Cor. 3 : 21-23). "To him, to God who alone is wise, glory is given from age to age, through Jesus Christ, Amen" (Rom. 16 : 27). "Honour and glory through endless ages to the king of all the ages, the immortal, the invisible, who alone is God" (1 Tim. 1 : 17). This chant of praise runs joyously through the epistles (2 Cor. 4 : 15; 8 : 19; Phil. 4 : 20; 2 Tim. 4 : 18, etc.). It seems to find its fullest expression in the solemn opening of the letter to the Ephesians where the blessings of the redemption are seen to be prepared for all eternity by the Father, merited by the blood of Christ and granted to believers in the gift of the Spirit for the praising of God's superabundant grace:

> Blessed be that God, that Father of our Lord Jesus Christ, who has blessed us, in Christ, with every spiritual blessing, higher than heaven itself. He has chosen us out, in Christ, before the foundation of the world, to be saints, to be blameless in his sight, for love of him; marking us out beforehand (so his will decreed) to be his adopted children in Jesus Christ. Thus he would manifest the splendour of that grace by which he has taken us into his favour in the person of his beloved Son. It is in him and through his blood that we enjoy redemption, the forgiveness of our sins. So rich is God's grace, that has overflowed upon us in a full stream of wisdom and discernment, to make known to us the hidden purpose of his will. It was his loving design, centred in Christ, to give history its fulfilment by resuming everything in him, all that is in heaven, all that is on earth, summed up in

him. In him it was our lot to be called, singled out beforehand
to suit his purpose, (for it is he who is at work everywhere,
carrying out the designs of his will); we were to manifest his
glory, we who were the first to set our hope in Christ: in him
you too were called, when you listened to the preaching of the
truth, that gospel which is your salvation. In him you too learned
to believe, and had the seal set on your faith by the promised
gift of the Holy Spirit; a pledge of the inheritance which is ours,
to redeem it for us and bring us into possession of it, and so
manifest God's glory (Eph. 1:3–14).

The fullness of the doctrine contained in this passage is
nowhere surpassed. Besides linking the divine gifts with
the mystery of the Trinity,[3] and showing that they constitute a share in the very life of the divine persons themselves,
it illustrates more than any other passage, St. Paul's insistence
on the glory and praise of God as the supreme end of the
redemption of mankind. This is a truth which we might regard
as elementary and self-evident, but it is stimulating to see it
placed in a new light at the summit of St. Paul's thought.
God wants our happiness and our salvation, but our salvation
works for his glory by showing in the highest degree his
mercy and his love (Eph. 2 : 4-6). And if we are able to
understand this, desire for God's glory will penetrate and, as
it were, absorb our own desire for the eternal reward.[4] If it has
been possible to claim that the living man is God's glory,
gloria Dei vivens homo, what are we to say of redeemed man?
"He whose power is at work in us is powerful enough, and
more than powerful enough, to carry out his purpose beyond

---

[3] It is worth while pointing out once more how fully Pauline theology is Trinitarian (see end of chapter 10). Nevertheless, the great
mystery is revealed to us less on its own account than in relation to the
redemption. Immediate knowledge of it is reserved for the meeting
with God face to face in the eternal vision (1 Cor. 13 : 12).

[4] See the end of chapter 16.

all our hopes and dreams; may he be glorified in the Church, and in Christ Jesus, to the last generation of eternity. Amen" (Eph. 3 : 20-21).

The glory and praise of God should constitute the chief preoccupation of any Christian worthy of the name in his pursuit of salvation, penetrated as he is with the love of God and of the Saviour. He lives in Christ in a perpetual thanksgiving for divine mercies, anxious not to reject his cross and to please Christ in all things. His attitude is one of determined and joyous optimism about the struggles that lie ahead and the difficulties that remain to be overcome. He is always busily at work glorifying God and showing himself worthy of God's call (2 Thess. 1 : 11-12).

We are bound to be seized with admiration and gratitude as we look upon the unfolding of the world's history and the various stages of salvation—Adam, Abraham, Moses, Christ, the Church and the Parousia. We can only repeat what St. Paul wrote to the Romans after having outlined for them the intentions behind God's temporary rejection of Israel and the calling of the heathen to the faith: "How deep is the mine of God's wisdom, of his knowledge; how inscrutable are his judgements, how undiscoverable his ways" (Rom. 11 : 33). But however deep the mystery of salvation, it is evident that God turns all things to the good of those whom he loves and that so great are his gifts that he must be praised and glorified in them. After having delivered his own Son on our behalf, God has given us everything with him (Rom. 8 : 32). In truth, with Christ there has not been hesitation between Yes and No; in him all the promises have found their Yes and through him we will say Amen to God's glory (2 Cor. 1 : 19-20). This will be the eternal praise delivered by the redeemed who have achieved final salvation and live for ever in Christ. With him and in him, they will send up towards the Father the hymn of the eternal liturgy: "All things find in him their origin, their impulse, the centre of their being: to him be glory throughout all ages, Amen" (Rom. 11 : 36).[5]

[5] See Spicq, *Vie morale et Trinité Sainte selon saint Paul* (Lectio Divina), Cerf, 1957, 29-32; 87-9.

INDEX

Abraham, 72-3, 126.
See: Justification
Adam, 67-72, 100, 120; Christ as the new Adam, 40, 72, 120, 171.
Angels, inferior to Christ, 188
Antichrist, 272-3
Apostasy, morally irreparable, 131, 220; prelude to Parousia, 272-4
Apostle, 210-2
Asceticism. *See:* Redemption

Baptism, united to the death and resurrection of Christ, 80, 133-41, 145, 148; for the dead, 37
Bishop, 213-5.
See: Episcopacy, Presbyters

Celibacy, 225-6
Charismata, 150, 156-7, 176-9
Charity, 131-2, 157-8, 166, 178, 187
Chastity, 224
Christ. *See:* Jesus Christ
Church, 108, 127; as spouse of Christ, 225; baptized on the cross, 135; hierarchical form, 213-26; infallibility, 216-21; marks of, 207-10; and Mystical Body, 140-1, 175-6, 204-7, 228
Communion of Saints, 205, 240
Covenant, 66, 89, 98, 173
Cross, 93 et seq. *See:* Jesus Christ

Deacons, 213
Death, bodily death and eternity, 239-44; consequence of original sin, 67-72; defeated by Christ, 263-5; and judgement, 239-49; last human generation exempt from death, 256-8; to sin, 240-1

Episcopacy, 213-5
Epistles, authenticity, language, etc., 35-9
Eucharist, 193-203